Home and School Partnerships in Exceptional Education

Carol T. Michaelis, Ph.D.
Associate Professor of Special Education
Northwestern State University of Louisiana
Natchitoches, Louisiana

AN ASPEN PUBLICATION®
Aspen Systems Corporation
Rockville, Maryland
London
1980

Library of Congress Cataloging in Publication Data

Michaelis, Carol T.
Home and school partnerships in exceptional education.

Includes bibliographies and index.
1. Exceptional children—Education. 2. Home and
school. I. Title
LC3969.M52   371.9   80-23920
ISBN: 0-89443-330-X

Library of Congress Catalog Card Number: 80-23920
ISBN: 0-89443-330-X

Printed in the United States of America

1 2 3 4 5

To Mother, who showed me how to be one,
and to Dick, Blaine, Jim, Neil, and Trish
for allowing me to practice

Table of Contents

Foreword

The passage of Public Law 94-142, which has as its overriding goal an education for all handicapped children and youth, has been termed one of the few occasions wherein modern professional ideologies and technologies have—in one bold stroke—been codified into federal law and thus into a national policy. This national law and resultant national standard of educational policy, because of the sweeping realignments it demands in the traditional home-school relations, has underscored the pressing need for new guidelines in the responsibility of our primary-secondary educational system to our handicapped young citizens and their parents. In this volume, Dr. Michaelis provides guidelines in a way that is at all times pragmatic in its direct bearing to the realities of day-to-day provision of modern educational services for handicapped children and youth—including their major support system: their mothers and fathers!

In the past, much of the major legislation on behalf of exceptional children and youth in the United States has been dissipated by the lack of both an organized advocacy group and a firm financial base. An educated body of parent and professional advocates was needed to demand modern programs and, in turn, energetically lobby at the local, state, and federal levels of government for resources that would finally provide a financial base for maximizing the rights of exceptional children. The groups who fought so valiantly for the passage of P.L. 94-142 demanded modern programs for the optimal development of all handicapped citizens. The modern definition of who is to be helped and specific mechanisms for delivering that help via individual education programs have received the full support of the large advocate groups that strongly supported the P.L. 94-142 legislation at all levels of its development.

The challenges related to the full service implementation and monitoring of P.L. 94-142 have slowly begun to unfold. Importantly, those working at the educational "front lines" of the classrooms and their monitoring groups have clearly recognized the types of approaches that will successfully implement the noble promises

ix

that P.L. 94-142 contains. Especially vital are the roles and interrelations between handicapped citizens, parents, and professionals, which must be orchestrated in an efficient and fair manner. It is toward the enhanced understanding and effectiveness of all these groups that this book directly addresses itself.

Insight is provided into the most commonly noted sets of dynamics in parents of the handicapped, which range from overprotective modes of parental caregiving to disinterested personal preoccupation. The perspectives and vicissitudes of siblings, as well as effective parental participation in the education, care, and management of their handicapped child, are also discussed. In dealing with these complex issues, Dr. Michaelis initially takes a hard look at communication—the stuff of which human transactions (and strife) are made. The problems of communication, at home or in school, that often develop are direly in need of the helpful resolution strategies so clearly presented in this book. The variety of parental interactions with their handicapped child are clearly presented. Throughout this book, there are recommended approaches and/or techniques that help parents and professionals to aid handicapped children effectively. For example, there is a definitive analysis of the recurrent challenge to professionals to distinguish clearly the hallmarks of crisis counseling from developmental approaches that embody the long-term needs of families and their handicapped youngsters. Similar management challenges (and excellent guidelines for their successful resolution) are repeatedly stressed in this book and represent a major contribution to this field of endeavor. These challenges and similar current-future topical areas are fully discussed by this experienced author.

In summary, Dr. Michaelis succinctly presents the major communication/ organizational pitfalls of home-school interrelationships that must be resolved in order to maximize the developmental potentials of our handicapped citizens and lighten the burdens of their parents. At all times, the information and resultant guidelines reflect modern ideologies and excellent management principles.

It is a pleasure to write the Foreword to this book, because I believe it is the harbinger of new ways to implement modern special education and a clear exposition of how, when, and where to utilize fully creative professional technology and knowledgeable approaches for helping our handicapped citizens of today and tomorrow.

FRANK J. MENOLASCINO, M.D.
Professor of Psychiatry
and Pediatrics
University of Nebraska
Medical Center
Omaha, Nebraska

November 1980

Chapter 1

Due Process with or without a Hearing

IN LOCO PARENTIS

Almost everyone can remember calling the teacher "Mother." It is embarrassing, but it is an easy thing to do. Teachers sometimes act like parents act. In the grammar schools where most of today's teachers were students, the teacher operated under the common law in loco parentis, in place of the parent. The teacher was instructed to act always as a parent would in the interests of the safety and welfare of the child. The appropriateness of teaching a particular fact or set of facts was to be the decision of the teacher. If the teacher had difficulty deciding, it was suggested that the supervisory staff and other experienced teachers be consulted for assistance in making the decisions. In loco parentis common law is no longer in effect; in fact, the teacher who does act in place of the parent may be compelled to explain that action as a witness at a due process hearing. Now the only person who has the right to act for the parent is the parent or a legally appointed, trained, impartial surrogate parent (Demars, 1964).

A due process hearing is in case all else fails. This book is about "all else" and how to keep it from failing.

THE HEARING

It is a quiet evening in the late spring. Inside, it is even quieter than outside. They sit across the table; there doesn't seem to be anything to say before the formal hearing begins. These parents, these teachers, the principal, and the psychologist have sat across the table from each other many times before. How many times no one really remembers, but they have been there before.

This time it is different; this is not an ordinary conference. The parents are not sitting there alone, but are accompanied by an attorney, a psychologist who has independently examined their child, and a member of the state child advocacy organization. The parents seem different, too. The mother has had her hair done, and the father is wearing a tie. (See Chapter 5.)

It hasn't been an ordinary day for the professional staff either. They have rushed home and back since school. Miss Jones has changed to a black suit, and Mr. Anderson is wearing his best tie. Days haven't been ordinary for some time. There have been meetings, conferences, statements to write, testimony to prepare, and copies to make and file.

In a few minutes the hearing officer will begin the hearing by saying something like, "We have come here to talk about an appropriate educational setting for Johnny." But they will really talk about how Miss Jones saw the problems, what she did to help Johnny learn, and how she explained all of this to Johnny's mother and father. They will talk about how well the principal explained the programs to the parents. "Now tell us about the problems that Johnny has been having at school," the hearing officer asks. "And what did you do about them?" "And, Mr. Anderson, have you explained these tests to Johnny's parents?" "And what other methods have you tried, Miss Jones?" Miss Jones and Mr. Anderson may not have wanted to come, but they had no choice. Johnny's parents have the right to compel them to be witnesses at the hearing.

The public hearing is a "trial" for the public agency to make sure that the "rights of handicapped children and their parents are protected" (*Federal Register*, 1977, p. 42474). The parents and the hearing officer listen as the agency defends its position and explains its activities. The hearing officer determines if all of the obligations to the family have been met (Goldberg, Thornburg, Weatherman, & Permuth, 1977). The public agency must defend its position and answer the questions that the parents and the parents' attorney ask. The questioning could go on for hours, or even days. The hearing is recorded, and the parents are given a copy of the proceedings if they desire it. If the agency cannot document all of the contacts, evaluations, or explanations, it is assumed that the child has not been proven to be handicapped and therefore belongs in the regular school program.

NOBODY WINS AT A HEARING

After all the testimony has been presented, the hearing officer makes a decision. If the decision favors the school's position, the angry and hurt parents are expected to comply. If the decision favors the family's position, the angry and hurt personnel of the public agency are expected to comply. Somehow, no matter what the decision, nobody wins. What the school really wants is the parents' cooperation in the school's programming. What the parents really want is an ally, not an enemy.

What the Hearing Costs the Public Agency

There are some obviously time-consuming activities that the public agency personnel must do to prepare for a hearing. The costs of updating the child's folder and the professional interaction required to prepare the necessary documentation can be measured in dollars and cents. Other expenses to the public agency are not so easy to measure, however.

Whenever the agency is involved in a hearing on the suitability of its programming for one child, it is likely that the appropriateness of services for other children will be questioned also. Requiring a school to assume a defensive position implies a negative evaluation of the competence of the professional staff, and the general satisfaction with school programming is likely to decrease.

Since most professionals have chosen to work in education because they are interested in the development and welfare of children, there can be a personal emotional strain to being questioned about the methods and activities used in the education of a particular child, especially if the professionals thought they were acting in the interests of the safety and welfare of the child, in loco parentis.

What the Hearing Costs the Family

Child care and family life routines are significantly altered while the family's emotional and financial resources are focused on one child's need. There is not the usual amount of time available to assist other children in the family. (See Chapter 6.) Work routines of the parents are interrupted both inside and outside the home.

In addition to the overt preparation for the hearing, the parents are likely to spend some sleepless nights being concerned about how to get the help that they feel the child needs without exposing family problems to public inspection. (See Chapter 4.) Very few parents can really afford the financial and psychological cost of a hearing. But if they are upset and hurt and do not understand what is being done in regard to the child, the parents may be willing to pay that awful price.

WHY HAVE HEARINGS IF THEY ARE SO EXPENSIVE?

The due process hearing is not imposed only on educational agencies. Due process is part of the democratic system of seeing that the rights of citizens are protected. No opportunity or right is to be taken from a citizen without due process of law. Whatever is available to one citizen must be available to all citizens. Since education is available to some children, education must be available to all children.

If the child is not to have access to the regular school system, the reason for this must be shown through an organized, specified process. If there is some question and the parents do not understand what is being done or said, they can ask that a hearing be held to evaluate whether or not the rights of the child and the parents have been protected. The public agency can also initiate a hearing, if they feel that the parent is not acting in the child's best interests. The agency must first prove that the circumstances have been explained to the parents and that the parents understand them.

Although the parents and the public agency both have the right to initiate the process, only the agency can set the stage to prevent a hearing by making sure that the parents understand and accept all evaluations, placement options, records, and programs designed for the child. The best way to cut down on the expense of a hearing is to know as much about the process of referral, programming planning, and parents as possible. Chapters 1 and 2 are about the law; Chapters 3, 4, 5, and 6 are about parents; and Chapters 7, 8, 9, 10, 11, 12, 13, and 14 are about ways to get the two together.

THE ORIGINS OF HEARINGS IN EDUCATION

Some children have been "excluded" from school because of "bodily or mental conditions rendering attendance inadvisable" (Weintraub & Abeson, 1976, p. 7). Other children have been placed in state schools and hospitals where education is not available to them. Parents seeking help for their children from the school agencies were refused, since the laws excluded the children from the education or did not provide directly for their education. The process in this society to interpret the law is to challenge in a court of law. Parents seeking help for their children initiated court cases. The judge ruled that "citizens residing in state schools and hospitals indeed have certain rights . . . which, of course, includes education" (Gilhool, 1976, p. 14).

In the case of *Pennsylvania Association for Retarded Citizens v. the Commonwealth of Pennsylvania,* it was found that education "cannot be defined solely as the provision of academic experiences to children . . . for children to learn to clothe and feed themselves is a legitimate outcome achievable through an educational program" (Weintraub & Abeson, 1976, p. 8). The Pennsylvania order defined the rights of the parents in placements to special settings. Much of the language of the court order later became the language of Public Law (P.L.) 94-142, Education for All Handicapped Children Act of 1975. Some of the requirements of this act are

"1. Providing written notice to parents or guardians of the proposed action.
2. Provision in that notice of the specific reasons for the proposed action and the legal authority upon which such actions can occur.

3. Provision of information about alternative educational opportunities.
4. Provision of information about the parent's or guardian's right to contest the proposed action at a full hearing before the state secretary of education or his designate.
5. Provision of information about the purpose and procedures of a hearing, including parent's or guardian's right to counsel, cross examination, presentation or independent evidence, and a written transcript of the hearing.
6. Provision for the scheduling of the hearing.
7. Indication that the burden of proof regarding the placement recommendation lies with the school district.
8. Right to obtain an independent evaluation of the child at public expense if necessary." (Weintraub & Abeson, 1976, p. 10.)

THE DEVELOPMENT OF P.L. 94-142

The court cases made the public more aware of the educational needs of handicapped children, but the beginnings of P.L. 94-142 are difficult to trace. Even those who worked on the concepts for "nearly four years of intensive legislative development" (Ballard, 1976, p. 113) were sometimes unsure of how or why certain events occurred (Weintraub, 1978). Personnel in the governmental relations unit of the Council for Exceptional Children (CEC) are collecting all the letters, memoranda, and other documents in their files that were generated during the development and passage of the law so that these materials will be available for further study (Weintraub, 1978).

The national office of the CEC is located in the Washington, D.C. suburb of Reston, Virginia, which makes it possible for staff members from the governmental relations unit to attend congressional committee hearings and interact informally with congressional staff on an ongoing basis. Congressional committees also receive input from the Office of Education's Bureau of Education for the Handicapped (BEH). Staff at BEH can present not only their personal professional experiences with handicapped children, but also information from projects that are funded through the bureau. During the development of P.L. 94-142, other testimony was presented to Congress by advocacy groups such as the National Association for Retarded Citizens (NARC), organized by parents of the mentally retarded. (See Chapter 13.)

Numerous revisions were made before the "conference agreement" was drafted and passed by Congress (Ballard, 1976). By then, an almost countless number of persons had given testimony to the legislators. The bill was signed into law by President Ford on November 25, 1975.

The law itself contains a brief statement of purpose:

The Congress finds that—

(1) there are more than eight million handicapped children in the United States today;

(2) the special educational needs of such children are not being fully met;

(3) more than half of the handicapped children in the United States do not receive appropriate educational services which would enable them to have full equality of opportunity;

(4) one million of the handicapped children in the United States are excluded entirely from the public school system and will not go through the educational process with their peers;

(5) there are many handicapped children throughout the United States participating in regular school programs whose handicaps prevent them from having a successful educational experience because their handicaps are undetected. (Ballard, 1976, p. 114)

OLDER LEGISLATION FOR THE HANDICAPPED

P.L. 94-142 is not the first law concerning the handicapped. In fact, legislation regarding education for the handicapped dates back to 1827 when P.L. 19-8, concerning a grant to the "deaf and dumb asylum" of Kentucky, was passed (LaVor, 1976). P.L. 94-142 is actually an amendment to P.L. 91-230, which was enacted in 1970 to expand programs of assistance to elementary and secondary education. P.L. 91-230 was also amended in 1974 by P.L. 93-380, which required states to make goals and guidelines for providing educational services to handicapped children. Over the years there have been some 195 federal laws for the benefit of the handicapped. Not all of the laws are about education; some concern civil rights and other services (LaVor, 1976).

P.L. 94-142 itself is a comprehensive law that includes not only educational provisions but also the civil rights of privacy, informed consent, and due process.

IMPLEMENTATION OF THE LAW

Laws do not contain specific guidelines for implementation, and governmental agencies prepare rules and regulations. Soon after the passage of the law, BEH contracted with CEC to develop "tape-slide presentations for use in describing the significance and implementation of Public Law 94-142" (*Federal Register*, 1976, p. 56966). Five hundred copies of the packets were disseminated to state educational agencies and advocacy groups.

In the early part of 1976, BEH sent over 1,000 copies of the law to consumers and agencies interested in the handicapped. Meetings were held with interested people to gather information about implementation. In June of 1976, a national writing group of approximately 160 advocates, parents of handicapped persons, and nonprofessionals from across the United States analyzed the comments made at the public meetings and prepared position statements. From these statements, proposed rules were developed and published in the *Federal Register* (1976). Comments were again solicited—at ten regional meetings held in 1977, through national conferences, and from interested individuals. Over 600 written comments were received (Peterson, 1978). Many of these comments are included in the final rules and regulations (*Federal Register,* 1977).

CONTENT OF THE REGULATIONS

The regulations for P.L. 94-142 are written:

(1) To assure that all handicapped children have available to them a free appropriate public education;
(2) To assure that the rights of handicapped children and their parents are protected;
(3) To assist States and localities to provide for the education of handicapped children; and
(4) To assess and assure the effectiveness of efforts to educate such children. (*Federal Register,* 1977, p. 42474)

P.L. 94-142 requires that the state educational agency provide each child with an education and other related services, such as counseling, therapy, recreation, transportation, and medical evaluation, at "public expense and under supervision and direction, without charge" (*Federal Register,* 1977, p. 42478). (See Chapter 2.)

Parent Participation in Annual State Program Plan

Providing education is a state responsibility. In order to receive funds to assist in the programming for exceptional children, each state is required to submit an annual program plan to the U.S. Commissioner of Education. Each program plan must include information about how the state is serving handicapped children and how the state plans to enrich that service. It is required that parents be included in the development of this plan.

Each state educational agency is to establish a panel to advise the state educational system on the unmet needs of handicapped children, to "comment publicly on the State annual program plan" (*Federal Register,* 1977, p. 42501), and otherwise to assist the state commissioner of education. At least one member of that advisory panel must be a parent of a handicapped child.

In order to comply with the regulations of the law, the plan must show that parents of handicapped children were consulted during the preparation of the state plan for services to the handicapped. The state educational agency must show that other groups as well have had "an opportunity to participate fully in the development, review, and annual updating of the comprehensive system of personnel development" (*Federal Register,* 1977, p. 42492). In addition, the state must "provide for making the application and all documents related to the application available to parents and the general public" (*Federal Register,* 1977, p. 42487).

As part of the plan "to develop materials or disseminate information" (*Federal Register,* 1977, p. 42492), the state agency may enter into contracts with institutions of higher education and other organizations, including parent organizations, to carry out the training of personnel engaged in the education of handicapped children.

The Local Program Plan

The state program plan is in part a collection of the program plans of each of the areas of the state. Planning on the local level is similar to planning on the state level. The local district must develop a plan with documented assistance of the citizens in that area. An advisory panel to assist in the planning of services is to be formed, and the panel is to have at least one parent of a handicapped child as a member. Public hearings are to be held locally in connection with the plan for each area.

Monitoring for Compliance

The state educational plan and the implementation of that plan are monitored by the federal educational agency. The local program plan and implementation of that plan are monitored by the state educational agency. One of the things monitored is parent participation in the planning and in-service training process.

HOW THE PARENT SEES THE PROCESS

Federal regulations don't read with the continuity of a novel. In order to describe one regulation, it is necessary to know how that regulation is related to other regulations. The register is full of cross references that make it difficult to describe the due process without referring to other sections many times. Although it is important to know the interrelationships of the regulations, any individual parent measures the process only by "what happened to *me.*"

THE PROCESS

Benefits of Education with Other Children

All communication with the parent must be based on the assumption that the child has normal learning capacity. Even though the child may have obvious clinical symptoms of a handicapping condition that is associated with learning problems, the school is to assume that the child has normal learning capacity unless there is documented evidence of learning problems that the parent fully understands and recognizes.

Some parents may approach the school with an evaluation of the child's learning capacity already completed. This evaluation, or other evaluations that the parent has secured from independent agencies or from previous school agencies, "must be considered by the public agency in any decision made with respect to the provision of a free appropriate public education to the child" (*Federal Register,* 1977, p. 42494). Under certain conditions, an independent evaluation for the child could be at public expense. The public agency is required to provide to the parent "information about where an independent evaluation may be obtained" (*Federal Register,* 1977, p. 42494).

Even though there is documented evidence that the child has learning problems and the parent understands the child's problems, the law declares that the child should be educated in "the school which he or she would attend if not handicapped" (*Federal Register,* 1977, p. 42497), unless the plan for the child's education developed cooperatively with the parent indicates that another setting would be more appropriate. It is premature for the public agency to assume the child's need for services until the parent has been included in the total identification and planning process.

Informed Consent for Everything

Before the school can do any observation or evaluation of the child beyond the "basic tests administered to or procedures used with all children in a school, grade or class" (*Federal Register,* 1977, p. 42494), the proposed procedures must be explained to the parents, and the parents must approve. Consent must be obtained before a preplacement evaluation is conducted and before a handicapped child is placed in a program that provides special education or related services.

The notice requesting the parent's consent must be written, and the parent must be given a reasonable time to consider before the activity is requested. The notice must include:

(1) A full explanation of all of the procedural safeguards available to the parents;

(2) A description of the action proposed or refused by the agency, an explanation of why the agency proposes or refuses to take the action, and a description of any options the agency considered and the reasons why those options were rejected;

(3) A description of each evaluation procedure, test, record, or report the agency uses as a basis for the proposal or refusal; and

(4) A description of any other factors which are relevant to the agency's proposal or refusal.

(b) The notice must be:

(1) Written in language understandable to the general public, and

(2) Provided in the native language of the parent or other mode of communication used by the parent, unless it is clearly not feasible to do so.

(c) If the native language or other mode of communication of the parent is not a written language, the State or local educational agency shall take steps to insure:

(1) That the notice is translated orally or by other means to the parent in his or her native language or other mode of communication;

(2) That the parent understands the content of the notice, and

(3) That there is written evidence that the requirements in paragraph (c) (1) and (2) of this section have been met. (*Federal Register*, 1977, p. 42495)

The school must have written records showing that the parent was contacted, that the parent understood, and that the parent consented to the activity. The record must also show that "the granting of consent is voluntary on the part of the parent and may be revoked at any time" (*Federal Register*, 1977, p. 42494). (See Chapter 12 for examples of how this may be documented.)

Educational Records

Parent Access

It should be assumed that everything written about the child is written for the parent. Parents have the right at any time to read anything that has been written about their child by anyone. Parents are to be allowed to study and have copies of the child's records made at any time. They can also have someone study the child's records with or for them. The regulations read:

(a) Each participating agency shall permit parents to inspect and review any education records relating to their children which are collected, maintained, or used by the agency under this part. The agency shall comply with a request without unnecessary delay and before any meeting regarding an individualized education program or hearing relating to the identification, evaluation, or placement of the child, and in no case more than 45 days after the request has been made.

(b) The right to inspect and review education records under this section includes:

(1) The right to a response from the participating agency to reasonable requests for explanations and interpretations of the records;

(2) The right to request that the agency provide copies of the records containing the information if failure to provide those copies would effectively prevent the parent from exercising the right to inspect and review the records; and

(3) The right to have a representative of the parent inspect and review the records.

(c) An agency may presume that the parent has authority to inspect and review records relating to his or her child unless the agency has been advised that the parent does not have the authority under applicable State law governing such matters as guardianship, separation, and divorce. (*Federal Register,* 1977, p. 42498)

If the parent objects to something that is in the child's records or if the parent "believes that the information in the educational records collected, maintained, or used under this part is inaccurate or misleading or violates the privacy or any other rights of the child" (*Federal Register,* 1977, p. 42498), the parent may request that the records be amended. If the agency refuses to amend the records, the parent may request an impartial hearing officer to examine the information.

Confidentiality of Records

Any records that include the child's name, address, or personal characteristics are to be maintained in confidentiality and must not be disclosed to anyone except participating agencies without the parent's permission. A list of those who inspect the records is to be kept by the agency.

Individual Education Programs

The heart of the whole process is the concept that the child does not have to fit into the assembly line of education in order to receive an education. The assembly line of education puts the child on a slow-moving conveyor belt. As the child moves past, the kindergarten teacher puts on color recognition and counting; the first grade teacher adds letter sounds and simple addition. The second grade teacher adds sound blending and subtraction. The third grade teacher puts on sentence structure and multiplication, and the fourth grade teacher adds paragraphs and long division. The fifth grade teacher puts on fractions and outlining; the sixth grade teacher adds decimals and the use of the library. When the child has moved along the conveyor belt, the child has been given what a child "of that age" presumably needs.

It is not always possible to preplan what children will need or how long it will take them to learn a concept or skill. The concept embodied in P.L. 94-142 is that the child with learning problems should be allowed to move along the conveyor belt with other children and be given whatever fits his or her needs, no matter what the other children are getting.

In order to create this customized education, all the people who know the child must collaborate in designing an appropriate production plan and monitoring the production very carefully. This is called an Individual Education Program (IEP). The parents must be part of the collaboration, since they have known the child longer than anyone else. (See Chapter 4.)

Gathering the Information for the Individualized Program

Since parental consent must be secured for each test and procedure administered to the child, it is important that the interaction with the parent about the school findings, both formal and informal, be an ongoing process. (See Chapter 12.) Important information about the child's out-of-school development can be obtained by gathering a social and developmental history from the parent and by making a home observation. (See Chapter 7.) After all the information about the child's development has been gathered, the agency is ready to schedule a meeting or meetings for the development of the IEP. It is the responsibility of the agency to include the parents in the scheduling and interaction of the IEP meeting or meetings.

(a) Each public agency shall take steps to insure that one or both of the parents of the handicapped child are present at each meeting or are afforded the opportunity to participate, including:

(1) Notifying parents of the meeting early enough to insure that they will have an opportunity to attend; and

(2) Scheduling the meeting at a mutually agreed on time and place.

(b) The notice under paragraph (a) (1) of this section must indicate the purpose, time, and location of the meeting, and who will be in attendance.

(c) If neither parent can attend, the public agency shall use other methods to insure parent participation, including individual or conference telephone calls.

(d) A meeting may be conducted without a parent in attendance if the public agency is unable to convince the parents that they should attend. In this case the public agency must have a record of its attempts to arrange a mutually agreed on time and place such as:

(1) Detailed records of telephone calls made or attempted and the results of those calls.

(2) Copies of correspondence sent to the parents and any responses received, and

(3) Detailed records of visits made to the parent's home or place of employment and the results of those visits.

(e) The public agency shall take whatever action is necessary to insure that the parent understands the proceedings at a meeting, including arranging for an interpreter for parents who are deaf or whose native language is other than English.

(f) The public agency shall give the parent, on request, a copy of the individualized education program. (*Federal Register,* 1977, pp. 42490-42491)

In addition to the parents, the teacher, and a representative of the agency, anyone else that the parents wish to attend and the child, if it appears to be appropriate, are included in the IEP meeting. A meeting to create a plan must be held within 30 days after it has been determined that the child needs special education or related services. The plan must be reviewed at least once a year, more often if the parents request.

Although the plan can contain anything that the group decides is necessary, it must include:

(a) A statement of the child's present levels of educational performance;

(b) A statement of annual goals, including short term instructional objectives;

(c) A statement of the specific special education and related services to be provided to the child, and the extent to which the child will be able to participate in regular educational programs;

(d) The projected dates for initiation of services and the anticipated duration of the services; and

(e) Appropriate objective criteria and evaluation procedures and schedules for determining, on at least an annual basis, whether the short term instructional objectives are being achieved. (*Federal Register,* 1977, p. 42491)

Related Services to Children

If the exceptional child is to ride along the conveyor belt of education with the other children, it will be necessary for the child to have some help that is not traditionally given through the school system. These services might include audiology evaluation and training, counseling services, medical services, occupational therapy, physical therapy, psychological services, recreation and leisure training and services, social work services, speech pathology, adapted physical education, vocational education, and transportation to and around school. The IEP should also include any special arrangements necessary for the child to have access to nonacademic and extracurricular activities, such as meals, recess, and athletics. (See Chapter 2.)

Surrogates for Parents

For those exceptional children who do not have a parent, the law provides for the "recruitment and training of surrogate parents" (*Federal Register,* 1977, p. 42491). The state is required to discover the whereabouts of a parent, if possible. When a parent cannot be found or the child is a ward of the state, the "duty of a public agency . . . includes the assignment of an individual to act as a surrogate for the parents" (*Federal Register,* 1977, p. 42496).

Criteria for selection of the surrogate parent include that he or she:

(i) Has no interests that conflict with the interests of the child he or she represents; and
(ii) Has knowledge and skills that insure adequate representation of the child. . . . A person assigned as a surrogate may not be an employee of a public agency which is involved in the education or care of the child. (*Federal Register,* 1977, p. 42496)

The public agency treats the surrogate parent in the same way that it treats the natural parents since one of the responsibilities of the agency is to provide training for those individuals who are selected as surrogate parents.

IF THE PARENTS ARE DISSATISFIED

If the parents don't understand the explanation, consider the explanation incomplete or inadequate, believe that they have not been notified of all that is happening to the child, or are dissatisfied with the implementation of the plan and no one in the agency seems willing or able to help with the problem, the parents can request a hearing.

If a hearing is requested, the public agency must hold a hearing within 45 days. The "oral arguments" must be conducted at a time and place which is reasonably convenient to the parents and the child involved" (*Federal Register,* 1977, p. 42496). Regulations for the conduct of a hearing include:

> (b) The hearing must be conducted by the State educational agency or the public agency directly responsible for the education of the child, as determined under State statute, State regulation, or a written policy of the State educational agency.
> (c) The public agency shall inform the parent of any free or low-cost legal and other relevant services available in the area if:
> (1) The parent requests the information; or
> (2) The parent or the agency initiates a hearing under this section. (*Federal Register,* 1977, p. 42495)

The officer selected for the hearing must be a qualified person who has no personal or professional interest in the child or the school and who has received training to be a hearing officer.

At a hearing the parents have the right to:

> (1) Be accompanied and advised by counsel and by individuals with special knowledge or training with respect to the problems of handicapped children;
> (2) Present evidence and confront, cross-examine, and compel the attendance of witnesses;
> (3) Prohibit the introduction of any evidence at the hearing that has not been disclosed to that party at least five days before the hearing;
> (4) Obtain a written or electronic verbatim record of the hearing;
> (5) Obtain written findings of fact and decisions. (The public agency shall transmit those findings and decisions, after deleting any personally identifiable information, to the State advisory panel. . . .
> (b) Parents involved in hearings must be given the right to:
> (1) Have the child who is the subject of the hearing present; and
> (2) Open the hearing to the public. (*Federal Register,* 1977, p. 42495)

Material presented at the hearing by the public agency includes documentation of the consent procedures, evaluations, and the reasons for the decision on the IEP.

The parents must be given a written decision. If they are dissatisfied with the hearing officer's decision, they have the right to appeal and have it reviewed. A copy of the appeal decision is to be sent to the parents. If the parents are dissatisfied with the decision of the hearing appeal, they have the right to bring a civil action in court.

IF THE PARENTS DON'T CONSENT

It is possible to design a program for the child even if the parents refuse to consent, but the first step is to provide the proof of contact. Although the hearing may be difficult, it can be a means of documenting parent contact and information exchange. The public agency must provide written proof that the parents were contacted, that the procedures were explained, and that the parents understood the explanation.

If all the parent contacts have been made according to proper procedures, the public agency may request a hearing to resolve conflicts about funding, placement, and content of the IEP. In each case, the agency cannot be granted a hearing unless the professional responsibility of providing information to the parent has been fulfilled.

A hearing may also be held to determine if material in the child's record that a parent requests be amended must actually be amended.

PRETEND THERE MIGHT BE A HEARING

It was never intended that a due process hearing would enhance the child's educational program or facilitate communication between schools and families. But knowing what happens at a hearing might. The hearing is a public display of whether the professional responsibility of the school has in fact been carried out. The process of prior notice and consent are part of a package the school must accept.

In order to implement the communication responsibility, professionals must understand both the responsibility and the parent. The best way to avoid a due process hearing is to think of each decision to be made about the child's education as the parent's decision and to think of each discussion with the parent as being recorded at a hearing and monitored by a hearing officer. Only then is there assurance that the quiet spring evenings will not be interrupted by the loud discord of a hearing.

REFERENCES

Ballard, J. Education for All Handicapped Children Act of 1975. In F.J. Weintraub, A. Abeson, J. Ballard, & M.L. LaVor (Eds.), *Public policy and the education of exceptional children.* Reston, Va.: Council for Exceptional Children, 1976.

Demars, E.T. (Ed.). *School organization and administration for Utah teachers.* Salt Lake City, Utah: University of Utah, 1964.

Federal Register. Vol. 41, No. 252. Dec. 30, 1976.

Federal Register. Vol. 42, No. 163. Aug. 23, 1977.

Gilhool, T.K. Education: An inalienable right. In F.J. Weintraub, A. Abeson, J. Ballard, & M.L. LaVor, (Eds.), *Public policy and the education of exceptional children.* Reston, Va.: Council for Exceptional Children, 1976.

Goldberg, M.B., Thornburg, T.K., Weatherman, R.F., & Permuth, S. *Insuring the rights of handicapped children in school. A compliance procedures manual.* University of Minnesota College of Education, 1977.

LaVor, M.L. Federal legislation for exceptional persons: A history. In F.J. Weintraub, A. Abeson, J. Ballard, & M.L. LaVor (Eds.), *Public policy and the education of exceptional children.* Reston, Va.: Council for Exceptional Children, 1976.

Lichter, P. Communicating with parents: It begins with listening. *Teaching Exceptional Children,* 1976, *8* (2), 67-71.

Peterson, W. Personal communication, Aug. 7, 1978.

Weintraub, F.J. Personal communication, Aug. 3, 1978.

Weintraub, F.J., & Abeson, A. New educational policies for the handicapped: The quiet revolution. In F.J. Weintraub, A. Abeson, J. Ballard, & M.L. LaVor, (Eds.), *Public policy and the education of exceptional children.* Reston, Va.: Council for Exceptional Children, 1976.

Chapter 2

Translating Public Law 94-142 into Educational Action

APPLYING THE GESTALT

The educational ideas, concepts, and theories embedded in the regulations of Public Law (P.L.) 94-142 are magnificent, comprehensive, and abstract. In order for the ideas, concepts and theories to have meaning, however, they must be applied to the day-to-day, hour-to-hour school life of each child. If the personnel of the public agency are to be able to interpret the concepts to the parents, these concepts must be applied not only to the individual child's program, but also to the total fabric of the educational system, the state plan, and the local plan. But to each parent the only really important application is to the school life of his or her child.

THE REFERRAL PROCESS IS THE DUE PROCESS

In essence, the due process hearing is a determination of whether the process of identification, educational planning and placement of the child into an alternate school program has followed a careful procedure of back and forth communication with the parent, i.e., notification of the proposed action and written consent for the action for each step. Each school agency will have its own forms and procedures for getting them and filling them out. (See Chapter 12.) The filling out of the forms, however, is not the referral process. The process is the careful, sensitive contact with the parents (Figure 2-1).

Who Initiates the Referral?

The Parent Refers

The process of identifying a child for special educational services can be begun by the parent. The parent may request that the child be given special educational services because the child has been evaluated by medical personnel or because the

19

Figure 2-1 The Referral Process

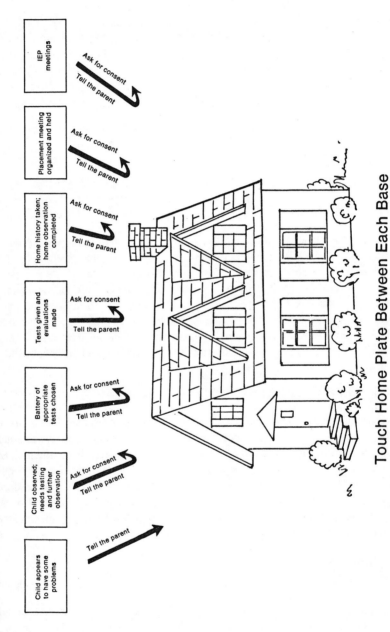

Child appears to have some problems

Tell the parent

Child observed; needs testing and further observation

Ask for consent
Tell the parent

Battery of appropriate tests chosen

Ask for consent
Tell the parent

Tests given and evaluations made

Ask for consent
Tell the parent

Home history taken; home observation completed

Ask for consent
Tell the parent

Placement meeting organized and held

Ask for consent
Tell the parent

IEP meetings

Ask for consent
Tell the parent

Touch Home Plate Between Each Base

child has a congenital defect or an early childhood condition that usually requires additional services. The parent may approach the school with the records of previous evaluations and requests that the child receive special services since the child has problems. The parent may request that the school "do something" for the child since the parent has been experiencing difficulty in the home training of the child. Whatever evaluation that the parent brings to the school is to be used in the planning for the child. Since many parents have asked for help and been refused (see Chapter 4) it may be difficult for parents to refer the child even though they are very much aware of the child's learning problems.

Screening To Find Children

Included in the regulations is a requirement that the public agency search for children who may be in need of special services and may not be receiving them. The children may be in the regular school system or so young that they do not yet attend school. A child may be identified as needing further evaluation studies through a generalized screening program. Although it may seem that permission for further evaluation is implied, it is important that anything discovered in the screening process be discussed personally with the parent so that the parent understands the process well enough to give informed consent for further evaluations. Parent contacts to explain the testing materials and the results of the screening must be documented.

The Teacher Refers

If the child is not having severe problems, the parents may not even notice that the child is not "keeping up" with the academic and social learning of other children of the same age. The child may be experiencing difficulties with the abstract symbol system of the school, but not the concrete routine of out-of-school activities. It may be necessary for the teacher to convince the parents that the child is indeed having difficulty with the school's world of symbols. In many cases, this may be very difficult, since the parents themselves may not be comfortable with the symbol systems. The school agency then has the double responsibility of recognizing the child's difficulty and explaining that problem and the fact that the problem needs special attention to parents who may be trying to deemphasize the problem in order to feel good enough about themselves to continue to face the routines of daily life. (See Chapter 4.) By seeking an opportunity to discuss the child's inadequacies with the parent, the school may appear to be forcing the parent to open the closet and expose the skeleton. (See Chapter 4.) The intent of the referral system is not to see that the forms are filled out, but to see that the parent is told about the child's needs in a sensitive manner (see Chapter 9) and in language understandable to the general public (see Chapter 11).

Explaining the Need for Evaluation

The referral must include a firm, definite explanation of the problems that the child has been experiencing and the methods and procedures that have been used to help the child. Specific anecdotes on the child's behavior, including dates, are part of the information that is to be included in the referral statement. Indicating that Johnny was not able to "do the work" is not a sufficient referral statement. The description of the problem must be more exact and more complete. For the documentation of parent contact it is also important that the referral statement include the interaction with the parent during the time that the decision for a referral was being made. For example, a referral statement regarding a fourth grade student who is having difficulty with math might be:

9/20: Johnny was not able to do the multiplication problems in today's assignment. He has not been able to complete any of the math assignments since school began. I realized that he did not understand the rationale for multiplication so I spent some time with him showing him that multiplication means groups of groups. He did not seem to understand the explanation. I talked with Johnny's mother, Mrs. Smith, about Johnny's work, and she said that she had noticed that Johnny has had trouble with math.

9/30: I have been explaining the concept of groups of groups to Johnny for several weeks. He appears to need material that is easier. I talked to Mrs. Smith about it and told her that I would borrow a second grade workbook and try Johnny in that book.

10/5: I have been working with Johnny on two place addition in the second grade workbook. He smiles and writes the answers when I work them out with him, but he cannot do them alone. I contacted Mrs. Smith about Johnny's work, and she was pleased that I had tried the second grade workbook and asked me to try the first grade workbook.

10/10: I borrowed the first grade workbook and have been trying to show Johnny how to add single figures. He can do it only when he has popsicle sticks to count and I am there to verify the accuracy of the count. I explained this to Johnny's mother and indicated that maybe he needs more help than I am able to give him.

10/15: Johnny appears not to understand one to one correspondence and perhaps needs to work with concrete objects to learn that concept. It is difficult for me to provide in the fourth grade classroom the tutoring that Johnny seems to need to understand math. I talked to Mrs. Smith about having Johnny evaluated to see if he would be eligible for additional help. She indicated that she would like to have this done.

The interaction required in the process of referral is not a one time signature of forms, but a repeated, open-ended discussion in which the parent feels free to ask questions and express concerns. (See Chapter 7.)

INTERACTION AND CONSENT

Continual interaction with the parent is important, because parental consent must be obtained for even the preevaluation observation. There is both a practical and legal reason for this contact. If the parent has been part of the identification process, it is much easier for the parent to accept the need for a more formal observation of the child: the evaluation. If the parent feels that he or she has been part of the search for help, there will be less shock and disappointment when the help is classified as "special education." (See Chapter 3.) In order to comply with the due process of the referral process it is important that the parent be fully informed during each development of the process. The concept of consent is discussed more thoroughly in Chapter 12, which discusses compliance.

EVALUATION: WHERE IT ALL BEGINS AND ENDS

Identification of the child as handicapped implies that the child has been compared to other children and found to be lacking in certain skills and abilities. For the parent, the evaluation of the child's abilities is an evaluation of the parent's worth as a person. Parents are highly concerned about the testing situation and whether the child has had an opportunity to do his or her best. Parents of children who do not speak standard English are likely to be even more concerned.

(a) Tests and other evaluation materials:
(1) Are provided and administered in the child's native language or other mode of communication, unless it is clearly not feasible to do so. . . . (*Federal Register*, 1977, p. 42496)

Although parents are not as interested in the qualifications of the person who tests their child as the expertise and experience of that person, the agency is required to be certain that the individual is qualified by having passed certification requirements.

The test selection criteria includes the suitability of the test for the skills to be measured. Regulations for testing include that the tests:

(2) Have been validated for the specific purpose for which they are used; and

(3) Are administered by trained personnel in conformance with the instructions provided by their producer;

(b) Tests and other evaluation materials include those tailored to assess specific areas of educational need and not merely those which are designed to provide a single general intelligence quotient;

(c) Tests are selected and administered so as best to ensure that when a test is administered to a child with impaired sensory, manual, or speaking skills, the test results accurately reflect the child's aptitude or achievement level or whatever other factors the test purports to measure, rather than reflecting the child's impaired sensory, manual, or speaking skills (except where those skills are the factors which the test purports to measure);

(d) No single procedure is used as the sole criterion for determining an appropriate educational program for a child; and

(e) The evaluation is made by a multidisciplinary team or group of persons, including at least one teacher or other specialist with knowledge in the area of suspected disability.

(f) The child is assessed in all areas related to the suspected disability, including, where appropriate, health, vision, hearing, social and emotional status, general intelligence, academic performance, communicative status, and motor abilities. (*Federal Register,* 1977, pp. 42496-42497)

Although most parents are not familiar with all types of tests given to children, they are aware of the intelligence quotient (IQ) test and will be dreading to hear the "bad news." (See Chapter 8.)

Independent Evaluations and Reevaluation

The regulations require that the public agency inform the parents where an independent evaluation can be obtained, and making parents aware of other sources for evaluation is a good practice. Even if the parents choose not to have another evaluation, it will make them feel that the public agency has faith in their own evaluation procedures and conclusions if the agency tells them where a second opinion can be obtained.

Telling the parents that the child will be evaluated again later to determine how the child has changed will also be a comforting thought to the parents. The intensity and total impact of the child's handicapping condition is difficult for parents to see at one time. It is necessary for the parents to feel that the child or the situation may improve if they are to continue to provide the intense parenting that most handicapped children need. (See Chapter 5.) The regulations require that the agency will reevaluate the child every three years, or more often if the parents or the teacher requests. Knowing this may help the parents accept the results of the current evaluation.

Placement Can Only Follow Evaluation

The child can be placed in a special education setting only after a careful evaluation that includes not only formal testing, but also informal evaluation, developmental/social history, and other information from the parents. (See Chapter 7.) The data gathered from the parents can help the school gain a more thorough understanding of the child, and participating in the process of data gathering helps the parents to become more satisfied with the school program. See Chapter 10 for suggestions on how to conduct formal and informal interaction with the parents.

CONFIDENTIALITY OF INFORMATION: A MEANINGFUL TRUST

Access Rights Protected

In 1974, the Family Educational Rights and Privacy Act made it necessary for the public system to open all children's educational records to their parents. This requirement includes the opening of the records of children who are suspected of being handicapped as well as students who are progressing comfortably through the school system. The educational record of a child who is successful in school usually contains a brief summary of the work accomplished each year and the scores of standardized tests given at various age levels. The file is likely to be slim, easy to understand, and very similar to the information that the parent has been given during the "your child is doing fine" conferences.

Since these parents are not particularly interested in the paper documentation of the child's success, there are likely to be few requests to examine records by parents of children who are doing well in school. Parents of children who are not doing well in the school system will be fearful of what has been written in the school's records concerning the child. (See Chapter 8.)

Making the Records Understandable

Parents are likely to disagree with any report about the child that they do not understand or any report about the child that is written in the shorthand of educational or psychological terminology. Knowing that at some point everything in the child's educational records may be read by the parent implies a simple solution. Everything in the child's record should be written as if it were written to the parent. This means that the reports and observations are written in language understandable to the general public rather than in the professional jargon that must later be translated to the parent.

Making It Unnecessary To Ask for Access or Amendment

A simple, practical way of ensuring that the parent will not request that the records be opened for examination or that some of the information in the folder be removed or amended is to make a practice of never putting anything into the child's record without showing and explaining it to the parent.

Each document could have written on it the date on which the information was explained to the parent and a summary of the parent's comment or concerns. The names of the agency and the individual who talked to the parent could also be included. Both the parent and the public agency staff member could sign the paper. In order to make the process an even simpler one, the agency could have a rubber stamp prepared with spaces for the information, similar to the stamp that some businesses use to record information on the back of a check (Exhibit 2-1). If the parent questioned the information later, it would be easy to trace the information and see exactly what he or she had been concerned about at that time.

Confidentiality Protected

Especially if the degree of the child's handicap is severe, the child's difficulties invade almost every facet of the family's daily life. It is important to the family that the details of the child's difficulties are known only to those people who have some right to know. The only persons who have the right to know about the child's problems are those professionals asked by the parent to work with the child privately and those formally assigned to work with the child in the public educational system.

Exhibit 2-1   Information for Stamp on Child's Records

Written by _____
Date written _____
Date discussed _____
Signature of those present

_____
_____

Parent comments _____

_____
Parent signature

Many professionals need to talk with each other about the intensity of their day-to-day work with children. Although this might contribute to the mental health of the professionals, it is not fair for children to have their difficulties and inadequacies discussed and rediscussed with individuals who have no professional responsibility toward the children. If the teacher, psychologist, administrator, or other professional needs to discuss a child's needs with someone else, it is important that the first "someone else" be the child's parent. The parent can then give permission (consent) for other professionals to observe the child rather than just receive a summary of an evaluation by a "stranger."

If the parent has agreed to have other professionals look at the records and offer educational suggestions, then the record of who did, in fact, look at the records will not be a source of contention. Teachers in training have for some time had open access to the child's records. Although it may be important for them to have the information that is in the records, it should only be given to them with the full knowledge and consent of the parents.

WRITING AN INDIVIDUAL EDUCATION PROGRAM

Setting Priorities for Goals

Learning the one-two-three process of writing behavioral objectives is simple. Three questions must be answered: (1) what behavior do you want the child to learn? (2) under what circumstances should the child do the activity? and (3) how should the activity be measured? The process has been simplified by lists of ready-made goals (Fairfax, 1979). The difficult part of goal writing for exceptional children is not the writing of the goal but choosing the most appropriate goal.

Handicapped children need everything that nonhandicapped children need— and more. Yet, because of their learning or behavioral problems, they will probably learn less. Knowing enough about the child and the child's learning or behavioral problems, as well as the family and the family's life style, to choose what the child needs most takes much more than a one-two-three process. Without honest, comfortable parental input the educators are likely to take the easy way out and write the goals about some traditional rote skills of the regular classroom. Although they may be easy to teach and measure, the child will probably not have the prerequisite understanding of the concept or the ability to transfer the learning to daily life activity.

The law emphasizes the legal right of the handicapped child to attend school with the nonhandicapped child. Perhaps the most vital reason for this is so that the handicapped child can learn to be with other children and be part of the give and take of childhood interaction. Goals that include student-to-student interaction may produce more valuable life skills than the memorization of the multiplication tables; learning to handle the self-care routines and social interaction can be of more value to the child than learning word attack skills (Michaelis, 1979a; Michaelis, 1979b).

Children who have known emotional problems need goals that relate to the development of skills that will remedy or alleviate their problem. Children who have known learning disabilities need goals that help them learn how to organize themselves more than they need the rote facts of the conveyor belt education. (See Chapter 1.)

There is a temptation for school officials to identify the problem, evaluate it, place the child in a special setting, and then continue to teach the regular curriculum. There is considerable evidence that the regular curriculum may not be appropriate for the child with developmental learning problems, even when it is watered down and analyzed into small pieces (Brolin & Kokaska, 1979).

When an Individual Education Program (IEP) for a child is written, it is important that the parents participate fully in setting goals and prioritizing them for the child. It is the surest method of writing a program that will continue to be acceptable to the parents.

Planning, Not Merely Approving, the IEP

Parents must be consulted about when the planning meeting will take place so that they have time to arrange to be away from work and for someone to care for the child, unless they wish to bring the child to the meeting. The parents also have the option of bringing anyone else to the meeting that they wish. Some parents may want to bring an educator or a psychologist; other parents may want to bring an attorney or a nurse. Some parents may want to bring a grandmother or grandfather; others may simply bring a friend.

Although there may be more questions to answer during the planning sessions if there are more people present, it is to the advantage of the public agency to have the parents ask about the things they are thinking. If the questions are not asked in the meeting, they will be asked later when the school is locked and there is no one to answer. Dissatisfied parents talking about their dissatisfaction to one another can create more dissatisfaction. (Chapter 10 contains checklists, and Chapter 12 contains summary sheets to facilitate interaction in the IEP process.)

RELATED SERVICES

The heart of the IEP planning process is to determine what services would help the child to be successful in the school setting. Planning and choosing those services is the purpose of the IEP planning meeting. One of the reasons that an administrator is to attend the IEP meeting is that the administrator is responsible for seeing that the related services needed for a child are delivered to the child. Although it may be that the school will not actually perform the medical, social, or other services to the child, the administrator is responsible for the coordination and scheduling to make sure that the child does, indeed, get the services and that the services are at no cost to the parent. (See Chapter 1.)

Social and medical services are usually available at no cost to parents with low incomes. Middle income parents are sometimes excluded from welfare clinics, however. If the child needs the service and there is no other no cost service available, it may be necessary for the school administrators to assist in the bending or changing of the rules for clinics funded with public monies.

The careful selection and possible methods of delivering related services are the prime reasons for the careful evaluation of the child and the group input during the IEP planning meetings. For any one child, the need for related services may vary from a ride to the special school to intensive physical therapy. Any experience that is not traditional teaching is considered a related service. Related services that are suggested for handicapped children are:

(1) "Audiology" includes:

(i) Identification of children with hearing loss;

(ii) Determination of the range, nature, and degree of hearing loss, including referral for medical or other professional attention for the habilitation of hearing;

(iii) Provision of habilitative activities, such as language habilitation, auditory training, speech reading (lip-reading), hearing evaluation, and speech conservation;

(iv) Creation and administration of programs for prevention of hearing loss;

(v) Counseling and guidance of pupils, parents, and teachers regarding hearing loss; and

(vi) Determination of the child's need for group and individual amplification, selecting and fitting an appropriate aid, and evaluating the effectiveness of amplification.

(2) "Counseling services" means services provided by qualified social workers, psychologists, guidance counselors, or other qualified personnel.

(3) "Early identification" means the implementation of a formal plan for identifying a disability as early as possible in a child's life.

(4) "Medical services" means services provided by a licensed physician to determine a child's medically related handicapping condition which results in the child's need for special education and related services.

(5) "Occupational therapy" includes:

(i) Improving, developing or restoring functions impaired or lost through illness, injury, or deprivation;

(ii) Improving ability to perform tasks for independent functioning when functions are impaired or lost; and

(iii) Preventing, through early intervention, initial or further impairment or loss of function.

(6) "Parent counseling and training" means assisting parents in understanding the special needs of their child and providing parents with information about child development.

(7) "Physical therapy" means services provided by a qualified physical therapist.

(8) "Psychological services" include:

(i) Administering psychological and educational tests, and other assessment procedures;

(ii) Interpreting assessment results;

(iii) Obtaining, integrating, and interpreting information about child behavior and conditions relating to learning.

(iv) Consulting with other staff members in planning school programs to meet the special needs of children as indicated by psychological tests, interviews, and behavioral evaluations; and

(v) Planning and managing a program of psychological services, including psychological counseling for children and parents.

(9) "Recreation" includes:

(i) Assessment of leisure function;

(ii) Therapeutic recreation services;

(iii) Recreation programs in schools and community agencies; and

(iv) Leisure education.

(10) "School health services" means services provided by a qualified school nurse or other qualified person.

(11) "Social work services in schools" include:

(i) Preparing a social or developmental history on a handicapped child;

(ii) Group and individual counseling with the child and family;

(iii) Working with those problems in a child's living situation (home, school, and community) that affect the child's adjustment in school; and

(iv) Mobilizing school and community resources to enable the child to receive maximum benefit from his or her educational program.

(12) "Speech pathology" includes:

(i) Identification of children with speech or language disorders;

(ii) Diagnosis and appraisal of specific speech or language disorders;

(iii) Referral for medical or other professional attention necessary for the habilitation of speech or language disorders;

(iv) Provisions of speech and language services for the habilitation or prevention of communicative disorders; and

(v) Counseling and guidance of parents, children, and teachers regarding speech and language disorders.

(13) "Transportation" includes:

(i) Travel to and from school and between schools,

(ii) Travel in and around school buildings, and

(iii) Specialized equipment (such as special or adapted buses, lifts, and ramps), if required to provide special transportation for a handicapped child.

(20 U.S.C. 1401(17).)

Comment. With respect to related services, the Senate Report states:

The Committee bill provides a definition of "related services," making clear that all such related services may not be required for each individual child and that such term includes early identification and assessment of handicapping conditions and the provision of services to minimize the effects of such conditions.

(Senate Report No. 94-168, p. 12 (1975).)

The list of related services is not exhaustive and may include other developmental, corrective, or supportive services (such as artistic and cultural programs, and art, music, and dance therapy), if they are required to assist a handicapped child to benefit from special education.

There are certain kinds of services which might be provided by persons from varying professional backgrounds and with a variety of operational titles, depending upon requirements in individual States. For example, counseling services might be provided by social workers, psychologists, or guidance counselors, and psychological testing might be done by qualified psychological examiners, psychometrists, or psychologists, depending upon State standards.

Each related service defined under this part may include appropriate administrative and supervisory activities that are necessary for program planning, management, and evaluation. (*Federal Register,* 1977, pp. 42479 and 42480)

Services in Short Supply

In addition to an insufficient number of trained teachers, many areas have a scarcity of several types of related services. Transportation and therapy are in short supply in many places, for example.

Transportation Services

The additional transportation needs of handicapped children are frequently difficult to meet. Since the children are scattered throughout the school district, bus routes may be complicated, and the child may be required to ride the bus for unusually long periods of time. Children in some centers are on the bus longer than they are in the classroom. Some state and local regulations prohibit busing arrangements that require the child to be on the bus for long periods. In order to use the child's educational time more wisely and the school's transportation budget more efficiently, more localized services may be necessary. This would be in line with the requirement that the child be educated in the school he or she would attend if not handicapped. If planning is done carefully, some handicapped children can be absorbed into other programs and long, complicated busing will not be necessary.

Therapy Services

Since educational systems have not until recently dealt with the physical needs of the students, there are not enough physical and occupational therapists to provide the therapy services that are needed by many children. Some school districts have purchased services from centers already operated by United Cerebral Palsy and Easter Seal Society. Others have provided some service with the use of a consultant. If the school is unable to provide the service properly, it is important to tell the parent and enlist the parent's help in securing the professional expertise required to implement the service. The parent may know someone who knows someone. . . . If parents share the knowledge of the problem, it is not only possible that they might help, but also it is less likely that they will become critical. The message must be sent in a straightforward, accepting manner with the genuine desire for whatever ideas the parents may have. (See Chapter 7.)

Related Services for Parents

The school is responsible for the child only for a few hours each day on weekdays. It is highly important that the child's developmental needs be met during other times, since the child's work in school is somewhat dependent on the continuity of the life experience. The law provides for counseling and training experiences to be delivered to the parents in order to facilitate better school adjustment for the child.

MAINSTREAMING AND THE LEAST RESTRICTIVE ENVIRONMENT

Mainstreaming, perhaps the hottest word associated with P.L. 94-142, isn't really in the law. What is written in the regulations is "least restrictive environment," and "the child is educated in the school he or she would attend if not handicapped" (*Federal Register,* 1977, p. 42497) and that "each handicapped child participates with nonhandicapped children . . . to the maximum extent appropriate to the needs of that child" (*Federal Register,* 1977, p. 42497).

> (b) Each public agency shall insure:
> (1) That to the maximum extent appropriate, handicapped children, including children in public or private institutions or other care facilities, are educated with children who are not handicapped, and
> (2) That special classes, separate schooling or other removal of handicapped children from the regular educational environment occurs only when the nature or severity of the handicap is such that education in regular classes with the use of supplementary aids and services cannot be achieved satisfactorily. . . .
> In providing or arranging for the provision of nonacademic and extracurricular services and activities, including meals, recess periods, and the [other] services and activities. . . , each public agency shall insure that each handicapped child participates with nonhandicapped children in those services and activities to the maximum extent appropriate to the needs of that child. (*Federal Register,* 1977, p. 42497)

Convincing the Parent To Use the Least Restrictive Setting

The concept of nonhandicapped children and handicapped children attending school together may not be palatable to many parents of handicapped children. Mothers, especially, are accustomed to providing the extra care that an exceptional child needs and frequently believe that the child needs a more protected environment than others think the child needs. (See Chapter 5.) Fathers, on the other hand, may want the child in the regular programming, even when the child can not be successful with the regular tasks. (See Chapter 5.)

Continuum of Placements

The law requires that there be alternate placement situations for handicapped children.

> (a) Each public agency shall insure that a continuum of alternative placements is available to meet the needs of handicapped children for special education and related services.

(b) The continuum required under paragraph (a) of this section must:

(1) Include the alternative placements listed in the definition of special education. . . (instruction in regular classes, special classes, special schools, home instruction, and instruction in hospitals and institutions), and

(2) Make provision for supplementary services (such as resource room or itinerant instruction) to be provided in conjunction with regular class placement. (*Federal Register,* 1977, p. 42497)

Although the "continuum of placement" options may have similar labels, the regulations and practices may vary in different schools. In some schools, a resource teacher takes the handicapped children half of the day; in other localities, the resource teacher helps the regular teacher and doesn't remove the students from the regular class. In some regions the resource teacher operates a room full of teaching equipment; in other areas, the resource teacher works with the leftover ditto carbons.

In order to meet any specific child's needs it is important that the stereotypic "models" are looked at as just models. The ideal for any child is a tailor-made schedule and routine. It may be that the least restrictive place for Johnny to have math is with the second graders in Miss Smith's room, the least restrictive place for social studies is in the fifth grade room with Mr. Brown, and the least restrictive lunchroom setting may be in the classroom with the special teacher.

Although the model may specify a certain number of hours, the amount of time that the handicapped child can be with nonhandicapped children will vary considerably according to the activity, according to the child's immediate emotional/mental state, and according to the skills and wishes of the child's teachers and parents. It is important to talk about all the variables for each child with each teacher and all others involved. There should also be a way to report the immediate circumstances to the parent immediately. (See Chapter 8.) With the promise of close monitoring, teachers and parents will be more confident and willing to try new arrangements.

Administrators, too, must be creative and cooperative. It may be that a child needs to spend part of the day in a self-contained program and part of the day at the regular high school, at the technical high school, or even on a job placement. Arranging details of programming in more than one building and under more than one administration takes more sophisticated cooperation, but it allows for a broader program without dual budgets.

Creating an individualized program that translates P.L. 94-142 into educational action for each child requires the creativity of a composer and the tact of a diplomat.

REFERENCES

Brolin, D.E., & Kokaska, C.J. *Career education for handicapped children and youth*. Columbus, Ohio: Charles E. Merrill Publishers, 1979.

Fairfax County Public Schools. *IEP Manual*. Fairfax, Va: 1979.

Federal Register. Vol. 42, No. 163, Aug. 23, 1977.

Michaelis, C.T. *Self help skills: Adaptive behavior, melodies to teach personal care routines*. Long Branch, N.J.: Kimbo Educational, 1979. (a)

Michaelis, C.T. *Socialization: Adaptive behavior, melodies to assist social interaction*. Long Branch, N.J.: Kimbo Educational, 1979. (b)

Chapter 3

Discussing More Than Grades: The Whole Child and Family

MORE THAN A REPORT CARD

The back and forth communication with the parent required by Public Law (P.L.) 94-142 is more comprehensive than a carefully marked report card sent home four times a year and returned the next day with a parent's signature on the back. The communication required for consent is dynamic; it must flow with the parent's moment-to-moment concerns. Since the teacher no longer stands in loco parentis, it is necessary to communicate frequently with parents and determine how they feel about the little as well as the big things that occur at school.

KNOWING THE PARENT

The idea that teachers should get to know parents is not new. Teachers used to know the parents of their students personally. Gordon and Breivogel (1976) mention the old time schoolmarm, now seen only on TV, who was brought to town by the citizens of the community—the parents, to teach the children. As the schoolmarm lived in their home, there was plenty of time for the parents and the teacher to get to know each other. There was time for the schoolmarm to show the family how to do the homework, and there was time for the parents to show the teacher how they wanted the child to behave.

One schoolmarm, working in northern Utah in the late 1920s, remembers eating cookies that tasted of kerosene each time she stayed in a certain home one winter. Kerosene had spilled on a 100-pound sack of sugar the family was bringing to the isolated farm. Not only were goods scarce, but also there was no money to replace the sugar. "Eat and be thankful you have something to eat!" the father said in a commanding voice; the young teacher ate (Tingey, 1960)! After learning to know the family (especially the father) that well, it is unlikely that the young teacher would dare make a decision without discussing it thoroughly with the parents.

Young, unmarried schoolteachers no longer live in the homes of their students. Consolidation of school districts, mobility of families, specialization of training for educators, and the acceptance of married women as teachers have caused the scene to change (Gordon & Breivogel, 1976). Teachers have finished at least a four-year undergraduate program. Even many beginning teachers have a master's degree. Teachers are no longer young and dependent, and teachers and parents seldom see each other except in formal situations.

Parents are not always pleased with a teacher that they seldom see and policies that they do not help make. Not only in the field of education for the handicapped, but also in regular education, there is a move by parents for more input in the planning for the schools: what budgets contain, how curriculum decisions are made, how bus routes are determined, and which schools are closed (The American Education—Legal Defense Fund, 1976; Schimmel & Fisher, 1977).

PARENTS ARE SPEAKING UP

The National Committee for Citizens in Education was organized to help parents find ways to be heard within their own communities. The committee's toll-free information number receives calls each day from parents across the United States who want information on how to have an impact on the planning in their schools. Policies and procedures for the schools are the responsibility of the community (the parents), not the professional educator, and parents are learning how they can be more effective in making their wishes known.

Contact with Parents

A parent does not measure the school system by the impressive grouping of buildings and lists of degrees of the teachers and administrators but by how well the school helps the child with what the parent thinks the child needs. To a large extent, the parent feels that the child's needs are being met if someone at the school listens and responds when the parent wants to talk about the child's needs. (See Chapter 7.) The kind of contact that the parent needs in order to feel heard and understood is something far more involved than brief conversations in the classroom or a piece of paper that is sent home four times a year. (See Chapter 8.) Gallagher and Gallagher (1978), in describing the needs of parents of handicapped children, indicated that a "one-shot session" does not help the parents deal with "the adjustments that have to be made" and that the adjustments "come only gradually with experience" (p. 208).

Some projects designed for working with handicapped children have regular contact with the parents as a built-in feature. The Marshalltown project is one of these programs. The families of young handicapped children are visited weekly by a home teacher who works with the child in the home. Mother and teacher might sit on the floor with the child and see how the child holds a toy, moves, or talks. Sitting there on the living room floor together, it is easy for the teacher to establish rapport with the parent. They can discuss things that the child might be ready to learn and what the parent can do to help the child during the week. The parent may talk to the home teacher not only about the handicapped child, but also about other concerns involving the family. The home teacher from time to time can assist the family in getting services that the family might need from other agencies (Marshalltown, 1973).

After having discussed the child's needs while sitting on the living room floor together, the parent and the teacher are unlikely ever to meet on opposite sides of a due process hearing. It is much easier just to wait until the next week and talk about it together. Documentation for informed consent and Individual Education Programs (IEPs) can probably be obtained by having the parent sign forms during one of the home teacher's visits. There is generally no difficulty because the parent knows that the next week the teacher will be back in the living room and the two of them can change the plan if they wish. In fact, there is seldom any problem establishing an educational program for the child that will be acceptable to the parent in projects in which the parent is contacted regularly (Dmitriev, 1978; Gordon, 1977; Portage, 1978).

It isn't always appropriate to work with the child on the living room floor. For older children it may be more appropriate to arrange for a home visit or invite the parent to the school. (See Chapter 7.) Gordon and Breivogel (1976) suggest that parents should be invited to work in the schools in order to understand some of the "legal ramifications in the school setting" (p. 12), such as budgets and government requirements. One of the most effective ways to help a parent understand the needs and concerns of the school is to have the parent participate in the school program. Many parents have skills and ideas that could be used by educators.

Teachers and Parents As People

Perhaps the greatest advantage of having the parent in the school or the school go to the home is that the two become better acquainted. For the parent to learn that the teacher or the principal likes to sew, go fishing, or raise roses can help the parent see the professional as a capable, well-rounded person. If some of these interests are shared it is easier for parents to share their concerns about the child. One first grade teacher routinely tells her new parents each fall, "I will make a pact with you. I won't believe everything that your child tells me happened at home, if you won't believe everything that your child tells you happened at school." Then the experienced teacher goes on to tell the "back-to-school"-night parents that she would like them to call if there is anything that concerns them (Call, 1966).

WHO IS HELPING WHOM?

Particularly in the relationship between the professional and the parent of a handicapped child, there is an implied notion that the professional has some information and that the parent needs the information. It is assumed that it is the responsibility of the professional to "give" that information to the parent:

> Typically it is assumed that being an effective helper means giving advice. When friends or family members come to us with a problem, they will often ask, "What shall I do?" or "What would you do if you were I?" Rather than actively listening to the content and feelings implied by these kinds of questions, we all too willingly respond with advice: i.e., "If I were you, I would. . . ." (Lichter, 1976, p. 69)

Actually, the problems and needs of handicapped children are so complicated that the answers to many questions are unknown, even to professionals. Perhaps because of an implied role relationship, the professional does not usually tell the parent that the treatment has not been proven or that the reason has not been discovered. One parent in writing about "the parent-professional conflict" states:

> Recently a friend of mine who is a nurse and I took a youngster to a physician for some advice. We asked a particular question, to which the physician replied, "I don't know." The nurse looked at me and whispered, "Didn't that sound beautiful?" (Schultz, 1978, p. 32)

Educators, like physicians, are hesitant to reply that they do not have the answers, especially when they have just completed graduate degrees to prepare them for working with handicapped children. One resource teacher was almost intimidated by the principal's repeated remark: "Well, you should know how to handle Garth, you're the expert. I haven't had the training." Garth, who had been poorly programmed for his seven years of school, had learned to manipulate adults and was perhaps more of a mystery to the beginning teacher than to the principal, who was much more experienced. The teacher dared not say so, however, either to the principal or to the parents.

THE WHAT OF THE COMMUNICATION

Professionals frequently see a meeting with the parent as a time to tell or teach the parent something about the child. Actually, there is far more that the parent can tell the teacher about the child than the teacher can tell the parent about that particular child. The parents have been with the child longer and there are some things to be learned about the child before school, after school, on the weekends, and in the summer. The parent's relationship to the child began long before the school's relationship and will continue long after the child is too old for the public educational system (Figure 3-1). There are some things about the child that the parent understands better than the professional. Conversely, there are some things that the professional understands better (Exhibit 3-1).

Figure 3-1 Interaction with the Child

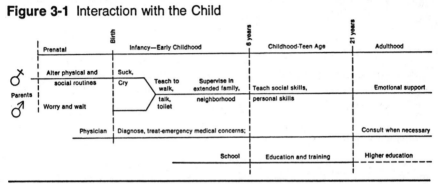

Exhibit 3-1 Information about the Child

What Parents Know Better Than Educators (About Their Own Child)	What Educators Know Better Than Parents (About Other People's Children)
A. Developmental history	A. Child development
B. Medical history	B. Evaluation techniques
C. Social and educational history	C. Behavior reinforcement
D. Favorite toys and activities	D. Medical and educational terminology
E. Amount of sleep and rest	E. Rules and policies of the school
F. Medication and diet needs	F. Problems at school

What Educators Know Better Than Parents

Child Development

Due to their training and experience working with many children, professionals usually know more than parents about the way children develop. The sequence of development that has been carefully observed by Piaget, Flavell (1963), Maslow (1954), and others is well known to professionals. Unless the parent has had some training in child development, it is unlikely that the parent is aware of more than the advice of Dr. Spock or Grandma.

Evaluation Techniques

Professionals have had training and experience in evaluation techniques. The reasons for standardizing tests, the various tests available, and how to interpret the results of tests are things that professionals are paid to know.

Behavior Reinforcement

Methods of directing the behavior of children were taught to each professional and practiced while a supervisor observed. Psychologists were trained in how to obtain a child's cooperation in testing. Teachers were taught methods of handling children during group activities, and principals have certainly had experience, if not training, in how to handle the child that is sent to the office.

Medical and Educational Terminology

Some concepts and conditions are summarized by the shorthand expressions that have been learned to label the condition or situation. Talking about the situation with the label implies a cluster of conditions. Professionals have memorized these clusters in order to pass college finals.

Rules and Policies of the School

Dates for the beginning of classes and the age levels of children in various programs are everyday information to educators. Although parents have access to this information, they usually only learn it in direct relation to their own child's program and know little about other programs in the system.

Problems at School

Professionals are much more aware of the problems that children encounter in school. They know that many children play in the lavatories, tease the younger children, copy answers from other students' papers, squirt water from the fountain, write spelling words on fingernails, and throw raisins when they are served for lunch. Professionals also know that children have difficulty understanding bases in math and vowel sounds in reading and spelling.

What Parents Know Better Than Educators

Developmental History

Because of the close contact that the parent has had with the child, the parent knows some things about the child that aren't written in any record. The parent knows the child's developmental history, including the prenatal period. The parent knows when the child learned to smile, to sit up, and to use a spoon.

Medical History

The parent knows about any complications in the pregnancy and the details of the delivery of the child. The parent knows whether the child took vitamins as an infant and when shots were given. The parent knows if the child has had the routine childhood diseases and if the child will chew baby aspirin. The parent also knows about any medication that the child has taken or is taking.

Social and Educational History

The parent knows how the child responds to new people and if the child went to a nursery school. The parent knows how the child interacts with other children and adults in Sunday school. The parent knows who the child prefers as a sitter and which other children the child likes to be with.

Favorite Toys and Activities

The parent knows about the tricycle that the child likes to ride, even before breakfast. The parent knows about the teddy bear that the child still takes to bed at night. The parent knows about the Saturday morning cartoons and "Walt Disney Presents" on Sunday. The parent knows about the child's fascination with airplanes, boats, doll clothes, or marbles.

Amount of Sleep and Rest

The parent knows the child's sleep patterns. The parent knows how much rest the child needs and when and where the child is used to resting.

Medication and Diet

The parent knows what medication the child has taken or is taking and the amount that seems to be appropriate. The parent knows the foods that "agree" with the child and which ones are not liked or tolerated well. The parent knows how much the child is used to eating. The parent knows about the peanut butter and jam sandwiches and the chicken gumbo soup.

The Home History and Information Form (Exhibit 7-1) and the Home Observation (Exhibit 7-2) are designed to help the professional gather this information in a form that can be used for educational planning.

THE WHY OF THE COMMUNICATION

Parents' Progress toward Trust

Most parents face the school system with some leftover reactions from their own school days: sit still, walk in a line, do not use the lavatory during study time, do not chew gum in the library. The junior high school girl who was required to stay after school and write "I will not chew gum in the library" 1,000 times because she was chewing gum in the library (P. Michaelis, 1975) is unlikely to enter the library again without remembering the cramped hand and the smudgy paper. Most people have similar memories of authoritarian teachers and strict administrators. Even those who were not actually punished themselves can remember hearing the sound of the paddle or seeing the ruler slapped across the hands of "disobedient" students. These memories can make the parents uncomfortable about sending their children to school.

Parents of children who are experiencing difficulties in school are even more likely to feel uncomfortable about the whole concept of school (Gorham, 1975). In order for the parents of a handicapped child to be comfortable about the school setting, they must learn to know the school personnel and they must feel that their child is welcome in the school. (See Chapter 8 for suggestions about positive messages to the home.)

After many rejections and negative advice one mother wrote:

> When she finished examining her, she told me of a couple of options we would have for treatment and said, "I'd really like to work with her." Those words were like music to me. (Burke, 1978, p. 89)

Sending a Child to School

Sending a child to school is an event for any family. One only has to read the August newspapers to know that even the department stores get into the act. There are sales on jeans, sweaters, and coats; drug stores even stock the long-lost cigar boxes covered with pictures of pencils and rulers to sell for "school boxes." There is a place for a name and a grade on each box.

Sending a child to school who may have difficulty knowing what to put in the grade blank on the school box is more of a strain for the parents than merely finding clothes that fit, wash well, and are like those the other kids are wearing. The thought of sending the handicapped child to school reawakens the concern that the parents try to forget now and then so that they have energy for the rest of the family and for other responsibilities. (See Chapter 6.)

Although summer days mean the living is easy, that isn't so for mother. The end of the summer for most mothers signals a chance for the relief of having the children supervised by someone else for part of the day. A parent who has not been too successful in finding baby sitters or recreational activities for a handicapped child (see Chapter 4) may be uneasy at the idea of sending the child to someone else for part of the day. Will that person really be willing to do what is necessary to make the child comfortable and also able to learn? For the parent of a handicapped child, the end of the summer does not bring relief; it brings concern. It is not that the parent doesn't want to trust the school; it is that they know how much they and the child need from the school (see Chapter 4). With that intensity of concern comes anxiety.

ATTITUDES OF PARENTS OF HANDICAPPED CHILDREN TOWARD SCHOOL

Parents' attitudes generally follow a progression toward understanding and acceptance (Figure 3-2).

Apprehension

The sister of a profoundly handicapped child watched her brother through the one-way observation window as the teacher helped him feed himself. "My mother didn't want Don to come to school," she said. "She was afraid that the teacher would hurt him." "Mrs. Wilson would never hurt Don," the counselor who was watching with the nine-year-old girl replied. "Oh, Mother knows that now, but she didn't at first" (Fuller, 1976).

Although most mothers are not afraid that the child will be physically hurt, many are afraid that the child will be punished for not being able to do the things that the other children are able to do. Not being sure that the child will be accepted by the school system that sent naughty boys to the principal and slow ones to the corner can be a frightening experience for the parents of a child who may not be able to "keep up" in academic or social skills. "I always hate for school to start," one mother said. "My children don't do too well in school."

One of the reasons that parents have accepted segregated schools for handicapped children is that they were not sure that the formal educational systems that

Figure 3-2 Parent Attitudes toward School

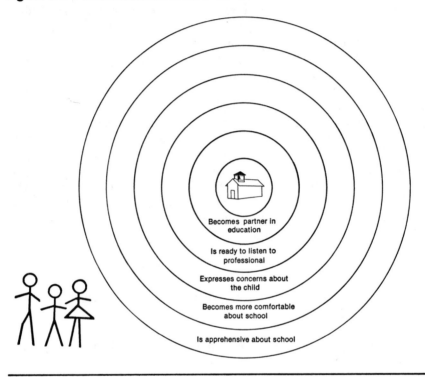

Becomes partner in
education

Is ready to listen to
professional

Expresses concerns about
the child

Becomes more comfortable
about school

Is apprehensive about school

they remember as students could adjust to the needs of their children. A more restrictive environment was thought by many parents to be a more protective environment, one in which the children would not be subjected to name calling by either teachers or students. Many parents worked to help create the "special" schools.

The parent of a handicapped child has some other real concerns about the child's ability to adjust. New situations and new people are difficult for all of us. For a child with learning problems, finding the lavatory, learning to use the fountain, or even finding the classroom in an unfamiliar building can be a devastating experience.

One retarded boy was allowed to attend a special school on a trial basis for one day. The school refused to admit him because "He didn't say a word." The boy, usually verbal, needed time to become accustomed to his surroundings, but even the special school expected immediate adaptation. Frequently, handicapped children are "evaluated" either formally or informally in a new setting before they have had time to find their way around.

When faced with new situations, any child may have unexpected problems. Children with learning problems may have adjustment problems simply moving to the room next door or having a different teacher. Parents of handicapped children send their children to school wondering whether they will respond to the stress with bedwetting, having daytime accidents, refusing to eat, becoming withdrawn, or having tantrums. The fear that the child will be too uncomfortable in the school environment to learn causes many parents to face school days with a great deal of apprehension.

Becoming Comfortable

When it comes to services for their children, all parents "come from Missouri." Even parents of normal children go to school the first day to get a look at the kindergarten teacher. "She looks so young. Do you think that she will be a good teacher?" "The principal was gruff to me. What do you think he will do to my child?" "I don't like the way the playground faces the busy street. What if one of the kids runs into the street and gets hurt!" "I think we need more crossing guards." Parents are relieved of this stress only when they see that whatever they worried about isn't happening.

Parents of handicapped children become comfortable with the school only after the child becomes comfortable in the school. If Johnny happily gets up in the morning, gets himself ready for school, and hurries off to "show this to Mrs. Brown," the parent will like the school. If Mary can do something that she couldn't do before, the parent will like the school. One teacher of profoundly handicapped children says that after he toilet trains the child, the parents will "do anything" for him (Wexler, 1978). If the child comes home from school happy and more skillful, the parent will like the school.

It may take some time for the parent of a child who learns slowly to become comfortable, and there is no way to hurry the process. Don had been in the classroom for almost a year before the family began to believe that Mrs. Wilson would not hurt him. Chapter 14 describes the roles that other personnel in the school play in helping the parent become comfortable with the child's schooling. Even when the parent has become very comfortable with the teacher, the parent may not trust the way the young bus driver drives on rainy days. Apprehension has the tendency to spill over to other areas.

Expressing Concerns

One highly competent speech pathologist states that he does not expect the parent to tell him anything about the child for some time. He just works with the child until the parent feels like saying something about the child (Rooney, 1975).

Most people discuss their deep concerns only with people they trust. Parents of children who have learning problems, particularly, do not want to discuss these problems except with trusted friends. Since schools for years have excluded the child who had "bodily or mental conditions rendering attendance inadvisable" (Weintraub & Abeson, 1976, p. 7), parents were not likely to tell of the child's inadequacies for fear that the school system might exclude the child. Personal, emotional issues discussed in Chapters 4, 5, and 6 can also cause the parent to "not want to talk about it."

Ready To Listen

Even after parents are ready to talk about their problems, they may not be ready to do anything about them. (See Chapter 9.) It may be some time before the parent has been able to deal with the problems well enough to want to hear anyone else's response to the problems. For the mother who was afraid the teacher might hurt her son, it was over a year before she felt comfortable enough to ask the teacher for some help with the child.

Until the parent asks for advice, there is no reason to give it. The advice will not be heard. (See Chapter 7.) The surest way to know when the parent is ready to listen and wants to know what the professional thinks, is to wait for the parent to ask for help with a certain problem. When the parent asks, it doesn't mean that everything should be discussed. It means only that the parent wants to know that specific piece of information. Educators are familiar with the "teachable moment," that moment when the child has the prerequisite skills and is ready for the presentation of a new stimulus. Parents have teachable moments, too. If too much information is presented at once, the parent may be overwhelmed and the apprehension stage may last longer.

Partner in Education

The parent is expected to work with the educators in the development of an IEP for the child. Some parents may not be ready to do this, however. They may not feel comfortable enough to respond to the objective criteria for evaluation and goals to be completed in the specified amount of time. Parents may be deeply concerned about other child-related problems, but may not feel comfortable expressing these at the conference. (See Chapter 7.) Educators, anxious to get on with it, have assumed the leadership in the plans for the child:

> For many years the schools have assumed the sole position of authority in making decisions about testing and placing children; parents were not accorded much status in the decision making process. (Nazzaro, 1976, p. 35)

The intent of the notice to parents and the written response from the parent is to see that the professionals take enough time to make the parent feel free to express concerns, to listen, and to plan cooperatively. The burden of this relationship is given to the professional through the requirements of "informed consent"; the school cannot coerce the parent into signing the paper so that arrangements can be made quickly, but must work with the parent until the parent understands and participates in developing the plan.

One father of a young handicapped child signed the paper for placement of his son into a program that he felt was inappropriate because "That is the only thing they have available." After the father, an oral surgeon, started asking questions, the parents later requested that the school district change the child's program (Geinger, 1976).

THE HOW OF THE COMMUNICATION

Parents are not paid to be interested in information about other people's children as professionals are. The parent of a handicapped child will not be impressed by the professional's success with other people's children, unless the professional proves to be competent with this child. To the parent, the other children are rivals for the attention of the professional, not symbols of successful teaching. Parents of handicapped children are also keenly aware of the fact that their children need more or different things than other children. Even though the professionals may have been successful with hundreds of other children with similar handicaps, to the parent, the only success is the success with this child. "It's you and me against the world" and that includes the educational system.

Professionals can respond to parents' attitudes in several concrete ways (Figure 3-3).

Ask the Parent To Describe the Child

The first thing that a wise professional does with a parent is to ask the parent about the child and then listen to the answer—not with the idea that a message should be sent in return, but just listen, in a warm, accepting manner. (See Chapter 7.)

> The process of helping another person begins by accepting the total person in a non judgmental manner, communicating an attitude of acceptance as clearly as possible. One very direct way to communicate acceptance of others, particularly to those in stress, is to listen to their feelings and the ways in which those feelings are "coded" into language. (Lichter, 1976, p. 70)

Figure 3-3 Professional Response to Parent Attitudes

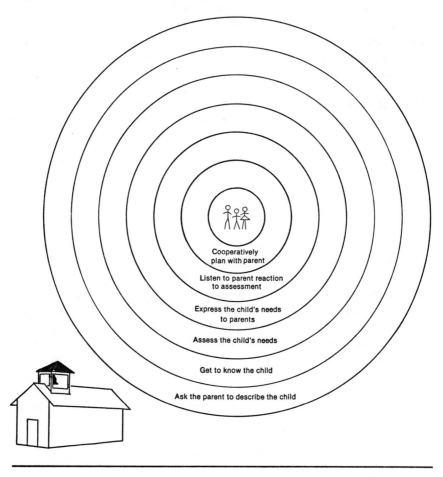

Get To Know the Child

Each child is different. Even Down's syndrome children, who frequently look alike and have similar movement patterns and similar grammatical structure (C.T. Michaelis, 1976), are very different in their likes and dislikes. Jim loves basketball and makes baskets about 18 out of 20 shots. Bob loves to swim, especially under water. Barbara doesn't like to swim, but she loves to ride the bus and go shopping.

One psychologist indicated that whenever he tests a "Mongoloid" (Down's syndrome, see Chapter 11) child, he tears up the test, writes 33 on the score sheet, and talks to the child till the parent comes back (LaPray, 1969). The significant educational variables about a Down's syndrome child are the child's interests, likes, and dislikes rather than the measured intelligence quotient (IQ). Knowing the child's interests and strengths and dislikes is a prerequisite to an appropriate evaluation of the child. But perhaps even more important, it is prerequisite to being able to carry on constructive conversation with the child's parents. Parents need to hear positive things about their child before they listen to the educational concerns. (See Chapter 8.)

Assess the Child's Needs

The professional responsibility, of course, goes far beyond noticing the child's pretty dress or the blue eyes. Professionals have the task of objectively evaluating the child's capabilities according to norm-referenced as well as criterion-referenced measures. It is important to use formal and informal evaluations. The law requires that each of these measurement techniques must be explained to the parent, along with the rationale of why this test is being given at this time for this child.

As part of her training to become a school psychologist, one "coed" who went back to school after her own children were in school asked to give psychological tests to the neighborhood children. All of the children were bright, active youngsters. It was a surprise to find that, without exception, the parents called or came by wanting to find out how their child did and if there was anything that the parent should know or do. The parents were all college educated and successful. The children were all successful in school, yet the parents were intimidated by the psychological examination process.

Parents of children who are not doing well or not expected to do well in school are even more concerned about how the child is doing compared to the other children and what is going to be done with the information. Since all records are open to the parent, professionals may want to share the information with the parent during the report-writing process. (See Chapter 7.)

Express the Child's Needs to the Parent

"Face it; you have a vegetable" is the phrase that one professional says he uses to tell parents the results of an evaluation that found the child to have low developmental skills. In a society in which intelligence, beauty, and personal autonomy are highly valued, such a message can be devastating. There is a great deal of evidence that even the children who function at the lowest level are not "vegetables," but can learn to clothe and feed themselves (Haring, 1978; Johnson & Werner, 1975; Meyers, Sinco, & Stalma, 1973; Sontag, Smith, & Certo, 1977).

If the professionals express the child's needs to the parent not in terms of what the child can't do, but in terms of what the child is ready to learn, the message could be more palatable. If the professional is able to say; "Well, we looked at Johnny and it looks like he could learn to close his lips to swallow if the lips were stimulated before he was fed. Having his lips closed not only will help him to eat, but also will make it easier for him to make sounds," the parents' reaction will be more positive than if they are told, "Johnny will never talk." "Having Johnny tell about something that he has been doing and writing it down for him will help him understand that these lines and circles that we write have the same meaning each time they are used" sounds better than "Johnnie cannot discriminate letters and will be a poor reader." Careful statements can describe the child's developmental skills without stressing the things that the child cannot do. (See Chapter 8.)

Frequently, the parents are the first to discover the child's problems (Cruickshank, 1977) and are aware of the things that the child cannot do. Most parents, however, hope that somehow the child will be able to master all the things that other children are able to learn in the public school system. Professionals know that this is not possible for many children who learn slowly, particularly if they have physical or mental conditions that inhibit learning certain skills. However, the parent may be hurt and react very angrily to a forceful, limiting statement about what Johnny can or can't do.

Listen to the Parent's Reaction to the Assessment

The professional must listen carefully to the parent's response to new information about the child or to old information in a new form. The parent needs an opportunity to say, "Yes, I would like to help Johnny learn to close his lips" or "Can't we just tip his chair back to feed him so it won't run out of his mouth?" or "Can't I get him some books from the library that are more interesting so he will be able to read better?" (See Chapter 7.)

Unless the professional listens to how the parent sees the child in each particular skill area, it will not be easy for the parent to accept the goals that the professional may establish in that area. The staff in one program, for example, decided to toilet train Don because he seemed to be ready. Checking with the home, they found that the father had just been in an accident and needed several operations on his legs. In addition, the family had only one bathroom, which was upstairs, and the boy did not know how to go up and down the stairs alone. Although the boy was ready for toilet training, the family was not. A year later, after the father was in better health and a bathroom was built downstairs, Don was toilet trained in only a few days. Insistence on the school-oriented goal at first would have caused the parents more apprehension. The home training would probably have been impossible for the grandmother who tended Don during the mother's frequent trips to visit the father in the hospital.

Cooperatively Plan with the Parent

Since the parent's consent for the IEP can be withdrawn at any time, it is wise to consider the IEP a dynamic outline to be changed whenever it seems appropriate. After the program is begun, it is the responsibility of the professional to keep the parent informed as to how the child is responding to the curriculum and management plan. (See Chapter 8.) The school should do whatever is necessary to help the parent feel free to contact the school or stop by for a visit. In order to be a little more organized during the visit, some schools prefer to organize regular visiting days to visit with parents without taking time from the children's programming. (See Chapter 7.)

RETURN OF UNCERTAINTY

Back to the Beginning

The growing trust of the parent in the school system can disappear almost suddenly, and the parent will be totally apprehensive once more. The accumulation of stress can be difficult for any family, but families of handicapped children live under constant stress (C.T. Michaelis, 1977). If there is additional sickness in the family or other types of family stress, the situation is reflected in the parent's concern for the child's schooling.

C.T. Michaelis (1975) describes her personal, emotional reaction to moving a handicapped child to a new area. The process of adjustment for the child and the family begins anew each time any change occurs in the child or in the family. Each new teacher means a new relationship, and the rapport developed with one teacher is not transferred automatically to another teacher. Professionals must expect the parent's anxiety to return and be ready to meet it over and over again without an emotional response of their own, "But we already decided that!"

Prepared Messages: Candy and Flowers with a Printed Card

One of the most effective ways to make a parent hesitate to trust the school with the fragile child is for the educators to give the parent one of the typical messages that are prepared for "parent training" at a "parent level." They are almost as effective as a printed valentine from "guess who." The prepared approaches may be described as state-of-the-art, group design, and graduate school messages. (See Chapter 13 for parent programs and Chapter 11 for language understandable to the general public.)

State-of-the-Art Message

Any graduate student is familiar with the state-of-the-art paper. Such papers are produced with regularity for course assignments. Each paper begins with a review of the literature in which all references to this particular topic that have been published in the "acceptable literature" are included, particularly articles by the "leaders" of the profession. The positions of these people are briefly summarized, and a statement is made that this information reveals the most valuable and significant way to train children who are having learning difficulties. The papers typically conclude with proposals for additional research that needs to be done before the programs can be implemented effectively.

Because of funding requirements, administrators must create position papers for the development of programs in their school district—or even the state. P.L. 94-142 itself requires that a plan be written about how the needs of the children in the state will be met. This type of program description and written documentation is necessary for funding and planning purposes, but it has little significance to the parent.

Every teacher and every administrator knows that promises of new teaching materials and more lavatories for next year do little to help meet the problems of this year. This is even more pragmatically important to the parents. What is good for one child may not be good for another, and the parents are not interested in the trends of the profession. Parents are interested in the pragmatic needs of their child. Parents are only tangentially interested in funding concerns or trends for the future. Parents are interested in the child's needs today.

One parent, a member of a parent organization, finds that even the parent organization works toward goals for the future and fails to meet the needs of the individual children today. She related it to medieval times when "men of great faith" built a cathedral

> knowing that it would not be completed until after they, and probably their children, had died. For many people the vision of progress for the retarded people is rather like this noble vision of eventual success, but individual parents and individual children cannot afford to sacrifice a personal vision while the universal vision evolves. (Bennett, 1978, p. 154)

Everyone wants the services that are created when parents complain, but no one wants to listen to the complaints. When the parent who complains about the lack of physical therapy, transportation, counseling, or in-home services is answered by being given a state-of-the-art message, the parent develops negative feelings not only toward the individual giving the message, but also toward the school system and the profession.

Group Design Message

Perhaps the greatest difference between regular education and special education is that regular education is designed to meet the needs of children in groups and special education is designed to meet the needs of an individual child. The concept of the IEP has evolved from a combination of the rights and needs of the child who has difficulty learning; the need for a one-to-one curriculum has been demonstrated by the child's difficulty with the curriculum and methods used for groups of children. Even though this concept has created a whole new specialty in the profession and has been an impetus for the development of services to the handicapped, the use of the class goals concept is still common, even for the special class. One mother was repeatedly told at parent conferences: "I know Jim has read this book before, but the others do not know how to read that well so we are going through it again." "I know Jim can tell time to the minute, but the others do not know how to tell time to the half hour, so that is what we are studying this year."

It is unrealistic to assume that a parent will have trust and feel comfortable about the child meeting the needs of the group. Parents are not very interested in group projects of the class, unless they are told how their child participated and have some reason to believe that their child has benefited from the experience in a direct way. Parents do not have the responsibility of other people's children in the classroom, and it is unrealistic to assume that a parent will be excited about having the child in the class unless the child's individual needs, as seen by the parent, are being met.

Graduate School Message

In a desire to appear well trained, educators sometimes answer a parent's question by telling the parent all that they know about learning problems similar to the one that the child has. It is a little like the child who asked where he came from. The father proceeded to tell the story of the birds and bees. The child listened patiently and then replied; "Oh, Billy said he came from St. Louis, and I wanted to know where I came from."

For the most part, parents are not concerned about all the problems of visual discrimination that children have or the sequence of motor development. They want to know only what their child is ready to learn. Educators are responsible for knowing as much as possible about all children; the parent is not responsible for knowledge about "other people's children." It is more useful for the professional to find out how much the parent knows than to use the parent as an audience for all the information that was memorized for the comprehensive examination.

DISCOVERING AND RESPECTING THE PARENT'S ATTITUDE

Parents have a variety of feelings as a result of the personal experiences that they may have faced before they came in contact with the school system. Many parents have uncomfortable feelings about the school environment and how their child will fit into it. Although parents may not be able to describe the child's learning problems in graduate school terminology, they have informally compared their children to the other children in the extended family and to the children in the neighborhood. They know that the child has trouble "keeping up," and the knowledge is painful.

Educators today have long, intensive preparation that the schoolmarm didn't have. Part of the preparation should be the development of the ability to understand and respect the unique life experiences of each person who happens to be the parent of a handicapped child.

REFERENCES

The American Education—Legal Defense Fund. *Beyond busing: Some constructive alternatives.* 1976.

Bennett, J. Company, halt! In A.P. Turnbull & H.R. Turnbull (Eds.), *Parents speak out: Views from the other side of a two-way mirror.* Columbus, Ohio: Charles E. Merrill, 1978.

Burke, J. Face to face in times of crisis and over the long haul. In A.P. Turnbull & H.R. Turnbull (Eds.), *Parents speak out: Views from the other side of a two-way mirror.* Columbus, Ohio: Charles E. Merrill, 1978.

Call, B. Back to School Night. Presentation, Salt Lake City, Utah: Howard R. Driggs School, 1966.

Cruickshank, W.M. *Learning disabilities in home, school and community.* Syracuse: Syracuse University Press, 1977.

Dmitriev, V. Normal and delayed development in young children. In N.G. Haring, (Ed.), *Behavior of exceptional children* (2nd ed.). Columbus, Ohio: Charles E. Merrill, 1978.

Flavell, J. *The developmental psychology of Jean Piaget.* New York: D. Van Nostrand, 1963.

Fuller, M. Personal communication, June 17, 1976.

Gallagher, J.J., & Gallagher, G.C. Family adaption to handicapped child and assorted professionals. In A.P. Turnbull & H.R. Turnbull (Eds.), *Parents speak out: Views from the other side of a two-way mirror.* Columbus, Ohio: Charles E. Merrill, 1978.

Geinger, K. Personal communication, October, 1976.

Gordon, I.J., & Breivogel, W.F. *Building effective home-school relationships.* Boston: Allyn & Bacon, 1976.

Gordon, R. Special needs of multi-handicapped children under six and their families: One opinion. In E. Sontag, J. Smith, & N. Certo (Eds.), *Educational programming for the severely and profoundly handicapped.* Reston, Va.: Division on Mental Retardation, Council for Exceptional Children, 1977.

Gorham, K.A. A lost generation of parents. *Exceptional Children,* 1975, *41* (8), 521-525.

Haring, N.G. *Behavior of exceptional children* (2nd ed.). Columbus, Ohio: Charles E. Merrill, 1978.

Johnson, V.M., & Werner, R.A. *A step-by-step learning guide for retarded infants and children.* Syracuse, NY: Syracuse University Press, 1975.

LaPray, T. Personal communication, November, 1969.

Lichter, P. Communicating with parents: It begins with listening. *Teaching Exceptional Children,* 1976, *8* (2), 67-71.

Marshalltown Project. 570 Anson Street, Marshalltown, Iowa, 1973.

Maslow, A. *Motivation and personality.* New York: Harper & Row, 1954.

Meyers, D.G., Sinco, M.E., & Stalma, E.S. *The right-to-education child.* Springfield, Ill.: Charles C. Thomas, 1973.

Michaelis, C.T. We've Moved to Iowa. *The Exceptional Parent,* 1975, *5* (6), 19-24.

Michaelis, C.T. The language of a Down's syndrome child. Unpublished manuscript, University of Utah, 1976.

Michaelis, C.T. Imperfect child—Cause for chronic sorrow. *Special Children,* 1977, *4* (1), 39-48.

Michaelis, P. Personal communication, October, 1975.

Nazzaro, J. Comprehensive assessment for educational planning. In F.J. Weintraub, A. Abeson, J. Ballard, & M.L. LaVor (Eds.), *Public policy and the education of exceptional children.* Reston, Va.: Council for Exceptional Children, 1976.

Portage Project. 412 E. Slifer Street, Portage, WI, 1978.

Rooney, T. Personal communication, October, 1975.

Schimmel, D., & Fisher, L. *The rights of parents in the education of their children.* Columbia, Md.: National Committee for the Citizens in Education, 1977.

Schultz, J. The parent-professional conflict. In A.P. Turnbull & H.R. Turnbull (Eds.), *Parents speak out: Views from the other side of a two-way mirror.* Columbus, Ohio: Charles E. Merrill, 1978.

Sontag, E., Smith, J., & Certo, N. (Eds.). *Educational programming for the severely and profoundly handicapped.* Reston, Va.: Division on Mental Retardation, Council for Exceptional Children, 1977.

Tingey, L. Personal communication, 1960.

Weintraub, F.J., & Abeson, A. New education policies for the handicapped: The quiet revolution. In F.J. Weintraub, A. Abeson, J. Ballard, & M.L. LaVor (Eds.), *Public policy and the education of exceptional children.* Reston, Va.: Council for Exceptional Children, 1976.

Wexler, L. Personal communication, July 24, 1978.

Chapter 4

Getting to Know the Parents

UNDERSTANDING THE PARENT'S SUBJECTIVE EXPERIENCE

The role of the professional and the role of the parent are quite different. The professional, who *chooses* to work with handicapped children, receives pay checks, health insurance, retirement benefits, paid vacations, and opportunities to enroll in credit unions and tax-sheltered annuities. The parent receives no monetary rewards for working with the child. On the contrary, parents are required to pay for the routine expenses of the child's development plus an array of additional expenses caused by the child's additional needs.

Professionals work with the child about 6 hours, 5 days a week, for 9 months a year for 12 years. Parents are responsible for the child during the other 18 hours each day, on weekends and holidays, and all summer for the child's entire childhood. For children with developmental delays, the childhood may last the entire life of the child.

Professionals Should Be Objective

Parents usually receive no training. One physician told a young expectant mother that she could not have the baby until she had read a stack of books that he gave her about the development and delivery of a baby. Both the physician and the young mother-to-be laughed, since they both knew that the baby would be born whether she read or not (Clark, 1952).

Professionals are not allowed to work with children until they do "read some books." Part of the training that professionals receive before becoming licensed to work with children is designed to help them master clinical methods and procedures. Observing and recording behavior as seen, without reflecting the personal feelings of the observer, are skills that are mastered in the training process. These skills are needed because one of the prime tasks of the teacher is to devise learning experiences and ways to measure whether the child has learned that activity (Stephens, Hartman, & Lucas, 1978).

Psychologists are taught to interact with children in a structured way, giving credit only for certain specified responses. The psychologist's reaction to the color of the child's eyes is not to be part of the clinical report that is prepared by standardized methods. During training, the psychologist's ability to give children standardized examinations is evaluated. How the examiner or the child "feels" is not to be part of the objective report.

It is frequently suggested in the professional's traditional training to work with parents that objective information should be given to the parent at conference time. The true meaning of conference is a "formal interchange of views" (Webster, 1970, p. 174). To do this, the sender and receiver must understand one another's position.

Parents Are Not Objective

A parent was told "I sense that you are becoming emotionally involved" (Lund, 1979, p. 18). When the executive director of one of the state associations of parents of handicapped children is told "parents are emotionally involved with their children," she replies, "Would you want one that wasn't?" (Henderson, 1976). Perhaps part of the reason that children living at home consistently have higher test scores than those living in institutions (Kirk, 1958) is that, in order to develop, children need someone to care about them (Berne, 1964; Harris, 1967; Maslow, 1954; Spitz, 1965; James and Jongward, 1971).

The parent has the right to expect that the professionals will not only have accurate, objective information for the parent, but also be "compassionate and have expert guidance" (Wolfensburger & Kurtz, 1969, p. 61). To do this, the professional must understand the personal experiences that the parent has had.

THE ROLE OF THE PARENT

There is something very magnificent and very wonderful about having a child. Having a child means there is someone who could have and be all the wonderful things that you wanted to be. Children themselves seem to know this and make statements like "When I grow up, I'm not going to make my kids go to bed early" and "I'm going to get my little girl a doll, just like this one."

When students in graduate education classes are asked to write what they would like their own children to be like, they use words like happy, outgoing, well adjusted, popular, bright, and able to work and enjoy it. Many of these students do not have children, but they know what they want their children to be like, if they ever do. Most parents are anxious to have their children be happy and enjoy success (Popp, Ingram, & Jordan, 1979).

Parents of Handicapped Children

There is something very magnificent and very wonderful about having a child . . . unless that child is handicapped. Parents of handicapped children face something that is not wonderful, not magnificent. Parents of a handicapped child face an undefined situation in which the family status is questioned and the family resources are strained (Michaelis, 1977a).

It is difficult for someone who has not personally experienced the adjustments that must be made in a parent's personal life to understand the role of a parent. One woman who was a psychologist for a number of years before she became a parent found mothering to be "demanding." I never imagined how "consuming it would be," she remarked (Foster, 1970). Child care and training, a 24 hour a day, weekend, holiday experience can be even more complicated when the child is handicapped. Understanding the additional complications of parenting for parents of handicapped children is an almost impossible task for someone who has only worked the 9:00 A.M. to 3:00 P.M. child care shift. It is not surprising that Heilman (1969) writes that it is doubtful whether the position of the parent is understood.

The Disappointment

There are many interrelated reasons why people have children. It may be to prove adult status, to decrease personal loneliness, or to conform to an expected life style in the family or in the church (Ross, 1964). Whatever the reason, prospective parents do not begin the pregnancy with the expectation that the child will be handicapped. Even couples who have received genetic counseling and know that there is some chance that their child may be handicapped do not plan to lose in genetic roulette. Knowing the possibilities, parents hope to win and have a child that is normal. One young expectant mother explained that, even though all the male children in her family have a rare inherited disease and her four-year-old son was handicapped, she and her husband decided to have another child in the hope that the child would be normal.

Unlike the professionals, who choose to work with children who have problems in development, the parents did not choose to have a handicapped child.

Searching for Help

Religion As a Source of Support

One of the reasons for organized religion is to meet the needs of people under stress, but families experiencing stress caused by the birth of a handicapped child have received little guidance from religion (Wolfensburger & Kurtz, 1969).

Philosophies under which it is held that God is perfect and any thing not perfect cannot be of God have led some religious organizations to avoid direct contact with families who have a handicapped member (Boyd, 1969).

The Bible, considered to be scripture for many western churches states:

> And Jesus passed by, he saw a man which was blind from his birth. And his disciples asked him, saying, Master, who did sin, this man, or his parents that he was born blind?
>
> John 9:2

The scripture continues to say that the man was blind so the "works of God should be made manifest in him."

The philosophy of "sons of the fathers" continues to be prevalent in some religious doctrines (Hoffman, 1969). Farber (1960), in his study of selected families of retarded children, found that only when religion was combined with birth order and sex of the child was religious affiliation of any significance to the family adjustment. Parents whose first son is retarded have better adjustment in some religions than in others.

Many handicapped children are not able to participate in the regularly organized religious meetings. One family takes their severely handicapped son to a residential facility to spend each Saturday night. The family attends church before they stop by to pick David up on Sunday afternoon. This is the only way the family can attend church together (Diekman, 1975). Many parents take turns going to church or attend services at different hours while one parent stays with the handicapped child.

It has been suggested that churches organize to provide for learning disabled children who can not "benefit from routine religion" (Tarnopol, 1969), but such special services are available in few churches. In a booklet "published as a cooperative effort of many religious denominations," Perske (1973) suggests attitudes that parents may acquire. The written material contributes little to the practical problems that the family faces. Most church members are uncomfortable around handicapped children, and many of the religious programs for handicapped children are organized and implemented by the children's parents. A few fortunate families are able to have their handicapped child participate in a church group led by a professional educator who volunteers to work with the children.

The Medical Diagnosis

If the child is born with a congenital abnormality or if the handicap is the result of an accident, it is the physician who should tell the parents that the child is handicapped. Many times, however, the physician does not do so. The parents may have the child examined to see if there is something that can be done to help the child. "Worst of all," writes Dr. Spock, "I hated to be the one to tell the parents that their fears were justified" (Spock, 1961, p. 5).

In order to be of help to the family, the pediatrician must "come to terms with his own feelings" about the handicapped child (American Medical Association, 1965). For many doctors, this is not an easy task. Instead of telling the family directly that they had a Down's syndrome baby, one family doctor kept saying, "I think maybe we'll have a specialist look at this baby." But he didn't say why. When the young mother had heard the diagnosis from a specialist, she told the family doctor, "You should have told me." "I didn't want to worry you if it wasn't true," he said, as he turned his eyes away (Preston, 1957). Even though Down's syndrome infants can be identified at birth, the family doctor was too uncomfortable to tell the parents himself. Some doctors continue to have difficulty being straightforward with new parents (Boggs, 1978).

Other physicians react in more aggressive ways. One doctor refused to do eye surgery on a Down's syndrome child and wrote "mongoloid" across the child's chart with a felt tip pen (Michaelis, 1974). Other avoidance activities include telling the parents that the child will "outgrow" the problem (Akerley, 1978) or suggesting that the family send the child to an institution. Ann Landers, a popular newspaper columnist, wrote that the family doctor could make an objective decision for the family (Schrieber, 1970). There are many cases in which the doctor "prematurely" decided that the child needed to be institutionalized, however (Wolfensburger & Kurtz, 1969). Most parents of moderately to severely handicapped children have been told to institutionalize the child by at least one physician. Perhaps the decision to institutionalize a child should not be "objective" but should be tempered by the feelings of all the people involved. Although many physicians may be honest in their recommendations that the child needs to be institutionalized, implied also in that message is that the child is unwelcome as a patient.

Although the physician may be the individual who provides the bulk of the counseling for the family early in the child's life (Tarnopol, 1969), the physician is poorly prepared to describe the child's educational needs. Many of them do, however. One pediatric neurologist guesses children's IQs by asking the child to name the states and their capitals. Parents have no way of knowing that the medical evaluation of the child does not measure learning potential.

Physicians who have been trained to "cure" people may be frustrated with handicapped children who cannot be "cured." Much of the medication given to these children may be given because the physician has nothing else to give. One mother of a handicapped child explained to the school that she had changed doctors because the old one "didn't listen" (Fuller, 1975). Not "listening" may have been the doctor's way of reacting to his own discomfort. Another young mother was thrilled when she was told that a new pediatrician was interested in treating children with epilepsy (Thompson, 1976). Usually described as an avoidance tactic of parents (Smith, 1969), the "doctor shopping" may be initiated by the doctors themselves as they communicate their discomfort with the child to the parent through both straightforward and hidden messages.

The Extended Family

One of the greatest sources of support for most young families is the grandparents. In the gift shop of some hospitals is a bumper sticker that reads, "Ask about my grandbaby." It is concrete evidence that the child belongs to more than just the young parents.

Whenever a car is sporting such a bumper sticker, one thing is certain: the grandbaby is not handicapped. Grandparents have perhaps more of a concern with the family tree than do the parents. After all, it has been their family longer. One grandmother said to her daughter-in-law, who had just given birth to a handicapped child, "This hurts us a lot more than it hurts you. It really does, you know" (Pieper, 1976, p. 8). Parents dream and wish for good things for their children; grandparents may wish for even better things for their grandchildren.

One young mother said, "I don't take Mom [husband's mother] along with me to Graham's evaluations any more. When I do, I have to take care of her, too. She starts to cry sometimes and she keeps asking why and wants to play with Graham when he needs to be sleeping" (Geinger, 1975). Other grandparents have suggested that institutionalization would be best for the child. One grandmother arranged for someone to tend a retarded boy during his uncle's wedding reception. Apparently, she thought the boy's presence would spoil the family celebration (Michaelis, 1974).

Perhaps the greatest approval that anyone can receive is the approval of his or her parents. Having a handicapped child shakes the whole family tree (Michaelis, 1977a). Frequently, one or both sides of the family blame the other side for "bad blood" (Pieper, 1976). Disappointment is the natural response for grandparents of handicapped children, but it can deprive the parents of one of the strongest means of support that parents have, i.e., the approval of their own parents.

Neighbors and Friends

Neighborhoods develop when people of similar interests, income, and life style move close to one another. Children play with the other children in the neighborhood, and adult friendships grow. Adults also tend to keep some friends from school days and make new ones at work. These sources of support are important to busy parents, especially if the friends and neighbors are also raising children. Outgrown clothes and toys can be exchanged, and car pools can be arranged.

For the parent of the handicapped child these sources of support may not be available. Neighbors may not want the handicapped child in their yard. Potential neighbors may choose not to move into the neighborhood because they fear the handicapped child might be "mean" (Michaelis, 1974). Some parents of normal children do not want the handicapped child to wear their children's outgrown clothes, nor do they want their children to have anything that belonged to the handicapped child—if any of the child's things survive the additional wear that handicapped children usually give their personal belongings (Michaelis, 1972).

Handicapped children are frequently excluded from the ordinary activities of the neighborhood children, and car pools for the activities of handicapped children are not easy to organize. It is difficult to get phone numbers and addresses of other children because, in the interest of confidentiality, agencies do not release lists of children, even to other parents. The children are usually so scattered that it is easier for the parent to drive each day. In addition to the extra time this takes, the family car is in use and the activity is less fun for the parent and the child; they do not have the opportunity to visit with other children on the way and with other parents when the children are picked up and brought home.

A favorite pastime of young mothers is talking about the activities of their children. They brag to one another about the developmental achievements of the children as well as their creative mischief. When one mother mentioned that her retarded son had done something similar to what a friend's normal son had done, the friend replied with a long look that seemed to say, "How could you compare Jim to Brent?" (Michaelis, 1974). One stepmother was told that her friend's husband found the retarded boy "depressing," and the mother realized that her son was not welcome at the friend's home anymore (Turnbull, 1978). At a conference of parents one father told how a friend sent a sympathy card when his Down's syndrome son was born (NARC, 1978).

The center of social life in many neighborhoods is the supermarket. Most shoppers ignore children's requests for a cookie or more ice cream bars. But children who do not speak well and try to show what they want by doing something attract attention, and other parents look as if to say, "I wouldn't allow my child to act that way; what's the matter with you?" (Morton, 1978). For parents of handicapped children, taking the child on the mundane errands of the household is not fun but a crusade into "enemy territory" (Michaelis, 1978). Stopping for a hamburger is not a treat for the family of a child who looks different and eats poorly. Many handicapped children are not able to sit long enough for their parents to finish the meal.

Although suburban shopping centers are billed as the homemaker's answer to "cabin fever," trips to shopping centers with a handicapped child in tow are not the delightful breaks for the family that they are for other families. One teacher in training who went to a shopping center with the family of a profoundly handicapped child pushed the adapted wheelchair. Although she had done this before, during the school week, she found that the Saturday crowd responded differently as she walked with the family. Adults perceived as teachers are treated in a way differently from the way those perceived as parents are treated. Teachers receive smiles that seem to say "you're a brave one;" parents receive stares. Families with handicapped children can only "tackle" the outside world when they are physically and emotionally at their best (Michaelis, 1978; Morton, 1978; Turnbull, 1978).

The Additional Work

Brutten, Richardson, and Mangel (1973) tell parents:

> Your job is far more important than that of the teacher, the pediatrician, or the psychologist. Don't get discouraged; don't give up. (p. 141)

The advice is well directed. Parents of handicapped children can very easily become discouraged. Parenting is a difficult task under any circumstances. There is always another pair of shoes to buy or another batch of clothes to wash (Michaelis, 1972). For children who are having more than the usual difficulties, the work multiplies. Delayed children spill more frequently, lose more socks and jackets, and need more parental attention than normal children. One mother found that she needed 12 to 15 clean outfits a day during a period when the son was unable to eliminate wetting behavior (Turnbull, 1978). Another mother who counted the items in the wash for her retarded son and for the other children (three boys and one girl) found that there were the same number of pants, socks, and underwear for the retarded son as there were for the other four children put together (Michaelis, 1972). That was when the children were all under ten. The other children are all grown, but the retarded son still needs almost the same number of clothes washed as he did when he was under ten. Parents of children with cerebral palsy face saliva-stained clothes day after day. The care needs of handicapped children do not diminish as they do for other children.

Children who are having developmental difficulties take more time than other children to master each developmental milestone of childhood. There are more diapers (some are adult-sized), and more energy is spent on toilet training and learning to eat. More time is required for dressing, frequently with special clothes to make it easier (Michaelis, 1972). One retarded boy did not learn to tie his own shoes until he was 17. Others never do. It is the parents who tie all those shoes.

Bathtime can be a time-consuming experience for the parents of a child who "plays in the water," is not able to get in or out of the bathtub alone, or who cannot adjust the water temperature. Bathing for handicapped children and teenagers frequently takes as much of the parent's time as the infant's daily bath.

Prolonged Infancy and Childhood

Unlike normal children, handicapped children continue to be dependent into the teens. Boys frequently need help with shaving; girls, with personal hygiene during menstrual periods. Parents who have children who develop slowly must keep the "family treasures" hidden for many more years than do parents of children who learn more quickly. Some families are not able to keep anything that is breakable. The child handles all new items and frequently breaks them.

Dirty clothes, spills on the kitchen floor, wandering into the street—these problems and others usually associated with early childhood may last indefinitely for parents of handicapped children.

There are other demands on parents of handicapped children. In order to get the child to the services needed, the parent spends many hours transporting the child and waiting while he or she is served. One young mother takes her baby to therapy two mornings a week. She also bundles up the twin sister and leaves the housework to find time for the treatment. It costs a full day of her weekly energy. In order to help pay for the treatment, the busy mother gives piano lessons in the evening when the father comes home from his work; the father spends his evenings caring for the children (Freeman, 1978).

Since many of the children never learn to drive or ride a bicycle, the "pick up and delivery" lasts a lifetime. Even when transportation is provided, the parent is frequently required to meet the bus with the child (Montgomery, 1978).

In a most revealing journal, Greenfield (1978) describes the day-to-day activities with his son, Noah:

> They want us to bring him to school for one hour each day for three weeks. Then four hours each day, from 9:00 to 1:00. And it won't be until November that there'll be a 9:00 to 2:00 program. (p. 137)

Greenfield describes numerous trips to investigate programs for his son. No wonder that the father wrote in his journal: "While I am in the city, however, I often wish that I were still young and alone" (p. 21). A mother of retarded twins writes: "I am learning that it's all right to look forward to a time when I am no longer totally responsible for my handicapped children" (Evans, 1979, p. 139).

IEP Meetings Mean More Work for Parents

Even the opportunity to participate in the meetings to develop the child's IEP requires that the parent fit another time and energy-consuming responsibility into an already overwhelming schedule.

Educators can make provisions for the additional needs of handicapped children, e.g., smaller classes, more aides, and more related services. Although these arrangements may not be adequate, they are possible resources that parents do not have. Parents must maintain a relationship with a handicapped child that is appropriate for the child's mental or emotional age for an extended period of time with no additional resources.

Respite care has been proposed as a means of relief for the parent. Even if such services were available, they would be too expensive for routine use, especially for middle class families, and the parent would still have to prepare in order to leave the child in the care of another person. It is a little like getting a substitute teacher; it is usually easier to come to school sick than to prepare for someone who does not know the children well to carry on the program. Returning to care for children who have had their own way for a few days can be more difficult than just staying home and caring for them yourself, to say nothing of the condition of the house and the amount of clothes in the hamper.

The parenting experience for parents of handicapped children is prolonged and intense as it is for a young child. The difference is that the relationship lasts for many years, sometimes for the entire lifetime of the "child." Although many parents develop warm, accepting attitudes about their handicapped child (Michaelis, 1976, 1977b), there is no relief from the physical and psychological energy demands.

The Internal Experience (Feelings)

Some emotional shocks that do not come to the parents of normal children come to parents of handicapped children. In addition to finding the outside world rather cold and hostile to the needs of the child and the family, the parents feel an inner turmoil.

Brazelton (1969), whose medical practice includes decades of working with parents, writes that "each baby becomes a special experience to a mother. There are potentials for change and adjustment not only in the baby, but in the mother" (p. 2). When the "unique combination of characteristics" of the baby are *not* "within the broad spectrum of normal development" the adjustment that must be made by the mother and father are even greater. One mother who was a practicing physician before her handicapped daughter was born talks about how she felt:

> I felt like I was nobody. Any credits of self worth that I could give myself from any of my personal endeavors meant nothing. Graduating from college and a first-rate medical school, surviving internship, practicing medicine and having two beautiful sons and a good marriage counted for nil. All I knew at this point was that I was the mother of an abnormal and most likely retarded child (Ziskin, 1978, p. 75).

The sense of loss of self-worth is not unusual. The child is, after all, an extension of the parent, a literal, physical extension. Parents who have a handicapped child have a real reason to wonder if something is "wrong with them" or if there was something they could have done to prevent the child's handicap.

The child of one mother who went into convulsions during labor was injured during the slow birth process. If the child had been delivered by cesarean section, the child would not have been handicapped. "I can't blame the doctor," she said,

"I had already had three children without any problems, and I had never had a convulsion before" (Bourne, 1959). The mother didn't "blame the doctor" but how many times when she was taking care of her child did she. . . . It is not unusual for parents to read encyclopedias and medical books to find reasons for the child's condition and wonder if there might have been something that they did or did not do that caused it (Ziskin, 1978).

Teachers, educators, and foster parents can suggest methods, materials, and programming. Social workers can give suggestions on how to adjust, but no one, except perhaps another mother, can understand the feeling of a new mother who is trying to recover from the physical and emotional trauma of giving birth, only to learn that the gift was defective (Ross, 1964; Michaelis, 1977a).

For the parent of a more mildly handicapped child, the knowledge may come later, but the parent is usually keenly aware that the child is "deficient" even if the handicap is minor. Frequently, the parent is the first to know that there is something wrong (Cruickshank, 1977).

One of the early articles in *The Exceptional Parent,* ". . . a magazine created to deal with the issues that many of you [parents] have been struggling with so long and patiently," Schleifer (1971) writes to the parent:

> Ultimately, you are left with the feeling that you produced the child, you are to blame for the problems. After all, there would be no problems if there was no child. (p. 62)

The real difficulty in caring for a handicapped child for the parents is that they care so much.

Searching for Help from the School

What the parents of a handicapped child need is something to take away the stigma and the problems of their child's handicap. There is only one thing that the parents really need; they need for the child to "get better." Since the child is not sick, the kind of "getting better" that the child needs is to get rid of the "disadvantages that make achievement unusually difficult" so that the child can "develop naturally." The only real hope that the parents have is that the school system can somehow "cure" the child's learning problems and the child will somehow be successful in school. The occupation of childhood is going to school; if the child is successful in school, it is assumed that the child will be successful in life.

The parent who has been rejected in the other searches for help will approach the school with an unrealistic desire for the school to perform the miracle that makes the child like other children. For many parents, it is an almost frantic hope.

CHARACTERISTICS OF PARENTS OF HANDICAPPED
CHILDREN

Boggs (1969) writes that, as a group, parents of handicapped children are not homogeneous; they are drawn "from the ranks" of normal parents. Before they became parents of handicapped children they were no more or less prepared for parenthood than were any other parents (Heilman, 1969). One father describes it this way: "Before they became parents of autistic children, they are not different, but afterwards they may become different" (Warren, 1978, p. 180). The experience of having a handicapped child may make the parents "different."

Parents become different because of their personal reactions to the problems. Any number of events may alter the course of one's life, and certainly the birth of a handicapped child does this. In some measures the birth of any child alters the life style of any parent. For parents of handicapped children, however, the alteration is greater. "Our life style is different because of Jennie," one mother writes (Ziskin, 1978, p. 78). "If it weren't for Eddie, none of us would be enjoying this ride," another mother writes (Akerley, 1978, p. 39). A third mother stated, "If I had had an unretarded baby, I'd never in a million years have thought of volunteering for anything during that period," as she described her volunteer work with the Association for Retarded Citizens when her children were young (Bennett, 1978, p. 157).

Parents of handicapped children do become different than they were before the child was born, but each parent becomes different in his or her own way. For some parents, it is the beginning of a new way of looking at life and life goals (Michaelis, 1976).

The attitudes of parents determine the way the situation is faced (Adams, 1971). The total resources of the family are important in the way the family faces the problems. "With money you can do things," one mother writes (Bennett, 1978, p. 165). Some parents appear to need more help than others (Tarnopol, 1969). Single parents face a double set of responsibilities (Adams, 1971). (See Chapter 5.)

Some parents are themselves very limited and in need of social services before the child is born. In some families the parent is referred for help to a social agency before the child is referred (Begab, 1969). In some families several children in the family are referred for help and carried on the social service rolls (Begab, 1969).

Other families have ample financial and emotional resources. Handicapped children were born in the Kennedy family, the Humphrey family, the Roy Rogers-Dale Evans family, the Pearl S. Buck family, and other prominent families.

The traditional way of looking at the family of a handicapped child is to assume that the family will go through several stages and need certain services in the process of adjusting. Social service agencies are frequently designed to serve the parents' needs in certain order, oblivious to the possibility that the services may not be meeting the needs of this particular family (Beck, 1969).

Each family faces a unique situation, however. About the "stages of reaction" Searl (1978) writes:

> My own experience as the father of a retarded child did not fit this pattern. Instead, it convinced me that most people seriously misunderstand a parent's response to this situation. The standard view does not reflect the reality of the parents' experience or lead to helpful conclusions.
>
> Professionals could help parents more—and be more realistic—if they discarded their ideas about stages and progress (p. 27).

In his discussion "Three stages of the growth of a parent of a mentally retarded child," Boyd, himself the parent of a retarded child, described his own subjective experience of growth, but he did not suggest that his personal experience was similar to that of any other parent (Boyd, 1969). The theoretical generalization that all parents respond to a handicapped child in the same manner is unsound in implication. It appears that, because of a desire to make a very complicated situation understandable, an artificial order has been imposed.

The family and the way in which the family reacts to the "crisis" have been examined by Farber (1960) and Grossman (1972). Both studies were carefully designed and have a thoughtful perspective; however, each investigates a limited number of selected parents that do not represent all parents. Farber (1960) worked with families in which both parents were active members of the Association for Retarded Citizens. Parents who decided to divorce during the study were dropped from the study. Grossman (1972) studied families through the eyes of siblings who were college students that volunteered to participate. Individuals gave verbal answers to structured questions. There is no evidence that the topics in these studies were of interest to the parents or siblings or that these families could represent other families.

"Mourning the loss of the child" and making adjustments to the family structure are considered healthy responses to the additional responsibilities thrust on parents of handicapped children (Olashansky, 1969). The way in which parents respond to these situations is entirely an individual matter.

PARENTING EXPERIENCE OF THE PROFESSIONAL

Tarnopol (1969) suggests that many of the professionals who are giving advice to parents have had little personal experience with children. They have had professional training to work with the child in the clinic but have had no experience working with the child in the home (Akerley, 1978). One professional who became the stepmother of a retarded child stated that she had learned more about mental retardation attempting to meet his needs in the home than she had from her three degrees in special education (Turnbull, 1978). This message was echoed by another educator (Schultz, 1978). One elementary school principal says that he thinks that mothers make better teachers because they understand children better (Bailey, 1969). Mothers might understand parents better also.

When one college professor who trains teachers to work with the handicapped was asked by a parent for some advice about her retarded son, the professor replied that he and his wife (also a professional educator) gave advice to parents for years before they became parents. Since they had become parents, they realized that their experiences had not prepared them to know all the answers and they no longer gave advice to parents (Erdman, 1969).

Information written in professional literature about parents can be used for background understanding, but it is extremely foolish to expect the subjective experience of one parent or one group of parents to explain the needs of all parents. Each parent deserves to be known and understood for himself or herself. As one parent put it: "Awareness of our individual problems, our unique abilities, and our strengths" is necessary (Schultz, 1978, p. 36). Only by learning to know each parent well is it possible to develop an individual interaction program with each parent.

REFERENCES

Adams, M. *Mental retardation and its social dimensions*. New York: Columbia University Press, 1971.

Akerley, M.S. False gods and angry prophets. In A.P. Turnbull & H.R. Turnbull (Eds.), *Parents speak out: Views from the other side of a two-way mirror*. Columbus, Ohio: Charles E. Merrill, 1978.

American Medical Association. *Mental retardation: A handbook for the primary physician*. Washington, D.C., 1965.

Bailey, J. Personal communication, 1969.

Beck, H.L. *Social services to the mentally retarded*. Springfield, Illinois: Charles C. Thomas, 1969.

Begab, M.J. Casework for the mentally retarded—Casework with parents. In W. Wolfensburger & R.K. Kurtz (Eds.), *Management of the family of the mentally retarded*. Chicago: Follett, 1969.

Bennett, J. Company, halt! In A.P. Turnbull & H.R. Turnbull (Eds.), *Parents speak out: Views from the other side of a two-way mirror*. Columbus, Ohio: Charles E. Merrill, 1978.

Berne, E. *Games people play*. New York: Grove Press, 1964.

Boggs, E.M. Pointers for parents. In W. Wolfensburger & R.K. Kurtz (Eds.), *Management of the family of the mentally retarded*. Chicago: Follett, 1969.

Boggs, E.M. Who is putting whose head in the sand or in the clouds as the case may be? In A.P. Turnbull & H.R. Turnbull (Eds.), *Parents speak out: Views from the other side of a two-way mirror*. Columbus, Ohio: Charles E. Merrill, 1978.

Boyd, D. The three stages in the growth of a parent of a mentally retarded child. In W. Wolfensburger & R.K. Kurtz (Eds.), *Management of the family of the mentally retarded*. Chicago: Follett, 1969.

Bourne, D. Personal communication, 1959.

Brazelton, T.B. *Infants and mothers: Differences in development*. New York: Dell, 1969.

Brutten, M., Richardson, S.O., & Mangel, C. *Something's wrong with my child*. New York: Harcourt Brace Jovanovich, 1973.

Clark, K. Personal communication, September, 1952.

Cruickshank, W.M. *Learning disabilities in home, school and community*. Syracuse: Syracuse University Press, 1977.

Diekman, B. Personal communication, October, 1975.

Erdman, R. Personal communication, Fall, 1969.

Evans, B. Letting Go. In T. Dougan, L. Isbell, & P. Vyas (Eds.), *We have been there*. Salt Lake City, Utah: Publishers Press, 1979.

Farber, B. Family organization and crisis: Maintenance of integration in families with a severely mentally retarded child. *Monographs of the Society for Research in Child Development*, 1960, *25* (1, Serial No. 75).

Foster, E. Personal communication, Fall, 1970.

Freeman, K. Personal communication, 1978.

Fuller, M. Personal communication, 1975.

Geinger, K. Personal communication, 1975.

Greenfield, J. *A place for Noah*. New York: Holt, Rinehart and Winston, 1978.

Grossman, F.K. *Brothers and sisters of retarded children: An exploratory study*. Syracuse: Syracuse University Press, 1972.

Harris, T.A. *I'm OK—You're OK: A practical guide to transactional analysis*. New York: Harper & Row, 1967.

Heilman, A.E. Parental adjustment to the dull handicapped child. In W. Wolfensburger & R.K. Kurtz (Eds.), *Management of the family of the mentally retarded*. Chicago: Follett, 1969.

Henderson, H. Personal communication, September, 1976.

Hoffman, J.L. Mental retardation, religious values and psychiatric universals. In W. Wolfensburger & R.K. Kurtz (Eds.), *Management of the family of the mentally retarded*. Chicago: Follett, 1969.

Holy Bible, King James Version.

James, M., & Jongward, D. *Born to win: Transactional analysis with Gestalt experiments*. Reading, Mass.: Addison-Wesley, 1971.

Kirk, S.A. *Early education of the mentally retarded*. Urbana, Ill.: University Press, 1958.

Lund, A. I sense you are becoming emotionally involved. In T. Dougan, L. Isbell, & P. Vyas (Eds.), *We have been there*. Salt Lake City, Utah; Publishers Press, 1979.

Maslow, A. *Motivation and personality*. New York: Harper & Row, 1954.

Michaelis, C.T. Why can't Johnny look nice, too? *The Exceptional Parent*, 1972, *1*(5), 24-27.

Michaelis, C.T. Chip on my shoulder. *The Exceptional Parent*, 1974, *4*(1), 30-35.

Michaelis, C.T. Merry Christmas, Jim, and happy birthday! *The Exceptional Parent*, 1976, *6*(6), 6-8.

Michaelis, C.T. Imperfect child—Cause for chronic sorrow. *Special Children*, 1977, *4*(1), 39-48.(a)

Michaelis, C.T. Responses to marriage and parenting: Issues for people with disabilities and their parents. *The Exceptional Parent*, 1977, *7*(3), 6-7.(b)

Michaelis, C.T. Don't leave home without it. *The Exceptional Parent*, 1978, *8*(3), 25-27.

Montgomery County Recreational Department Policy. Rockville, Md.: 1978.

Morton, K. Identifying the enemy—A parent's complaint. In A.P. Turnbull & H.R. Turnbull (Eds.), *Parents speak out: Views from the other side of a two-way mirror*. Columbus, Ohio: Charles E. Merrill, 1978.

National Association for Retarded Citizens. Regional Meeting. Green Bay, Wisconsin, March 10, 1978.

Olashansky, S. Chronic sorrow: A response to having a mentally defective child. In W. Wolfensburger & R.K. Kurtz (Eds.), *Management of the family of the mentally retarded*. Chicago: Follett, 1969.

Perske, R. *New directions for parents of persons who are retarded*. Nashville, New York: Abingdon Press, 1973.

Pieper, E. Grandparents can help. *The Exceptional Parent*, 1976, *6*(2), 7-10.

Popp, C.E., Ingram, V., & Jordan, P.H. Helping parents understand their mentally handicapped child. In W. Wolfensburger & R.K. Kurtz (Eds.), *Management of the family of the mentally retarded*. Chicago: Follett, 1979.

Preston, R. Personal communication, April, 1957.

Ross, A.O. *The exceptional child in the family*. New York: Grune and Stratton, 1964.

Searl, S.J. Stages of parental reaction. *The Exceptional Parent*, 1978, *8*(2), 27-29.

Schleifer, M.J. Let us all stop blaming the parents. *The Exceptional Parent*, 1971, *1*(1), 3-5.

Schrieber, M. *Social work and mental retardation*. New York: John Day, 1970.

Schultz, J. The parent-professional conflict. In A.P. Turnbull & H.R. Turnbull (Eds.), *Parents speak out: Views from the other side of a two-way mirror*. Columbus, Ohio: Charles E. Merrill, 1978.

Smith, E.M. Emotional factors as revealed in the intake process with parents of defective children. In W. Wolfensburger & R.K. Kurtz (Eds.), *Management of the family of the mentally retarded*. Chicago: Follett, 1969.

Spitz, R.A. *The first year of life: Normal and deviant object relations*. New York: International Press, 1965.

Spock, B. *On being the parent of a handicapped child*. Chicago: National Society of Crippled Children and Adults, 1961.

Stephens, T.M., Hartman, A.C., Lucas, V.H. *Teaching children basic skills: A curriculum handbook*. Columbus, Ohio: Charles E. Merrill, 1978.

Tarnopol, L. *Learning disabilities*. Springfield, Ill.: Charles C. Thomas, 1969.

Thompson, B. Personal communication, October, 1976.

Turnbull, A.P. Moving from being a professional to being a parent: A startling experience. In A.P. Turnbull & H.R. Turnbull (Eds.), *Parents speak out: Views from the other side of a two-way mirror*. Columbus, Ohio: Charles E. Merrill, 1978.

Warren, F. A society that is going to kill your children. In A.P. Turnbull & H.R. Turnbull (Eds.), *Parents speak out: Views from the other side of a two-way mirror*. Columbus, Ohio: Charles E. Merrill, 1978.

Webster's Seventh New Collegiate Dictionary. Springfield, Massachusetts: G. & C. Merriam, 1970.

Wolfensburger, W., & Kurtz, R.K. (Eds.). *Management of the family of the mentally retarded*. Chicago: Follett, 1969.

Ziskin, L.Z. The story of Jennie. In A.P. Turnbull & H.R. Turnbull (Eds.), *Parents speak out: Views from the other side of a two-way mirror*. Columbus, Ohio: Charles E. Merrill, 1978.

Chapter 5

Succeeding When Mothers Are Protective and Fathers Are Preoccupied

A successful "sender of information" makes sure that the information sent is about what concerns the listener. Because of differing contacts with the child, the interest of the mother of a handicapped child is likely to be different from the interests of the father of that child. Successful communicating in the school comes when the professionals understand the experience of the parent well enough to know that the mother is accustomed to protecting the child and the father is accustomed to providing for the child.

A professional communicator can see that the information sent to the home responds to the parent's need. Traditionally, the public agency and the teacher have prepared a single message for the home. Understanding the differing needs of the parents makes possible a multilevel communication that can be successful with "overprotective" mothers and "preoccupied" fathers.

WHAT IS A PARENT?

Fathers are not very much like mothers. Fathers have beards and broad shoulders. Mothers have breasts and carry babies. "Parent" means "one who begets or brings forth offspring." Notwithstanding the efforts to liberate women and offer equal pay for equal work, the begetting and the bringing forth of offspring are roles of entirely different magnitude and are highly differentiated. The father and the mother have experiences that do not become similar until the child acquires the necessary independence and self-sufficiency to achieve success in kindergarten. Since mothers and fathers have vastly different experiences being parents, the way in which they relate to the child is not the same, and the concerns that each has about the child are not the same.

The difference between the mother's experience and the father's is exaggerated if the child has a handicapping condition and does not develop independence at the rate that most children do. Mothering a handicapped child is a very different investment than fathering a handicapped child. Since a handicapped child has a prolonged period of dependency, mothers become accustomed to protecting the child. Since a handicapped child needs more goods and services, fathers become preoccupied with earning the means to supply them.

The mother's and the father's interests in the child are different. The public agency and the teacher must be aware of the parenting experiences of both the mother and the father in order to be successful in responding to the concerns of each parent.

THE ROLE OF THE MOTHER

The Parenting Experience for the Mother

Since no method of birth control aside from sterilization is entirely effective, a fertile woman faces the possibility of pregnancy each time she engages in sexual intercourse. Since this consequence is attached to the physical relationship, few women of childbearing age are able to participate freely in sexual intercourse without considering the possibility of changes in their personal life and in long-term goals. Perhaps the "double standard" is not one that is forced on women nearly so much as one that has been accepted by women as a reality. A woman who engages in sexual intercourse may be obligating herself to carry and nurture a fetus. If an unplanned pregnancy occurs, it is the woman that must alter her life to meet the child's immediate needs. Even if she chooses to have an abortion, the woman must have means to pay for it and the time for the procedure and recovery period.

Most women "know" that they are pregnant even before symptoms can be identified by a physician. One young mother said, "The next morning I just knew that I was pregnant. I just felt different."

Pregnancy

Women watch for the menstrual cycle from the grade school years. The "sex" films that fifth and sixth grade school boys and girls talk about are not about sexual intimacy at all; they are about the hygiene required during the menstrual flow. Young women growing up are reminded of the possibility of motherhood each month. For women growing up, the relationship between sex and pregnancy is part of their lives. They learn to carry purses large enough for an emergency supply of sanitary equipment and to plan their lives around the "red headed cousin" that visits each four weeks. If the menstrual period does not come, the woman knows what that probably means.

For many women, the nausea begins soon after the period is "missed," the usual foods become distasteful, and the mornings become miserable. Along with the nausea comes an almost uncontrollable desire to sleep, day and night. By the time the woman has chosen a doctor and made an appointment, she has already spent anxious and uncomfortable hours, almost always knowing what is happening to her and a little about what is ahead for her.

The call to the doctor's office for an appointment is usually answered by a young receptionist who asks, "What did you want to see the doctor about?" Somehow it seems almost sacrilegious to announce such private information to the voice on the telephone, but private information will be discussed by many people that the young woman never meets. Laboratory technicians and receptionists, as well as nurses and doctors, talk about such personal things as the weight and urine specimens of an obstetrics patient.

As the pregnancy proceeds, the private information becomes public. It seems that everyone feels free to comment, and even complete strangers ask when the baby is due. There is an almost continuous adjustment of clothes. Since pregnancy is one of the things that brings girls and women together, friends and sisters loan their maternity clothes to one another. It is not unusual for an outfit to go back and forth so many times that no one quite remembers who it belonged to in the first place.

The woman begins to wear maternity clothes at about the time that the baby begins to move. The child moves when he or she wants to move, even if the mother would prefer to relax. The pressure of the baby against the mother's diaphragm increases as the baby kicks.

Along with the maternity clothes comes the weight gain. Some of the weight is from the baby, some from the retention of fluid. All the extra weight interferes with the circulation in the legs and with the smooth operation of the bowels and bladder. As the pregnancy continues, the woman's usual physical activities must be modified. One young active woman wanted a child, but did not want to give up either her golf season or her skiing season. At least one "season" is affected.

The first trip to the doctor is followed by many more hours reading magazines in the waiting room. As the pregnancy progresses, the mother spends more time being weighed, measured, and "specimened." She also takes vitamin pills and does the exercises that will help in the delivery of the baby.

Delivery of the Baby

Since the pregnancy has curtailed the activities of the expectant mother, it is no wonder that she approaches the delivery with excitement and anticipation. Most expectant mothers have a suitcase packed for months with a toothbrush and some pretty nightgowns, ready to take to the hospital. The time and the day are uncertain so the prospective mother cannot make commitments.

The delivery itself can be long or short, but it is seldom private. People are busy preparing the mother on the table and getting the instruments ready. As the labor pains come closer together, anticipation increases. With all of this audience and with all the discomfort, the new mother delivers her child to be observed by whatever strangers are there. If she screams, cries, or fights, there will be an audience. One nurse remarked, "You ought to see how well she delivers," about a new mother. Yet no matter how good the "performance," it never gets the acclaim of a Sunday afternoon touchdown.

Only the oldest of the old wives spend much time talking about it, but the new mother has the discomfort of heavy flowing, tender breasts, and most likely stitches to heal. When she gets home, the things that she did not feel well enough to do before the baby came are still waiting for her. The carpet needs to be shampooed, and the windows need to be washed. Even though the energy level of the new mother is low, there are also exercises to be done to help the uterus go back to its normal position. The baby is no longer pressing against the bowels or the bladder, but neither works too well.

The mother has special foods to eat to increase the flow of milk if she nurses and other foods to decrease the milk if she doesn't. Perhaps the last straw, the old "pre-baby" clothes won't fit around the now empty, but still stretched abdomen. And, of course, all the visitors who come to see the baby also see the house in disorder, the clothes that don't fit, and the hair that needs to be "done."

Caring for the Newborn

In addition to all the changes in the mother, she has the additional responsibility of caring for the infant. Even women who plan to return to work spend the first few weeks after delivery in intimate contact with the baby. The mother learns to adjust her schedule to change the linen on the baby's bed and bottom many times a day, and night. The new mother must somehow adjust to this responsibility at the same time she is trying to adjust to the physical and emotional excitement that she has just experienced.

It is during these months in which the baby and the mother share the intimacy of meals and sleep, before and after birth, that they develop a very close tie to one another. Almost all mothers have sat holding the tiny newborn after the feeding just to look at the little fingers and the tiny nose. During these months of intimacy the mother and the child learn to understand one another: they learn how to respond to each other, they learn to fit into each other's patterns.

Sharing with Other Mothers

The experience of becoming a mother is so overwhelming that most mothers want to share that experience with someone else who has had the experience. This can't be the child's father because he has not had the experience. It usually is the mother's mother or the mother's sister or the mother's girlfriend. These women purchase or make baby clothes with tiny flowers and careful stitches.

As the baby gets older the new mother frequently prefers that her mother tend the child when she must do something else. Mothers go shopping with friends who have babies. They sit in city parks on good days and around the kitchen table when it rains; they talk about their babies and their pregnancies. As their babies grow up and no longer share the intimacy, mothers still talk to each other about when their children were babies. The intimacy of early mothering is a bittersweet experience, since the joy of being needed compensates for the consuming experience of mothering.

The Rewards of Parenting for the Mother

Additional Attention

Baby books have a place to list the gifts that were given to the baby. Even when family and friends have limited finances, a new baby is given new clothes and toys. The gifts, of course, are not opened by the tiny infant. The gifts are opened by the mother and she touches and admires the pretty little things. The baby shower is not for the baby at all. The baby shower is for the mother and it can be as exciting an adventure as a bridal shower, even if the child is not the first child in the family. Gifts for the new baby sometimes come from people who do not know the family well, but are interested in babies. One little old grandmother knits booties for each of the new babies in the church congregation. Some of the new mothers she hardly knows, but they receive booties for the new baby.

In addition to the tiny little things that the mother makes or purchases or receives as gifts for the baby, she also gets new clothes for herself. Some may come from the mother-to-be shop with a mannequin in the window that appears to have a basketball stuffed in the front of her dress. Or maybe the new clothes are the special clothes loaned to her by a friend. Sometimes smocks and dusters and caftans are sewed for the mother by a friend or by her mother. Even when she sews them herself, the new mother has a choice of new materials and colors and designs. The new mother probably needs some "flat" shoes and new stockings and a new robe to wear at the hospital and. . . .

Even before there are any concerns for the child, the doctor is concerned about the mother. How does she feel? Does she sleep well? Is she getting enough of the right kinds of foods? Is she getting time to relax? There are usually vitamin pills to take and as the pregnancy progresses mild exercises that may mean setting aside time for a walk. The doctor takes a medical history and examines the mother and monitors her weight and urine. Having someone "care" can be a rewarding experience, even when the "care" is a purchased service.

As the time for delivery comes, there is more information given to the mother and she is prepared for the "big event." In the delivery room the mother is, of course, the focus of attention, until the child is delivered. Then directions for the care of the infant are given to the mother. The calls to the doctor with questions and concerns about the child are a little like a "help line," because the mother has access to the expert ear whenever she needs help. Even though many of the doctors are not easily reached on the telephone, the nurse or answering service is usually available and, if there is an emergency, everyone listens.

Famous mothers have their pictures taken and printed with their infants. The picture of a mother and a child is considered a work of art and a little like a madonna in the art galleries. Since the mother has taken care of the child for months without being able to see and touch the child, the caring for the infant is a little like the childhood days of playing dolls. Mother can try the new clothes on the baby, and see how they fit. She can look at the ruffles on the bassinet, and the animal pictures on the wall. She can hold the soft pastel blanket with the baby in it close to her cheek. The nighttime feeding, whether sitting on the mother's bed or in the rocking chair, can be a little like the stillness of Christmas morning when the promised gift has arrived. To be able to show the baby to friends and relatives wrapped in the blanket that was given at the shower is a special delight. New mothers have been known to dress the baby in the dress that grandmother sent when grandmother comes. Some families have used the same christening dress for generations; the dress is carefully preserved for the next child in the family. Families also save cribs, bassinets, and baby bathtubs.

Mother-Infant Bonding

Anyone who has ever taken care of someone else's child has had the deflating experience of having the child cry because the mother was leaving. Even children who have not been treated well will cry when the mother leaves. Although this relationship can be a demanding one, it is also a source of joy for the mother. The mother can be absolutely sure that someone cares about her, that someone needs her, and that someone wants to be with her. It is the mother who can get the baby to eat the cereal. It is the mother who can train the baby to sleep through the night. It is the mother who knows what the baby likes, the minute details of what the child is used to doing, and how the child responds to different things.

Although notes can be left for the baby sitter to tell all the important things about the child, the only really important note is the one that contains the telephone number where the mother can be reached. It is useless for the sitter to call the doctor. The doctor will not be interested in the baby sitter's problems with the baby, even if the sitter is the father. If father is the sitter he frequently needs to find out where the extra night clothes are, or the special soap, or the cereal, or what food to feed the baby first, and only the mother knows. The mother may never have had complete control of anything, but while the child is an infant, the mother has complete control. The satisfaction of complete control can be a rewarding one.

New Meaning to Old Relationships

When the new mother returns to work or goes out with friends she is treated like a "new woman." The first few trips out have a holiday air. There is a new respect for her in the office, at the party, or in the meeting. The new mother is particularly respected by other mothers and other women. She does not need to announce to the world with cigars; one look and everyone knows. People say, "You look good." The message actually means "You look different than you did when you were pregnant," but the intent is warm and accepting.

The father, who realizes that he is to play a supporting role at first, begins to support the mother and do things to "thank" her for the gift of the "son" (even when he turns out to be a daughter). The birth of a child frequently brings a feeling of purpose to relationships and to family goals. It is not unusual for a husband to call his wife "Mother," after she is one, of course.

Complications of Parenting for the Mother of a Handicapped Child

Unplanned Child

"I didn't want to have a child, I had already raised three sons, now God is punishing me for how I felt," one mother of a Down's syndrome child said. Down's syndrome children and other handicapped children are frequently born to mothers who are over 35. Many of these mothers have raised children and do not particularly want to assume the responsibility of raising another. Handicapped children may be born to mothers who have experienced several miscarriages or whose earlier children have died in infancy. A mother does not forget the baby that she lost. The handicapped child reminds the mother even more.

Pregnancy

In the case of a high-risk pregnancy, the mother's condition must be followed carefully. The discomfort experienced by the mother during a high-risk pregnancy is greater than that of the mother who faces pregnancy in good physical and mental health. There are more trips to the doctor and more tests, and there is more anxiety as the mother waits for the results of the tests. Genetic counseling includes a discussion of all the skeletons in the family closet and can be emotionally traumatic.

The mother frequently needs even more sleep, experiences more nausea, and sometimes must follow a rigid diet. Bed rest may be prescribed. None of these is particularly pleasant for the expectant mother.

Spotting or flowing later in the pregnancy is not unusual during at risk pregnancies. Frequently, the mother feels even more fatigue and must undergo even more tests. The diet must be monitored more carefully; salt intake must be limited, and certain foods must be avoided. Bed rest is ordered for some women who threaten to miscarry. False labor pains plague many at risk expectant mothers, and the prevention of premature delivery is a matter of concern to many of the physicians. Trying to continue a semblance of normal life and even a few enjoyable activities is almost impossible when the pregnancy is a "difficult" one.

Delivery

Frequently, the delivery of a handicapped child involves a prolonged labor. Sometimes the labor stops when the child is only partly delivered. Sometimes the child's position is such that the child cannot proceed easily through the birth canal, which may cause severe injury to the child, as well as additional trauma and pain for the mother. Sometimes the mother needs more drugs during the delivery because of her delicate condition or the condition of the infant.

One of the reasons a new mother usually recovers quickly from the stress of childbirth is the presence of the beautiful child. When the child has some kind of problem, the mother has a difficult time organizing her resources to recover from the trauma that she has experienced.

Facing the Stress

Facing the infant's condition is a tremendous physical and psychological strain in itself, but frequently the child needs to have immediate surgery or other care for which the mother must give consent. For those decisions, more medical and social history must be taken, and the child's condition must be evaluated by other specialists.

The mother may not be given the care and emotional support that she needs at this time, since everyone is concerned about the needs of the infant. The staff may make comments about the child, and some can be very upsetting. "What are your plans?" one young mother was asked by a nurse. "Surely you are going to institutionalize her." The mother had learned only a few hours before that her child was seriously retarded and was certainly not ready to talk about it to a total stranger (Houghton, 1975). But having a baby is a public experience for a mother, and the condition of that child is common knowledge.

Religious decisions must be made quickly, for at risk newborns and their mothers are often visited in the hospital by clergymen or other religious leaders who offer to baptize or bless the child. Although the intent is to "help," the offer may cause the new mother more stress. Relatives and friends come, not with gifts and congratulations, but with concern and more questions.

Caring for the Newborn

The closeness that the mother has experienced with the child may be abruptly interrupted if the child needs oxygen or other special equipment. If the child is isolated from the mother, the mother does not have the soothing, healing experience of holding her child and watching the tiny fingers curl tightly around her finger.

If the child is able to go home, there is concern about being able to provide proper care for the child. At risk children usually need more frequent feedings, more burping, and more clean clothes. There is frequently not time even to sit down between feedings. At risk children need frequent trips to see the doctor, which means that the mother must bundle up the child; take medication, food, and extra clothing; and sit in the doctor's waiting room even more often. As she sits there, she sees the beautiful babies of the other mothers.

If infant intervention services are available, the mother takes the child there, too. Each such appointment diminishes the time that the mother has to complete her routine work at home or to spend on herself. One family kept a record of the time that was spent taking their handicapped child to the doctor. They marked the calendar with X's when at least half a day was spent getting services. There were two or three X's for each week that first year (Lichter, 1975).

Since the child needs so much of the mother's care there is not time for the mother to rest or take care of herself between the care routines that the child needs. There certainly is not time to go to have her hair done or to pretty herself and the house before the husband comes home.

Mother-Infant Bonding When the Child Is Handicapped

People sometimes speak of a face that "only a mother could love." Mothers of handicapped children frequently have to learn to love that face. She must deal with the child's condition and the role that she may have played in the deformity, which is extremely difficult. If the infant who was for some time part of her own body is deformed, the shock is great. If the mother had never seen any children with such severe physical handicaps before the child was born, the shock may be even greater.

If the baby cannot respond when the mother attempts to care for the child and touches and talks to the baby, the care-giving situation can become one that the mother does not enjoy (Michaelis, 1978). Some handicapped children not only do not respond, but also do not allow themselves to be handled. Forming a bond with these children is an emotionally exhausting task. Children who are seriously delayed may not develop the ability to respond for years. The state of infancy for them is prolonged.

Sharing with Other Mothers

Handicapped babies are seldom passed around from one mother to another. Most people are uncomfortable holding a baby who does not look and behave like other babies. The mother of that child finds herself trying to hold the baby and write checks, warm bottles, feed herself, and even comb her hair. Baby sitters are difficult to find; even grandmothers are often uncertain about how to care for the child and may not be as available to take care of the child as they might be.

The children themselves do not win friends since frequently they do not learn to smile at strangers for some time and continue to cling to the mother. The sharing of children's clothes that usually follows the sharing of maternity clothes may not happen. Sometimes the baby is so small and physically impaired that the clothes do not fit; other times friends do not choose to share their children's clothes with the handicapped child.

Additional Attention

The additional attention received by most new mothers is not given to the mother of a handicapped child. Friends do not rush to the hospital with gifts for the child. Since the child frequently does not leave the hospital after the usual few days, friends assume that the baby can't use the new clothes and they do not know what else to give and frequently do not come to congratulate the new mother by giving her gifts for the child.

The condition of the child is stressful not only to the parents but also to the physician and other medical personnel. Since they do not have "good" news, they sometimes avoid seeing the new mother. When they do come, they come with subdued messages (Spock, 1961). The interaction with the physician may not be open and supportive but full of messages such as "we will have to wait and see." To the new mother who has already waited for months to see her child, the additional emotional resources necessary to wait longer seem almost impossible to muster. Instead of comfort, contacts with the physician may produce additional stress.

The Uncompleted Task

Since the act of carrying a child and giving birth is often seen as an achievement for the mother, it is easy for her and for others to assume that something that she did or did not do caused the child's condition. In some cases this may be true. One mother who during her pregnancy took some medication that may have damaged her handicapped child has not told anyone. She is afraid that anyone who knows will not provide services to her child (Taylor, 1978). Other mothers are concerned because they did not quit smoking or because they contracted infections or diseases (Sharp, 1974). Some mothers of handicapped children feel that they have failed their families because they were not able to produce the normal child that the family wanted (Michaelis, 1977).

Almost all societies and all families have superstitions that an expectant mother's actions can cause the child to have everything from birthmarks to slurred speech. Admonitions include everything from reaching things on a high shelf to looking at spiders. For most mothers the "old wives' tales" can be dismissed. For mothers of children who have handicaps there are real and imaginary conditions that must be examined.

Continuation of Mother-Infant Bonding

Not only must the mother of a handicapped child learn to tolerate and hopefully enjoy the routine of caring for a child who does not respond and develop, but also she must maintain that relationship for a prolonged time. The "delayed" child can learn, but he or she learns more slowly. For the teacher, this means that skills of a lower developmental level must be taught to the child. For the mother, it means that the intense interaction of early infancy and early developmental years must be maintained for a longer period of time. It means that supervision of the child must be constant so that the child will not eat inappropriate objects, play in the street, handle sharp objects, etc. It also means that the bibs and diapers of infancy and early childhood must be washed well into middle or even late childhood.

Even children with mild learning problems tend to behave as if they were much younger. In the early preschool years the hyperactive child continues to behave much like the sensory-motor exploring child described by Piaget (Flavell, 1963; Michaelis, 1971). The behavior disorders of school age children are the behaviors typical of children when they are in the early toddler stage of development (Wheland, 1978).

The handicapped child needs more maternal attention and responds to that attention with less enthusiasm. The child does not learn to "interact with the mother" (Michaelis, 1976) and may not enjoy the cuddling that most children thrive on; however, the child still needs the intense attention of the mother to monitor the learning environment. For the mother of a handicapped child, the personal investment in bonding is greater.

The prolonged intense relationship can smother the mother and exhaust her potential to continue. The relationship can also become such a way of life for the mother that it is difficult for her to see when the child is ready or able to become more independent.

The mother-infant bond is broken by the normal child when he or she is capable of successfully interacting in a larger circle. For the child who does not develop autonomy in the same degree and with the same intensity, the need for maternal protection is an uncertain quantity. The child does not give the obvious cues to the amount of mothering that is required. Mothers of handicapped children continue to protect their children because they have learned to protect the child through a prolonged infancy and because the child's ability to interact without her help is uncertain.

Concerns That Mothers Are Likely To Have

Since the mother in most instances has provided for the child's personal needs through infancy and early childhood, she is used to being concerned about the child's personal and emotional needs. It is likely that the mother will be concerned about how the child feels at school and how the people at school feel about the child. It is likely that the mother will want to know about:

The Teacher

The mother is likely to be concerned about the training and experience that the teacher has had with "children like Joe." The mother will likely want to know how the teacher defines and manages misbehavior. The mother is likely to want to see the teacher and talk to the teacher about how to "take good care" of "my baby." The mother will probably want to know about the experience that any aides have had and how the aides will interact with the child.

Medical Services

The mother, who has cared for the child during numerous medical difficulties, will want to be sure that there is medical assistance available at school if the child needs it. The mother may be concerned about the services of a school nurse and how the child will be handled in case of illness or seizure. Many handicapped children take medication. Mothers are naturally concerned about how the medication will be given at school.

Other Children

Mothers are acutely aware of the isolation of the handicapped child and, having seen the behavior of the neighborhood children, may be somewhat worried about how the other children might treat the child. The desire for the child to have friends may be offset by the concern that the other children might tease the handicapped child. Even when handicaps are mild, the mother is likely to be extremely sensitive to the possibility that her child can be hurt physically or psychologically by other children. Despite the childhood chant, not only do sticks and stones break bones, but being called names *can* hurt! Mothers know that.

The School Curriculum

The mother, who has been responsible for the daily activities of the child, wants to know exactly what activities are available at school, what materials are used, and all the details of the school schedule.

Visiting the School

Because of the need to make sure that someone else can indeed meet the child's needs, the mother is likely to want to visit the child at school to see how the child is actually getting along in the school setting. This interest can be somewhat disconcerting to the teacher, who knows that unless the mother visits frequently the child is likely to "put on a show." (See suggestions in Chapter 8 for situations in which the mother can see for herself how things are going for the child without disrupting the program.)

THE ROLE OF THE FATHER

The Parenting Experience for the Father

It is possible for the father to see sexual intercourse apart from the parenting experience, since the father's heavy responsibilities of parenthood do not start until long after conception. Discussions of sex for growing boys do not center around the possibility of becoming fathers, but around the pleasure of the sexual experience. Since the identity of the father of the child cannot be immediately determined as it can with the mother of the child, the man can approach the sexual experience with less concern for impending pregnancy. No matter what the circumstances the man knows that he won't become pregnant.

Pregnancy

The mother of the child may not discuss the physical symptoms that she is experiencing and instead tell the father of her condition as a "surprise." If the father is around the mother, he may notice that she is behaving differently, but he only observes without participating.

It is possible for a mother to have a child without the father being present during the pregnancy. If the father is present during the pregnancy, he finds that his wife is more dependent and less interested in the usual activities. The additional responsibilities that she now has, i.e., to eat carefully, sleep well, and get medical attention, can interfere with the companionship that the father is used to having and make him feel isolated.

Fathers have been known to have headaches, back pains, and other symptoms similar to those of their wives during pregnancy. Some fathers have stopped smoking and drinking during the time the mother stopped for the health of the child. Fathers reschedule business trips, postpone transfers, and reduce the amount of time they spend on outside activities in order to be available to make the mother more comfortable. But the father does not actually participate in the pregnancy, except to support the mother.

The pending birth of a child is a time for the father to reevaluate his ability to provide for the family. It is frequently the time that the family decides to move to a larger apartment or a house. Families purchase station wagons and life insurance. The father must figure out how he will pay for the medical expenses and how the family will manage on one salary, at least for a while.

Delivery

Some fathers are allowed to be present in the delivery room while the child is being born. A few fathers have had training to help the wife relax during the delivery, but even in those cases the father is only an observer. He must rearrange his schedule at the last minute in order to be a supporting actor.

Father is usually the one who calls the grandparents to tell them about the arrival. He describes the baby and tells about the delivery. One father hung a large sign out of the upstairs window. It read, "It's a boy." The father calls friends and tells the neighbors and the other children at home. Then, after he organizes all that, he goes back to the office to pass out cigars.

While the mother is in the hospital, father is responsible for the care and running of the home and the care of other children and pets. He runs the routine errands for the household, gets the groceries, and buys all the last minute baby things from the drug and department stores. Sometimes he has the help of a mother-in-law or a person hired to help, but he still must supervise. After he finishes getting the things ready in the nursery he must catch up on the duties that he has been neglecting at work and make arrangements to pick up the mother and baby at the hospital.

A Baby in the House

When the mother and the baby do come home, things are not in their usual order. When the baby is new, and for sometime after, the mother is not able to keep up with the regular routines. "My blue heaven" can indeed be blue with a fussy baby and a mother who cries at the slightest provocation as new mothers are prone to do. Because of one mother's concentrated efforts to keep the *baby's* washing done, one father found that the only stockings that were clean for him to wear to work were a pair of his seven-year-old daughter's knee sox. He wore them. It is no wonder that fathers start educational funds for their infants. Until children are independent enough to no longer need intimacy with their mothers, fathers play only a supporting role.

Rewards of Parenting for the Father

To be able to impregnate a woman is proof of sexual maturity. The lyrics of a popular song in the early 1970s claimed that "having my baby is a lovely way of saying how much you love me," implying that the pregnant woman loved the man who had impregnated her and the public could see that affirmation.

Although society no longer needs to send out warriors and hunters to protect it and provide for it, a man still acquires a great deal of status in being able to provide material comforts for his family. A man must have children, and he must be able to show that what he gives to them is good in order to be a man among men. Great hunters have great herds (Goldberg, 1977).

Continuation of the Family Name

Although some career women are keeping their maiden names or hyphenating them with the husband's surname, most children use the surname of the father. In legal and in many religious circles the child is considered to be of the father's family. One of the greatest rewards of fatherhood is that the father will be honored because of the deeds of the child who carries his name. If children are successful, the local newspapers write that Mary, daughter of Mr. and Mrs. John Smith, has accomplished a certain thing. Many businesses are titled J.H. Smith and Sons, contractors or attorneys or. . . . The father is proud of the achievements of the grown child. Although the mother may look forward to interaction with the children's children, it is the father who looks forward to companionship with the grown child.

I Am a Man among Men

Since many people may be unaware that an expectant father is indeed an expectant father, he must spread the word when the new child arrives. He must also have, sitting on the desk or on the wall at the office, pictures of his wife and children. The man with the most pictures is assumed to be the most stable. Some businesses and agencies will not promote men unless they have families (Goldberg, 1977).

The greatest reward for the father does not come when the child is an infant or when the child is developing. It comes when the child develops enough skill for the father to feel pride in the child's accomplishments and share that pride with fellow employees and whoever reads the newspaper.

Complications of Parenting for the Father of a Handicapped Child

Learning of the Child's Condition

Some physicians tell the new mother about the child's problems and expect her to tell her husband. Other physicians tell the father and expect him to tell the mother. In either situation, the father is expected to perform some tasks that may be very difficult for him. He may be anxious to support and comfort his wife, but he does not have the information that would make that possible. In addition, the fact that the parents are separated by the mother's hospitalization deprives them of the best opportunities to communicate about such emotional concerns. The father is expected to attend to his responsibilities at work and in the community as if nothing has happened. He may be required to carry the information to brokenhearted grandparents, siblings, and friends and neighbors, but in each situation he must be strong and allow everyone to "depend" on him.

The father's personal needs are not met. He probably has concerns about the additional expenses involved in the care of the child and perhaps the care of the mother. He is probably concerned about getting some help at home for the mother, and he is probably concerned about how he will be able to do all that is needed and still function adequately in his job, which is now even more crucial for family solidarity.

Strain on the Father's Ability To Provide

Although Public Law (P.L.) 94-142 requires that handicapped children be provided a free appropriate public education (FAPE) and that such an education shall include related services to the children and their families, there are still additional expenses for the families of handicapped children. Many families need an additional car to transport the handicapped child to services. In order to allow family members time to participate in other activities, extra monies may be needed for help in the home.

If summer camp and other facilities can be found for the handicapped child, the fees are usually higher than those for camp services for nonhandicapped children. There are organizations with carefully trained personnel that offer short-term care for the handicapped child either in the family home or in some center, but the charge for such a service is higher than that for similar care services for nonhandicapped children.

With a handicapped child in the family, it is difficult for a father to feel that he has truly provided for his family. The handicapped youngster usually needs financial support from the father well into adulthood. Severely handicapped children may need dependent living facilities as they get older. Although some of the cost is offset by public agencies, the father still is required to finance much of it. It is not unusual for fathers of handicapped children to provide estates for the care of the adult handicapped child even when family resources do not allow funds for the creation of estates for all of the family members.

Ability of the Child To Mature

"Like father, like son" is seldom true when the child is handicapped. The son does not usually learn to do the things that the father enjoyed as he grew up. Even mildly handicapped children have difficulties playing ball and participating in other activities that are easy for fathers to do with their children.

One four-year-old physically handicapped boy who can't hold his head up lies on the family room floor and hits a piece of paper squeezed into a ball with his arms rigid. He does not have voluntary movement in his arms. The family puts a ball cap on him and calls it his ball game. Obviously, the father would rather play the game in the backyard with a real ball and a bat. Another father of a retarded boy coaches a basketball team for normal boys but does not find time to take his retarded son to a basketball game.

Some neurological conditions that make learning difficult for the child may be conditions that the father experiences also. In such situations the father may be distressed because the child is so much like him.

Fathers do not usually take their children with them as they go about their daily work activities. Fathers tell others about the beauty, brains, or talent of their children. The father of a handicapped child has little to share with coworkers, however. The child seldom achieves in relation to the accomplishments of other children of the same age. Men have learned to compete and achieve, and it is difficult for them to appreciate the accomplishments of children who are behind, even when they do their best. It is difficult for a father to accept a child who from the beginning is a "loser."

A father of a retarded girl says that the men he works with ask him about his son but do not mention his daughter. He says he doesn't bring it up either, "Are you going to brag about her learning to say her name? She is six now, and most six-year-olds have been saying their names for years" (Swanson, 1976). Another father, whose only child is handicapped, has nothing to say when the other fathers talk about the colleges that their children are attending. He is hoping to be able to get his daughter into a group home for the retarded, but somehow that does not seem like an appropriate topic of conversation (Schmidler, 1978).

Although fathers of handicapped children are required to provide more funds for the support of the child at least to some extent throughout adulthood, the reward for the support is not forthcoming, since the child does not achieve as well as the nonhandicapped child does with much less input.

The Father's Involvement in Daily Care

Since the handicapped child requires more care and attention for development, the father frequently assumes a care role that is not necessary when the child develops more quickly. Fathers frequently help bathe physically handicapped children and tutor children with learning disabilities. It is not unusual for fathers to assume a major role in the transportation of handicapped children. Greenfield (1978) gives a diary account of the energies that he has spent providing care for his son Noah at home and transporting him to various schools for service.

Other fathers completely withdraw from the care routine of the child. Since the needs of a handicapped child are more complicated than the needs of a nonhandicapped child, some fathers choose to leave the total responsibility of the child to the mother. These fathers do not participate in the care routine or search for services and appear too occupied with other things to be interested in the child. This may not be due to a lack of interest, however, as much as to an inability to express feelings. Fathers have not learned to express feelings or been encouraged to talk about disappointments (Montigue, 1974; Goldberg, 1977).

For some fathers, the lack of interaction with the child may be the result of a perceived inability to meet the child's needs. Since the mother receives most of the instruction about the child and attends most of the conferences, the father may not have the information that would allow him to be comfortable interacting with a child who has a handicapping condition. Although this inability may be a perceived inability rather than a lack of skill, it may actually make the father feel like an outsider in the mother-child and mother-child-school interactions. Because of the additional need for monies to provide for the child and the fact that, traditionally, interaction with the school has been with the child's mother, the father of a handicapped child may appear to be preoccupied.

Concerns That Fathers Are Likely To Have

Since the most rewarding part of fatherhood comes when the child is grown enough to participate in activities with the father, the father will be anxious for the child to develop in the same ways that other children do. The father is likely to be interested in the child's progress in:

Academic Skills

The father is likely to be interested in how well the child can read and do math problems. The father is likely to be interested in knowing if the child is at grade level in the academic skills.

Motor Development

The father is likely to be interested in how the child compares to other children in physical/motor skills. He will want to know if the child can physically keep up with other children and if the child has a chance to play ball and other activities with the other children. The father will probably want to know if the child can play as a member of a sport team.

Social Development

The father will likely wonder if the child is able to defend himself/herself and play and work with other children on an equal basis. The father is likely to wonder if the child follows the school rules and whether the child causes undue bother for the teacher and other school staff.

Supplementary Services

The father will likely be interested in knowing if the child has help on an individual basis to learn physical and academic tasks. The father is likely to want to know about tutoring and therapy for his child.

Fees

The father, who has been providing for the monetary needs of the child, is likely to be interested in knowing if the services provided require additional monies. The father will want to know if the child has all the equipment and materials needed at school and if all the fees have been paid.

The Father's Visits to the School

Although the father is interested in the child's daily interaction with other people, he is used to delegating this responsibility to someone else and is far less likely to drop in at school to "see what is going on" than the child's mother is. The father has been used to trusting someone else, usually the mother, to provide the daily activities for the child. Seeing the child in the school setting can help the father understand the capabilities of the child and the program of the school, however. The father is more likely to visit school if activities and open house programs are arranged. (See Chapter 13 for suggestions. Suggestions for involvement of the father in materials preparation and special activities are given in Chapter 8.)

RESPONSES TO PARENTS BY THE PUBLIC AGENCY

Respect for the Differing Needs of Mothers and Fathers

Under P.L. 94-142 the parents of a handicapped child are to be treated equally, but the public agency offering services to the child can facilitate the communication with the home by realizing that the parenting experiences and concerns of each parent are different. Mothers and fathers are likely to be interested in different aspects of the child's development and of the services delivered to the child by the agency. Recognizing this, the agency could organize communication to the parents according to the interests of each. If the agency assumes the responsibility of communication to each parent about all areas of interest to that parent, potential misunderstanding can be avoided. There are some things that the agency can do to facilitate the communication.

Scheduling Conferences and Home Visits

Fathers are typically not available to attend daytime conferences, and the regulations for the law require that an Individual Education Program (IEP) conference be set at a mutually agreed upon time. (See Chapter 2.) In order to clarify the meaning of the information, it is important that the receiver be allowed to ask questions. Messages sent to the father through the mother are colored by what she is interested in, and the father will not have the opportunity to clarify and ask other questions.

In order for one father, an attorney in the justice department, to attend his daughter's IEP conference he must take three hours out of his working day; the school is 45 minutes driving time from his office. During the conference, he must be concerned about getting back to other duties at work. It is highly likely that he will be preoccupied with the pressures of his other responsibilities during the conference (Schmidler, 1978).

Visits made to the home by public agency personnel make the parents more comfortable sending and receiving messages about the child. (See Chapter 8.) In order to gain full benefit from the visit, the visit should be scheduled at a time when the father as well as the mother is at home.

Providing Information That Fills the Needs of Both Parents

The information sent to the parents of a handicapped child is not required by law to cover such things as how the child is getting along with the other children or if the child has trouble finding someone to play with at recess. In order for each of the parents to become comfortable about the child's day at school, however, each of their individual concerns must be discussed. (Methods of information interaction are discussed in Chapter 7.) It is the responsibility of the school agency personnel to make the discussion open enough for the parents to feel free to request information that may be interesting to them (Lichter, 1976). Some of the information may be sent to the family through written communication, such as a newsletter. (See Chapter 8.)

Trying To Make the Father Comfortable

Because of the roles usually taken by the mother and the father, the mother is the parent who more frequently contacts the school and is contacted by the school. The father is not usually included in the mundane, routine interaction, and public agencies are not used to interacting with fathers. Even if the school has a male principal, most of the other school personnel are female and the content and organization of the interaction can be of the type in which women usually participate. In such a setting, it is rather natural for the conversation to include discussion of a new dress, a new recipe, or some other topic not particularly interesting to the father. The communication setting can be further complicated if the father is asked to sit on a child-sized chair or drink out of a dainty teacup. (See Chapter 10.)

Sending Messages to Each Parent Directly

If it is not possible to schedule a time when both parents can meet together to hear the results of evaluations or the planned program, arrangements should be made to discuss them with each parent separately. Asking one parent to explain the situation to the other is unrealistic. The parent who did not come to the conference is limited to hearing what the other parent perceived to be important. Each parent should hear the information straight from those who made the evaluations or recommendations.

Consent

School personnel should not attempt to get the signature from one of the child's parents without making sure that the other parent understands and agrees to whatever has been discussed. Parents at home must respond to the pragmatic needs of their children and seldom have uninterrupted time to discuss school problems. If the message goes to only one parent, the other parent may feel that his or her needs or concerns have been neglected. For instance, if the school wants the child to work on more math skills, it may be easier to get the father's permission than to get the mother's permission. Getting a signature from one parent will not be helpful if the parents disagree. Goals should be set that are important to each of the parents.

Counseling for Parents

If counseling for one or both parents appears to be warranted, it is advisable to tell the parents when they are together. If it is implied that the public agency considers one of the parents weak or unbalanced, communication that will enhance the development of the child is not facilitated. To imply that "You are all right, but we must get some additional help to deal with that mate of yours" can be a most harmful message.

RESPONSES MADE BY THE TEACHER

Evening and Weekend Conferences

Teachers are used to taking work home or going to school on Saturdays to run a stencil or fix a bulletin board. Although it may seem like additional work at the onset, conferences and home visits during evenings and weekends may be some of the most valuable preparation time that the teacher spends. The parents will be complimented by the teacher's commitment of her own time to understand their child better. The meetings and visits do not need to be lengthy unless there is some special reason. (See Chapter 7.)

Programs and Presentations

One of the episodes on "The Brady Bunch" television show concerned the discomfort of one of the children when she was given only one ticket to the school play in which she was a star. Since she could invite only one parent, she resigned her role in the play rather than exclude the other parent. If school performances and programs are given only during school hours, attendance for fathers and working mothers is almost impossible. Programs in which the children take part should be frequent, short, and held in a room large enough for not only both parents but also the entire family to attend. The programs should be distinct from other business meetings, and all family members should be invited. (See Chapter 13.)

Written Information Sent to the Home

Parents of school age children are busy people. Not only are they building their own careers, estates, and home skills, but also they are responding to the needs of dependent children. Children's needs tend to be spontaneous and immediate, even in the best organized homes. In order to meet all of these simultaneous demands, parents must plan the use of their time as completely as possible. Information sent to the home about the progress of the child can be studied in peace, even at midnight, if it is sent in writing. Personalized newsletters and diary notebooks can be most helpful. (See Chapter 8.) It is important that the teacher make sure that the information is of interest to fathers as well as mothers and that the information is about their child, rather than the school in general. Care must be taken to be sure that the information is written clearly in a nonthreatening tone. (See Chapter 11.)

Asking Mothers and Fathers for Help

One teacher of educable mentally retarded children found that their fathers were willing to build shelves and study carrells and that their mothers were willing to make costumes and cookies for school activities (Neal, 1972). Other parents serve as aides on the school bus, lunchroom monitors, and individual tutors. Fathers have wired language boards and made tote trays. Fathers who are businessmen can supply posters, packing boxes, and old ledger forms. (See Chapter 8.)

Care must be taken to ask each parent directly rather than ask one parent to ask the other parent. Expecting the mother to carry the messages to the father puts her in the position of being the mother of both the child and the father. Such a position is awkward for everyone.

SINGLE PARENTS

Although folklore indicates that children tend to make a marriage stronger, there is no evidence that this is true. The converse may be true, especially if the child has more than the usual problems developing. (See Chapter 4.) It is not unusual to find that one parent of a handicapped child does not participate in the parenting activity even though that parent is in the home. As the child gets older and remains dependent, for example, the mother may become exhausted from the intensity of the mothering or the father may not see ways in which he might interact with the child. The parent may withdraw completely and not interact with the child at all.

Regardless of how or why the parent is raising the child alone, the fact remains that one parent is doing the tasks that might overwhelm two strong, capable, well-adjusted, warm, interested parents. Care should be taken to make sure that the single parent is able to have his or her needs met.

A single woman raising a son may have a particular need for the boy, especially in his teen years, to interact with a strong male model. She may want someone to show an older boy how to shave or a younger one how to use the urinal. Single fathers of daughters may need help in explaining menstrual periods and feminine underwear to the girls. Children with learning problems frequently need a demonstration to learn, and a parent of the other sex is unable to demonstrate some of these biological differences.

The role of the single parent is sometimes complicated by the need to protect the child from exploitation by the other parent. P.L. 94-142 specifies that:

> (c) An agency may presume that the parent has authority to inspect and review records relating to his or her child unless the agency has been advised that the parent does not have the authority under applicable State law governing such matters as guardianship, separation, and divorce. (*Federal Register,* 1977, p. 42498)

The public agency and the teacher must conduct communication with a single parent carefully so as not to intrude into possible marital strife. Although professionals may provide services in the home in order to enhance the child's educational potential, intervention in the home situation for any other reason is not appropriate.

When the school agency or the teacher interact with the single parent, care should be taken to make sure that the single parent is not asked to do more than one person can do. Even when that person is capable and talented, the potential resources of a single person are never equal to the potential resources of two people.

STEPPARENTING: CHOOSING TO PARENT A HANDICAPPED CHILD

When marrying the parent of a handicapped child, the stepparent has the choice of sharing the new home with the child or supporting the natural parent emotionally or financially in a decision to have the child live in another "home." Neither situation is similar to that of the natural parent, who became the parent of a handicapped child without choosing to do so. One stepfather talks about his retarded son by saying to the parents of other retarded children, "I have a retarded son, just like you. I just didn't have the fun of conception. I keep trying to make up for it" (NARC, 1978). Along with the "fun" of conception comes the genetic responsibility of conception. The stepparent of a handicapped child in no way can be "blamed" for the child. In fact, the role is one of honor for self-sacrificing devotion to another person's child, particularly an imperfect child.

The honor comes from people of the community, but most importantly from the child's "real" parent. Whether the other parent died or chose to leave, the parent who is left with the responsibility of the child is likely to feel deserted. If there was a divorce, part of the reason could have been that the first husband or wife blamed the mate for the child's condition. After having been degraded for the birth of the child, the natural parent would probably find someone who would choose marriage with full knowledge of the child quite wonderful. One parent's comment, "From the beginning Jay was very much part of our relationship" (Turnbull, 1978, p. 132), shows a relationship quite different from that in which the child has interrupted the relationship and is the beginning of a continuing uncertainty as to what (or who) was responsible. The stepparent, after all, could not possibly be part of that what or who.

Freedom from Psychological Responsibility

Since the stepparent is not to "blame," the stepparent has no internal feelings of responsibility. The stepparent cannot be the parent who "sinned," ruined the family tree, produced the "bad blood" from their side of the family, drank too much during the pregnancy, failed to deliver the child properly, or. . . . (See Chapter 4.) The added physical responsibility of caring for a handicapped child is not the part of the situation that becomes heavy over the long haul. The heavy burden for the parent is doing all that work and still feeling that somehow, someway, "I should have done more."

Professionals and the Stepparent

The day-to-day practical needs of any youngster are legion. The needs of the handicapped child are even greater. The stepparent may have accepted the responsibility of the child in the rosy light of courtship and become tired of the responsibility in the disenchanting light of sleepless nights, mountains of dirty clothes, and perpetual school conferences.

It is important to include the stepparent in communication, but it is also important to remember that the stepparent's feelings about the child are not as intense as those of the natural parent. It may be easier to discuss the child's difficulties with the stepparent than with the natural parent. It may be that, because the stepparent's anxiety level is lower, he or she is able to work with the child better. On the other hand, the stepparent may lose patience with the child and vent frustrations on the child, especially in the case of common law stepfathers or boyfriends of the child's mother. It is doubly important that communication to stepparents include positive information about the child. (See Chapter 8.) It is essential that all communication to the family about the child include the natural as well as the stepparent.

The relationships between the mother and the child and the father and the child began before the child came in contact with the public agency and will continue after the child is no longer served by the agency.

Successful interaction comes in the school setting when the professionals are wise enough to understand the experience of each of the parents well enough to respond to the parent's needs rather than to label the mother as overprotective and the father as disinterested.

REFERENCES

Federal Register. Vol. 42, No. 163. Aug. 23, 1977.

Flavell, J. *The developmental psychology of Jean Piaget.* New York: D. Van Nostrand, 1963.

Goldberg, H. *The hazards of being male: Surviving the myth of the male privilege.* New York: Signet, 1977.

Greenfield, J. *A place for Noah.* New York: Holt, Rinehart and Winston, 1978.

Houghton, S. Personal communication, May, 1975.

Lichter, P. Personal communication, May, 1975.

Lichter, P. Communicating with parents: It begins with listening. *Teaching Exceptional Children,* 1976, *8*(2), 67-71.

Michaelis, C.T. *Concepts of Piaget as a basis for productive thinking activities for the retarded.* Unpublished manuscript, University of Utah, 1971.

Michaelis, C.T. *The language of a Down's syndrome child.* Unpublished manuscript, University of Utah, 1976.

Michaelis, C.T. Imperfect child: Cause for chronic sorrow. *Special children,* 1977, *4*(1).

Michaelis, C.T. Communication with severely and profoundly handicapped: A psycholinguistic approach. *Mental Retardation,* 1978, *16*(5), 346-349.

Montigue, A. *The natural superiority of women.* New York: Macmillan, 1974.

National Association for Retarded Citizens. Regional Meeting, Conference Proceedings. Green Bay, Wisconsin, March 10, 1978.

Neal, L. Personal communication, 1972.

Schmidler, K. Personal communication, September, 1978.

Sharp, E. Personal communication, 1974.

Spock, B. *On being the parent of a handicapped child.* Chicago: National Society for Crippled Children and Adults, 1961.

Swanson, T. Personal communication, 1976.

Taylor, P. Personal communication, December, 1978.

Turnbull, A.P. Moving from being a professional to being a parent: A startling experience. In A.P. Turnbull & H.R. Turnbull (Eds.), *Parents speak out: Views from the other side of a two-way mirror.* Columbus, Ohio: Charles E. Merrill, 1978.

Wheland, R.J. The emotionally disturbed. In E.L. Meyen (Ed.), *Exceptional children and youth.* Denver: Love, 1978.

Chapter 6

Working with Siblings in the School

SIBLINGS IN THE SCHOOL

It is not hard to recognize siblings in school. The Jones boys wear engineer boots. The Smith girls dress alike, except in different colors, like the Dionne quintuplets. The Andersons all carry lunch pails. Anyone who has worked in the school for years can spot siblings in kindergarten. It is not just the French braids or the lunch pail; sometimes it is literally the same dress that came to kindergarten two years ago! One elementary school had its own quiet black watchdog sitting on the steps each school day, just like Mary's lamb. The dog came to school for a dozen years while his "children" were in class.

Teachers, secretaries, principals, janitors, and bus drivers learn to know the children by the family they come from. "How is the Johnson boy doing?" one teacher asked another. "I had the other one, and he had a great deal of trouble with the multiplication tables. Is the younger boy having trouble, too?" "You have Bobbie in your class. Have him make a picture for the newsletter. All the Browns are good at art." Sisters are asked to account for brothers, and brothers are expected to do what the rest of the family has done. The basketball coach waited for Neil. His older brother had been a good basketball player.

Don was placed in a class for "slow learners" when he was in junior high school, because "all the Hills" are in special education. Now a director of special education for a school district, Don is just finishing a doctorate in educational administration. He had to prove that, although he is a Hill, he could manage the regular school system. He had to do it at the university.

There is a temptation to respond to each child in the family in the same way. Since they frequently look alike, dress alike, and have some of the same mannerisms and habits, it is easy to assume that children in the same family are alike. Wearing the older brother's outgrown coat may make Bobbie look like his older brother, but it doesn't make him learn in the same way.

101

Even when babies are first born, they have individual characteristics. Brazelton (1969) describes the observation made of identical twin boys in the Lying-In-Hospital where they were born. In the first week of the babies' lives, their mother and four doctors recorded a variety of impressions about the babies. The babies did not do the same things in the same way, even in the first week.

SIBLINGS OF HANDICAPPED CHILDREN IN THE SCHOOL

Since handicapped children are to be educated in the school that they would attend if not handicapped, if at all possible, it is likely that the handicapped child will attend the same school as the other children in the family. The parent's satisfaction with the IEP for the child who is having difficulties learning may be closely tied to the ability of the agency to implement that program without adversely affecting the other children in the family, particularly those attending the same school.

Almost hidden in the papers of one due process hearing was a comment that the student had made to the social worker. He did not like to be in the same room with his younger brother. The family was requesting funds to place the older boy in a private school. Perhaps the boy and the family would not have been so uncomfortable if the status of the older boy was not so threatened by the younger brother who could do the same school work as the older brother. The older boy was accustomed to doing work similar to that of younger children, but not his brother! What was not recorded in the official papers was the little brother's reaction or the interaction between the brothers about sharing a classroom. Most everyone has heard stories about what it is like when brothers share a bedroom.

Siblings of handicapped children have taken the lunch money to school, helped the handicapped child on the school bus, and taken notes to the teacher. Although using the services of the siblings to help implement the education program for the handicapped child may at first seem like an obvious solution, it may be the beginning of more problems for the school, the family, the siblings, and even the handicapped child. It is important that siblings are not expected to be their "brother's keeper" to the extent that their own social and academic learning is hampered by the responsibility.

Communication with the parents of a handicapped child includes communication with and about their nonhandicapped children. Frequently, it is difficult for the parent to separate the needs of their nonhandicapped children from those of their handicapped child. Teachers may have the same difficulty.

John is in a resource room program. When Mrs. Smith comes in to talk about John's problems in school, she usually begins to talk about the things that Joe does, too. It is difficult to keep to the point of the conference and not begin discussing the problems that Joe sometimes has on the playground. In order to comply with the legal requirements, however, the conference must cover the intended purpose.

Each afternoon Jane drops by the classroom to see if her brother, Tom, has any homework to take home. It would be easy just to explain the assignment to Jane and have her see that Tom completes it, but part of what Tom needs to learn is to complete his assignments independently. So if Jane takes the materials and responsibility home, it may not be good for either Jane or Tom.

The school usually sends information to the parent with the oldest child in the school. When the oldest child is handicapped, the information may not get home.

The easiest way to get Bob's lunch money is for his sister to bring it to school. Bob's Individual Education Program (IEP) includes experience with concrete numbers. Learning to count money and be responsible for it could be an excellent learning experience for Bob.

If the public agency can separate the work of each child in the family, ignoring the French braids and the engineer boots, it may be possible to help the parents feel that the public agency is meeting the family's needs for education of the children. Even though siblings do not share learning style and learning needs, they do share another important commodity: the emotional and financial resources of their parents.

FAMILY RELATIONSHIPS

In order to understand the complicated relationships of siblings of handicapped children to the handicapped child, the parents, and the school system, the relationship of siblings in any family and the complication of relationships when one of the children is handicapped must be examined.

Mother-Father-Child Relationships

Although families are generally described as parents and children, it is much more complicated than that. Farber (1959) described the family as a "series of triads, each triad representing a mother-father-child relationship." Farber believes that each child holds a unique position in the family composed of a number of mother-father-child triads. The relationship of a child to each of the parents may be entirely different than the relationships experienced by other children in the family.

The Sex of the Child

The oldest son has traditionally held the most esteemed position in the family. Families of certain times and cultures have measured their wealth by the number of sons in the family. Some families wait for a male child to give him a crown, a farm, or a business. Other families who have not had female children for several generations prize daughters. One little girl who has four older brothers has a room full of dolls, because her mother was tired of the boys trucks and baseball mitts. It is possible for one child to be prized by one parent and another child to be prized by the other parent; many expectant parents express a desire for a child of a particular sex.

The Strengths and Needs of the Child

Many people want children who are as much like themselves as possible. A child who can do what they did and continue their work is the desire of many successful people who are childless. Mothers and fathers may also prize a child who is something that the parent is not. A father may idolize a son who is tall and can play basketball. A mother may appreciate a son who participates in drama rather than football. Frequently, the characteristic that is valued by one parent is not valued, at least in the same degree, by the other parent. In this sense, mothers and fathers do have favorite children: the son who can do what I wanted to do, the daughter who is just like me.

The Position of the Child in the Family

In her book, *The Joy of the Only Child,* Peck (1977) describes the achievement of children who are the only child in the family. She contends that the family can concentrate resources and enhance the development of the first or the only child.

Even folklore suggests that the middle child does not usually achieve as much as the older or younger children. Sutton-Smith and Rosenberg (1969) found that middle children are less likely to go to college than either the older or the younger children in the family. Younger siblings are often more relaxed and less inhibited; younger siblings of famous people frequently have caused embarrassment for the well-known sibling.

Sutton-Smith and Rosenberg (1969) indicate that younger children learn not only from their parents, but also from each other. The position of the older child affects both the older and the younger child and creates expectations for both the children and for the family. The oldest child is expected by both parents and children to be a model for the younger children and to direct their behavior.

Circumstances When the Child Is Born

One father jokingly explains that the second son is taller than the first son since the father was still going to college when the older son was born and there wasn't enough food to feed him. When the second son was born, the father was no longer in college and there was more food. Obviously, this is not true, but the position of the family when the child is born does influence family relationships. Certainly, the availability of medical services and the health of the parents are factors in the development of a relationship. Children can take music lessons and go to summer camp only when the family income is sufficient.

Children born when the family has enough money for its needs may be more warmly welcomed than those who arrive at a time of economic famine, unless, of course, the cultural and economic patterns of the family include the belief that there should be many sons and daughters to work in the fields and to care for the parents in old age. One new mother shared the hospital room with another new mother whose migrant farm worker husband was thrilled because this time he could bring his wife to the hospital and the baby had survived. When he found that his wife's "roommate" in addition to the new baby girl had four sons at home he replied, "You're wealthy." To the migrant farm worker, wealth was measured in children, especially sons (C.T. Michaelis, 1961).

Family Planning

The amount of planning and preparation that the family does for each child varies. Children who are born to parents who had not planned to have a child have a different relationship with their parents than those who were planned. Joanne was told that she was the reason that her parents married, and whenever they quarrel, she feels guilty. One of the parents may be better prepared for parenting experience and more anxious to become a parent. Sometimes another child comes along after the parents have decided that they have enough children. Some parents have children because "it is expected," and they approach the task as an unpleasant duty.

The Size and Location of the Residence

When a new house was being built in her neighborhood, an eight-year-old commented on how large it would be. "And they only have two children," she said. A high school boy was considered by his friends to be "deprived" because, as the last child in the family, he lived with his parents in an apartment and he didn't have a family room in which he could have his friends over. Debbie was anxious for her sister to go away to college so she could have a room of her own. One boy had his friends drop him off at the corner and walked to his house because he didn't want them to see how small and run-down his house was.

Although the great American dream shows a happy couple carefully painting and decorating the nursery for the new child, the reality is often much different. One fifth child, when she was a baby, slept in the parents' room during the day and was moved into the kitchen when they were ready to retire at night. When family members stand in line to use the bathroom, it has to affect how they relate to one another. (If they have no bathroom, the effect can be even greater!)

Relationships of Siblings to One Another

In the Early Years

Just as young children have to learn to differentiate the self from the environ-ment, so they have to learn to separate themselves from their siblings. For children in a large family this may be difficult, since the parents frequently call their children by the wrong name. One woman insists that her parents always called her "Jean, Carol, Beth." Since her parents had learned to say the children's names in birth order and she was the third one, she claims that they could remember her name only by saying the first two.

Even when parents provide separate toys for each of the children, the play-ground is shared. The swing set, the sand pile and the backyard belong to the siblings together. If one child appears to get more than his or her sibling, there is usually a loud complaint. Frequently, the preschooler's toy box is full of toys that were at one time given to each of the older children but have long since become community property and are used by the child who is the strongest or most aggressive.

After lunch the older child is often expected to nap "so little Joe will," even though the other children of the same age in the neighborhood have long since outgrown their naps.

During the School Years

Just before she started kindergarten one little sister was solemnly told by her sixth grade brother that she could talk to him at home, but at school she was to act like she didn't know him. For a sixth grader to associate with people in the kindergarten wing of the school was just not "cool."

Another girl complained that she was never the only child in the family at the school that she attended. Because she had both older and younger siblings, there was always another Tingey in the same school. Of course, she had her own friends at school. Siblings attending the same school usually do. Otherwise, they would have to be the older, the smarter, the more responsible, or Dad's favorite, all the time, even when they are playing. Anyway, any school child knows that sixth graders are not at all like fifth graders and that seniors in high school are really lowering themselves even to talk to juniors, let alone have a junior for a friend.

Even though siblings frequently do not speak to each other at school, they are quick to tell the parents of any activities at school that appear suspicious. Siblings compete with one another during the school years. When June, a seventh grader, brought her report card home, she was quick to comment that Jane, her twin, got an F in physical education. She seemed to feel that the measurement of her work against Jane's was the only significant evaluation, since her grade was only a D.

In the Adult Years

The relationships between siblings begun in the early years continue. Even though they are both now grandfathers, Willis is Wayne's big brother and Wayne still tries to please him. Stone (1976) describes the surprising closeness that she found when she talked to her sister after not seeing her for several years. "We share something stronger than blood or ideology: the same view of childhood. She is a witness. She was there . . . we know . . . the same craziness" (p. 33).

Children in the same family share the same stories about parents. Two sisters in their 40s sat one evening reciting the poems that their mother had repeated to them as children. They could do it in unison, with the same rhythm patterns, yet they had never before talked to each other about even having listened to their mother recite the poems.

Children learn the family patterns: buy fabrics on sale, drive a General Motors car, live in the intermountain area, go to church on Sunday, take snacks to eat in the car, go skiing, have pumpkin pie with whipped cream for Thanksgiving, play touch football. It is difficult to change patterns, even with conscious effort.

COMPLICATIONS WHEN ONE CHILD IS HANDICAPPED

The family patterns of families with handicapped children are more complicated than those of families without children who have specific developmental needs. Farber (1959) describes the family as passing through stages in their life cycle:

    (a) The married couple.
    (b) The family whose youngest child is of preschool age.
    (c) The family with a preadolescent youngest child.
    (d) The family with an adolescent youngest child.
    (e) The family in which all children are adults.
    (f) The family in which all children are married. (Farber, 1959, p. 6)

The families of handicapped children do not complete the life cycle of the family. They do not raise all of the children to independent adulthood. The family of the mildly handicapped child comes closer to that goal, but even children with mild learning problems continue to have the same learning difficulties when they attempt to learn new skills as adults. They are, therefore, more dependent either on the family or the services offered by the society. One mother explains that, although her daughter has learned to handle the mild seizures that she began to have when she was a teenager, the family still worries about her being alone. This was especially true during a recent pregnancy. The young mother also does not drive and must have transportation for shopping and taking the baby to the doctor. The family of a handicapped child does not reach closure in the task of helping the child develop into independent adulthood.

The stress experienced by the family could be understood in the context of the mother-father-child triads described by Farber (1959). In any family there is a variety of relationships in these triads. One child is closest to the father; another, to the mother. Stone (1976) writes, "I take Daddy, and Ellen takes Toby [mother]" (p. 33). Since, in addition to help to deal with the handicap, handicapped children need everything that normal children need, the mother-father-child triad for the handicapped child is more intense. One reason for the intensity is that the child needs individual attention in order to learn not only school skills, but also the day-to-day routines of life. The family resources must be altered to meet this need.

The other children in the family are affected, too. Hayden, the sister of a deaf girl, puts it this way:

> All the members of my family are disabled. But most people recognize only the disability of my deaf sister. They do not realize that the disability of one member affects the entire family. Parents realize this to some extent because they themselves are affected—their attitudes, their priorities, their life styles. But sometimes they become so involved with the problems directly related to their disabled child they lose sight of the effect upon the other children. (Hayden, 1974, p. 26)

But the "other children," as Hayden calls them, know. The other children are aware of the things that they must do that their friends do not do.

One of the ways of increasing family resources is to expect all of the children to be the "oldest child" to the handicapped child. In most families the handicapped child eventually becomes the "youngest child." The more serious the handicap, the earlier this happens. All the other children, regardless of birth order, are expected to assume the responsibilities of the oldest child's role without ever having the additional attention and closeness that the real oldest child had. Playing the role of oldest child can be a consuming responsibility for a child. Needing the child to play that role can be a consuming responsibility for the parent.

From the Parent's Perspective

Any group of people living together share some common problems: a front door that must be pulled shut, a refrigerator that is too small to hold gallon milk bottles, and hot water that is always "gone." For families of handicapped children, the number of such problems is larger. It might include a school age child who:

- still needs help in the bathroom
- wanders around the neighborhood without telling anyone
- "uses" all the bottles of lotion, soap, or cleanser in sight
- examines the contents of all the purses that can be found

- does not understand verbal instructions
- takes things and puts them in other places without telling
- gets up at night and wanders around the house and neighborhood
- is clumsy, spills and bumps things
- eats almost everything—even nonfood materials
- gets clothes dirty easily
- cannot answer the phone and take messages
- cannot do the regular share of household chores
- cannot tell time and get ready for school alone
- cannot be left alone for even a few minutes
- gives bear hugs to acquaintances
- will not or cannot stand and wait for the school bus alone
- cannot count lunch money

With such a list and the endless number of items that could be added to it, the mother needs help—not just when the father may be available, but during the entire day. The natural person for her to ask to help is the oldest child. In homes of most handicapped children, the oldest child is all of the other children.

One mother gave her young children the title J.W. for Jim Watcher when they played in the back yard. Whenever Jim started to wander away from the group of neighborhood children in the back yard, the brothers were either to bring him back or to notify the mother. Later, when Jim no longer wandered, the mother labeled the children J.T. for Jim Teacher and asked the brothers to explain to Jim what they were doing and show him how to do it with them.

Another mother assigned each of her other five children the responsibility of coming home from school on a certain day and taking care of Tom in the house and neighborhood. That way she could continue to be active in church and community projects and keep the house in order (Cranston, 1979).

Hayden (1974) describes herself as a second mother for her sister while her father was in Korea for a year. Although mothers may not want to ask so much from the siblings, there is usually no other resource for meeting the additional needs of the handicapped child at the moment of need. Few families can afford live-in help to assist the mother with the bathing, feeding, dressing, and weekend supervision that the handicapped child needs.

Not only the mother, but also the father may expect siblings to assist with the additional responsibilities. Since the father usually must work additional hours to supply the income required for the extra needs of the handicapped child, he may be too tired to participate in the additional care that the handicapped child needs. Father, too, may expect the sibling to watch the handicapped child.

Parents also may expect the sibling to earn money for items that they might pay for gladly if their money was not needed to supply services for the handicapped child.

From the Sibling's Perspective

"I hate you" and "I wish you were dead" were things that Hayden (1974) shouted to her handicapped sister. A four-year-old boy expressed it more subtly: "I wish I was the 'tarded boy,'" he lisped (N. Michaelis, 1964). McGinley's poem (1935) *The Lament of the Normal Child,* although written about a peer rather than a sibling, expresses a similar feeling of jealousy. Some of the college students in Grossman's study of siblings of retarded children (1972) felt that they had been "cheated out of time, love and attention" because of the parents' preoccupation with the handicapped sibling (p. 116).

As the siblings grow up, there are three general areas of concern:

1. Why does everyone expect less from him/her than from me?
2. Why do I have to do all this extra work?
3. What will my friends think?

Siblings learn to see themselves and their needs apart from the handicapped child, but for most siblings the understanding takes years to develop.

In the Early Years

No one is born with an intact, confident personality; it must be developed. Each baby must have a "good start with his mother" (Brazelton, 1969, p. 21). The young child must feel important, loved, and wanted. Learning this may be difficult if many of the activities in the home center around the needs of just one of the children. One sibling described it this way: "They [his parents] didn't seem to want to talk very much about anything, let alone John" (Grossman, 1972, p. 131). Another sibling said, "I can remember Mom kinda helping her with walking or spending time with her, you know, helping her with her speech. This kind of thing I think I can remember a little bit from when I was pretty young" (Grossman, 1972, p. 131).

It is difficult for young children to understand why the handicapped sibling is not expected to do as much as the other children in the household, and the young child may wonder, "Why does everybody expect less from him/her than from me? Don't they like me?" and "Why do I have to do his/her work all the time? Is there something wrong or different about me?"

During the School Years

For most children, the school years are their first opportunity to observe role models outside the homes. Kindergarten teachers are idolized, and primary grade teachers are respected. In the upper elementary years the student begins to be very concerned about what the other students think—about everything!

For the siblings of handicapped children, this can be the beginning of a lifelong discomfort about how other people see their handicapped brother or sister. "When I was a kid all the other kids would laugh. . . . And to laugh at him [handicapped brother] didn't make any sense" (Grossman, 1972, p. 143). "With the advent of school, I began to have more and more associations with other children. But wherever I went, Mindy went, too. . . . I lost many playmates by having to side with Mindy" (Hayden, 1974, p. 27). For school age children, playmates are the richness of life.

To stop the questions, one little leaguer told the team members that his retarded brother was adopted. He was embarrassed by the bear hugs that his brother gave him when he hit one far enough to round the bases (C.T. Michaelis, 1974). Hayden (1974), too, was embarrassed by her sister Mindy's bear hugs. Another child describes one that came from her sister in the hall of Bates High. Handicapped children frequently express affection with bear hugs. For school age siblings, receiving a bear hug in front of their friends can be traumatic.

"Stephanie is retarded, too, isn't she?" a neighbor girl asked Stephanie's mother (Reicharts, 1976). Melody was so angry with her friend for making some comment about her handicapped brother that she no longer speaks to the girl and will not repeat the thing that the other girl said (Fuller, 1976). Yet Melody has some anger of her own, since she must share a bedroom with her brother and he continually spoils her things. He particularly likes her coat with a fake fur collar. He takes it out of the closet and sleeps with it.

Maria inspects her sisters' boyfriends. "You are ugly," she told one of them. Jim walked up to one of his brothers' girlfriends and looked at her with open admiration and said, "You're beautiful." Siblings of handicapped children are not comfortable about having their friends come to their home and see the undirected behavior of the handicapped child. The Wilson family institutionalized their two handicapped sons because the two normal children were embarrassed when the retarded boys followed them and their friends around the house.

In the Adult Years

"I am still angry about the way they treated him," one grown sister of a retarded boy says. "No one was nice to him, and I spent my childhood defending him" (Taylor, 1979). Maria's oldest sister plans to marry someone who could accept Maria into their home when her parents become too old to care for the younger sister.

Don's young wife is expecting their first child. Her mother is concerned about the possibility of the child being retarded, like Don's younger brother. Don is expected to offer assurances to the young mother-to-be and the grandmother-to-be. Dana has become a special education teacher. Her parents told her that, since her brother was handicapped, she should "achieve for two." Mrs. Jones has trouble discussing her son George's problems at school. It reminds her of all the time she spent as a child defending her brother, who had cerebral palsy, from the teasing of the other children at school.

Grossman's enlightening study of siblings of retarded children (1972) was conducted with college students. Even though they were no longer living in the home with the handicapped child, there were vivid descriptions of life in their homes. "She had to have attention the whole time. She'd yell unless you did, and you couldn't hit her to tell her no; she just didn't understand that too well. So we all had to play with her" (p. 66). When siblings of handicapped children remember the "craziness" of what they shared, it is likely to be actual madness rather than a situation comedy.

It Could Have Been Me

Whether the handicapped child's condition resulted from a combination of genes in the family pool or from some environmental influence before or after birth, the sibling has shared the same possibility that the condition could have happened to him or her. This is particularly true of twins. Tressa, Tom's twin, went to her mother in horror one day to say, "It could have been me!" "I know," the mother replied. "I kept telling you that you were lucky" (Cranston, 1979). "I feel sorry for him," one twin says about her profoundly handicapped brother. "I come home from college and play music for him. I think I will be a music therapist" (Diekman, 1975). Another 42-year-old twin employs his handicapped brother in his business.

Ten-year-old Blaine wondered about his retarded brother, two years younger, "How come him and not me?" he asked (B. Michaelis, 1970). "Why shouldn't we look alike? We're brother and sister," one student proclaimed (Grossman, 1972, p. 141).

Sometimes the normal sibling identifies strongly with the handicapped child. It is not unusual for the normal siblings to want to try out the wheelchair or the new glasses or go to the school to see what the classroom is like. Melody spent the day observing her profoundly handicapped brother's classroom. She wanted to be sure that he was being treated right (Fuller, 1976).

Because of this strong identification the normal child may feel responsible to help the handicapped sibling in order to justify the fact that he or she is not "the one."

Siblings of handicapped children may render service to the child because they feel that they "should." It is the dues that they must pay for not being "the one."

FAMILY CONCERNS

Maintaining a Balance

A few families have abundant financial resources, but all families have a limited amount of emotional and personal resources. All parents have a limited amount of time. The parents and the children must use their resources to obtain the maximum benefit. The resources used for the handicapped child must be weighed, measured, and balanced against the resources used for the other children in the family.

"Deborah [the handicapped child] is the least of my worries," one mother reported. "Her older sister refuses to get dressed for school in the morning and sometimes won't eat her breakfast. I know it is because we have spent so much time on Deborah's therapy" (Freeman, 1979). The parents are responsible for meeting the developmental needs of all their children and making sure that the normal child is not hurt by the handicapped child's requirements for material resources, emotional support, and much of the parent's time. Since all of the children's needs must be met simultaneously, the appropriate use of the resources is always a precarious balance. Balancing the uneven mother-father-child triads is a difficult task. There is no simple formula. The public agency can only serve the handicapped child by understanding the needs and concerns of the other children and how those needs affect the parents.

It is understandable why parents of a child who is having difficulties are reluctant to have the child labeled as handicapped. It serves no purpose unless labeling the child would make it possible to provide more services. Parents are justifiably unwilling to accept the label of "handicapped" for their other children or for themselves. It serves no purpose for the parents and siblings to carry the "handicapped" label.

Concerns That Parents Are Likely To Have

Although parents realize that the family's life style will probably be altered because of the additional needs of the handicapped child, parents are anxious for the siblings of the handicapped child to have as normal a childhood as possible. One of the major concerns of parents is likely to be whether the personnel at the school treat the sibling as if he or she were also handicapped. Giving a child more assistance than is needed may be harmful to the child. If the school personnel treat the normal child in a different way, it is likely that the other students will also. Feelings of isolation and anger aroused by special treatment when it is not needed will interfere with the child's schooling.

Parents are also likely to be concerned about the quality of schooling that the sibling receives. Although handicapped children can be helped not only to develop satisfactorily but also to achieve success, their achievements will never equal the achievements that they could make if some of their energies did not need to be spent to deal with their handicaps. Parents are anxious for the siblings to have the opportunity to use all of their talents and abilities. Since parents must be concerned about the quality of the educational experience for the handicapped child, they are likely to also be concerned about the quality of the educational experience for the other children. It is important to family solidarity that the other children are not handicapped by a lack of experience that might have been provided for them.

Mothers particularly (see Chapter 5) are likely to be concerned about whether the normal child will be teased about the handicapped child's problems. Most siblings are an integral part of the handicapped child's experience in the home, and they are often sensitive to the comments of other students in the school. Parents, especially mothers, will most likely be concerned about the "sticks and stones" and name calling that might occur because of "Janey's dumb brother."

A second concern that parents are likely to have is whether they will be recognized for their parenting efforts for the normal children. At one mothers' group the leader asked the mothers to tell about the other children first. Almost as a chorus they thanked the leader for the opportunity. "Usually," one mother commented, "no one talks about them, as if we are not capable of having 'real' children" (C.T. Michaelis, 1979).

Rewards for parents do not come often. One of the nicest and most coveted awards is for the school or the teacher, who knows many children, to comment about something outstanding that the child has done. Even if the outstanding event or activity is only a good math paper or an interesting picture, the parents feel that at least some of their parenting efforts have been worthwhile. Parents of handicapped children are anxious to hear that the balancing act that they are performing with family time and resources is successful in providing what the other children need also.

Concerns That Siblings Are Likely To Have

The role of oldest child and assistant mother is a comprehensive role, and the sibling may still feel some responsibility toward the handicapped child in the school setting. The sibling may wonder how the brother or sister is getting along. In fact, the sibling may have an even stronger feeling than the parent, since the sibling spends the day in the school setting, sometimes even in the same school.

It is likely that the sibling will wonder how the handicapped child is getting along with the teacher. Even adults can remember teachers who "crowned" poor learners with more than a dunce cap. Children are even more aware. The sibling may wonder how the teacher will treat the handicapped child when the child does some of the things he or she has done at home. Although siblings get angry at the behavior of a handicapped child, few of them would like to have a teacher punish the child for not being able to do the appropriate task.

Siblings may be concerned about how the other children will treat the handicapped child. Knowing how difficult it is to be patient with the child, the sibling, probably better than anyone else, knows how vulnerable the handicapped child is to the whims and teasing of other children.

The sibling is likely to wonder if the handicapped child will be able to make any friends. Since friends are such a valuable "possession" of childhood, a sibling, perhaps even more than a parent, would wonder if anyone would choose to be a "friend" of a child who has so many problems. Knowing how teasing can hurt, the sibling is likely to be acutely aware of comments such as "four eyes," the "retarded room," "crazy kid," and "running like a girl," which may be directed to the handicapped child.

The Sibling's Role at School

School age siblings are usually aware of how much the parents depend upon them for assistance with the handicapped child. Especially if the child attends the same school, the sibling is likely to be concerned about whether the handicapped child's teacher will be expecting the sibling to be a "brother's (sister's) keeper." The sibling is likely to wonder whether he or she will be required to miss some educational or social experience at school because of attention to the handicapped child. Conversation in the lavatory before school and in the back of the bus on the way home are socially important to the sibling.

Since the fun of teasing is to get someone "upset" and the sibling is already somewhat upset about the handicapped child, it is possible that the other children might tease the sibling, just as they tease the handicapped child. The sibling is acutely aware of this. For some siblings the school is a sanctuary away from the comments of the neighbors and the concerns of the parents. To change the school into a place where the peers can observe and comment on what is different about the handicapped child is likely to make it uncomfortable for the sibling at school (C.T. Michaelis, 1979b).

WHAT THE PUBLIC AGENCY CAN DO

The public agency can avoid friction by being concerned about the educational needs of the sibling as well as those of the handicapped child. Some of the concern could be directed to the parents, who need reassurance that all of their children are having appropriate educational experiences, and some could be directed to the sibling.

For the Parents

Confer about One Child at a Time

The conference called for the handicapped child should be about that child's problems and should not be related in any way to the problems that other children in the family may or may not be having. The success or failure of other children in the family should not be a topic for discussion during a conference arranged for one child.

If the parents want to discuss the needs of any of the other children or to compare their work, administrators could suggest that an appointment be made at another time for that purpose and maintain the integrity of the present conference. Of course, a conference about the sibling's work would only be appropriate if the sibling were currently being served by that educational agency and if those individuals working with the sibling were present at the conference.

This does not mean that the problems related to the handicapped child and the sibling cannot be discussed if they are pertinent to the educational needs of the handicapped child; however, they must be discussed in relation to the educational needs rather than to the general needs of either the handicapped child or the sibling. The conference may be an open-ended problem-solving session, but if the conference is to take that form, this, too, should be planned ahead of time and the topic must not focus on the strengths and weaknesses of the sibling.

Be Careful Not To Imply That the Sibling Is Also Handicapped

Although in some situations there may be reason to believe that the problems of the handicapped child are also problems of other members of the family, there is no reason to treat the sibling as if he or she were also handicapped. The inference that the sibling may have learning problems can come from statements made during the conference or from other interaction within the agency. Statements such as "We can have Mrs. Anderson evaluate Billy also" or "Does Barbara need help in the lavatory, too?" can be insulting to the parents and unfair to the child. Perhaps the most gross injustice is to "warn" the sibling's teacher that there "might be some problems." The warning might be sent as a formal message or as an implication in a remark such as "What can you expect from a Jones boy?"

These attitudes can be reflected by professionals who assign private tutors "in case you need some help," seat the child in front of the class, or assign the sibling to the only male teacher because he can "handle" the situation. Remarks might be made to the sibling in front of other children, "Maybe you need special education like your brother" or "You could read your brother's book."

Be Supportive and Positive about the Sibling's Accomplishments

Especially if there is some disagreement about the services to be delivered to the handicapped child, the sibling's work and behavior may be rigidly evaluated.

Since identification of learning problems focuses on the inadequacies in the work of the child, it would be natural for the personnel of the agency to scrutinize the work of the sibling to see if the sibling's work has some of the same "flaws." Frequently "honors" such as hall-person or tutor or monitor when the teacher leaves the room are conferred on students who are completing all of the regular assignments. Siblings of handicapped children may not be given the opportunity to do these special assignments.

It would be wise to make a conscious effort to ensure that the siblings of a handicapped child are given the opportunity to participate in the informal "awards" of the school system, i.e., to serve as lunchroom monitors, hall monitors, members of the safety patrol, chalk board cleaners, and pencil sharpener emptiers. Particularly if the sibling is helping the handicapped child in some way at school, it is natural to assume that there is no time for another "activity." One mother of a handicapped boy remembers fondly the month that three of his siblings happened to be chosen "citizen of the month" in their respective classrooms. It was an honor not only to the siblings, but to the parents. If the parent feels good about the sibling's experience in the school, it will influence the way the parent feels about the schooling of the handicapped child.

For the Siblings

Although the sibling of a handicapped child may be familiar with the behavior of the child and the problems that are caused in the home and school, frequently the sibling knows little about the characteristics of the handicap itself. An orientation to the problems encountered by the handicapped child could help the sibling see the situation in a more realistic light. Even a sibling who has been a student in the school for some time usually does not know exactly what will be done for the handicapped child that is so "special."

A time set aside for the sibling to observe the activities in the special classroom would be helpful. If a staff member accompanied the sibling, questions could be asked and answered. The sibling could see the teacher working, see the learning materials, and observe the methods that are being used. Sometimes siblings resent that the handicapped child is "playing" when they themselves have to work so hard. An explanation of the methods used with the handicapped child and the skills that are being taught will help make it possible for the sibling to be supportive rather than critical of the educational experience of the handicapped child.

Sibling School

Another way that the public agency could help the sibling understand would be to have a "sibling school" in which all siblings of the handicapped children were invited to an informal "milk and cracker" gathering to see the classroom and meet each other. Knowing that other children have to put up with a "dumb" brother can help the sibling be more tolerant and accepting of the handicapped brother or sister. John and Neil met because they both played on the high school basketball team, but they understood one another because they both had retarded brothers.

Although elaborate plans could be made for the agenda of such a sibling school, for most people who are used to being with children the agenda would almost create itself. (See Chapter 8 for suggestions about how parents and PTA could help.) A written invitation sent to each of the siblings individually would ensure that the siblings understood that the sibling school was organized especially for them. Name tags would be helpful, since the siblings may not know one another before the meeting. The siblings could make their own name tags, including both their name and the name and age of the handicapped child. The session could begin by having the principal introduce the teacher and perhaps the special services team. The teacher could give a general orientation and an explanation of how each item of equipment is used could be given by the teacher or therapist who used it. Then there could be a question and answer session in which students could ask about what they saw or anything else that interested them.

As the refreshments are being served, the siblings could walk around the room and visit. This type of interaction could be followed with sessions in which the siblings talked to one another about their problems and concerns. Such a group could be led by the school social worker, nurse, special education teacher, principal, or PTA volunteer. (See Chapter 13.) In this situation, as in other informal groups, it may be obvious that some of the members of the group need more in-depth counseling. (See Chapter 9.) Suggestions about counseling could be made privately at a later date to the appropriate persons.

In most cases it would be helpful to see the siblings alone also, so that personal questions could be asked and confidential information could be exchanged.

Discussion of the Sibling's Role with the Sibling

In private meetings with the sibling, the public agency personnel could describe the needs of the handicapped child to the sibling. As the needs were discussed, any services that the handicapped child might need in connection with the school could be discussed. If it seems that the sibling would be the appropriate one to help the handicapped child wait for the bus, bring the lunch money, or get the wheelchair in the lavatory in the morning, the sibling could be invited to be part of the IEP planning session. The need for the services could be explained and the sibling allowed to say whether performing these services would interfere with what he or she wanted to be doing at the time.

If handicapped children are educated in the school that they would attend if not handicapped, siblings probably attend that school also. There may be some reason to include the sibling routinely in part of the planning for the handicapped child when the two children attend the same school. Any school age sibling of a handicapped child is old enough to understand the handicapped child's need, perhaps even better than the parents, since the child is sharing the same child world.

WHAT THE TEACHER CAN DO

Since the sibling is aware of the needs of the handicapped child and assists with them at home, the sibling may volunteer to help the child at school, even when the service could be given by another or when delivering the service might interfere with the sibling's own schooling. Before the teacher accepts or asks the sibling for help, the situation should be discussed with the parents. The reason for the help and the way in which the sibling could be helpful should be discussed, even if the sibling has volunteered to help.

When the sibling gives service to the handicapped child at school, the teacher should compliment the parents on the accomplishments of the sibling. The parents have been concerned about how to train their children so that the needs of all of them might be met, and they need to know that others see the results of the training. If the sibling appears to be overly attentive to the handicapped child, the message should be sent carefully so that the parents see that the sibling's concern is seen as positive, even though the degree may not be appropriate for the needs of either child.

Especially if the teacher has had experience with the other children in the family, it is easy for the teacher to discuss the work of one child in relation to the work of another child. This can be particularly harmful to the children if one of them is handicapped.

For the Sibling

The teacher should be careful to recognize the sibling and respect the skills of the sibling. Anyone enjoys being called by name, but siblings of handicapped children especially appreciate not being known as "Larry's brother." Since the teachers of the handicapped child are important to the entire family and the sibling is sure to recognize the teacher, it is important that the teacher also recognize the sibling. It isn't necessary to call the name across the auditorium each day; sometimes just a smile is more effective.

Inviting the sibling into the classroom any time is important. Although formal sibling school fills one kind of need, the informal walk through the classroom after school fills another need. If the teacher is accepting, the sibling can actually gain status because he or she has "another room" at school. On the holidays that are usually accompanied by treats, the teacher is wise to prepare to have enough for the siblings, too. (See Chapter 8.)

Since well-adjusted school age children usually have a friend or two along, the friends of the siblings should be welcomed. Siblings of handicapped children are some of the best models for training the handicapped child, even at school. Their behavior also affects the behavior of the other students in the school.

Respect the Sibling's Personal Needs

Although there are times when the sibling welcomes the association with the "special teacher," there are also times when the sibling is not particularly anxious to have everyone know about the handicapped brother or sister. When the class is lined up for the field trip, when the sibling is busy with friends, or when the band concert is about to start, the sibling may not want to be singled out, even for a smile. The teacher will always be a reminder of the extra effort put into the life of the handicapped child. Sometimes the sibling would like to forget the handicapped business, just for a little while.

Be Available To Talk to the Sibling

Sometimes the sibling is more than a little "tired" of the handicapped child and could benefit from discussing these feelings with someone who could understand how heavy the responsibility seems. The teacher probably knows better than anyone, since the teacher has studied child development, has observed the activities of the sibling, and knows about the extra needs of the handicapped child as well as the needs of the sibling. Just listening now and then to the sibling could assist the sibling in the continuing adjustment. Sometimes the sibling has difficulty talking about the topic to the parents, either because they do not seem to want to discuss it or because the sibling is ashamed of these feelings. The teacher may encourage the sibling to develop open communication about the additional responsibilities in the family.

For the Handicapped Child

Education for handicapped children includes not just the development of academic skills, but the development of social and interaction skills as well. One of the concerns of special education personnel for some time has been how to facilitate the development of affective behavior.

One of the ways that teachers might accomplish this is to help handicapped children learn to understand their families. Lesson units planned to help the children understand their feelings toward siblings could be most productive. Although it is seldom discussed, it is highly likely that the handicapped child is envious of the skills and opportunities of the nonhandicapped children in the family. The environment of a nonhandicapped child is less restrictive than that of the handicapped child. Many handicapped children do not understand why.

Handicapped children live in a world focused on their needs. Since there are so many things that they need assistance with, having a tutor or other special help is almost a way of life for them. Children with cerebral palsy can use a communication board only if someone is patient enough to wait while they laboriously compose messages. Students with learning disabilities need time to approach the material again and again in several sensory methods. Blind children need assistance in securing large print or Braille materials. Since handicapped children are used to repeated attention, it is difficult for them to see that others have needs also.

Learning activities specifically designed to show the efforts that other children, particularly the siblings, must make in order to complete their tasks independently can be important eye openers to handicapped children. Handicapped children must learn that their siblings also have needs and must have time for their own development.

Other lessons could direct the handicapped child's attention to how the parents must plan and adjust family resources to meet the needs of the nonhandicapped children, as well as those of the handicapped child. It might be important for the handicapped child to know that nonhandicapped children need bicycles as much as children with cerebral palsy need wheelchairs and that somehow the parents must find a way to supply both needs.

SUMMARY

Since the mother-father-child triad for the handicapped child requires an intensive relationship for an undetermined length of time, the relationship strains family resources. Even though the sibling may not be older than the handicapped child, he or she is frequently called upon to serve the needs of the handicapped child in a manner similar to older children serving the needs of the younger child. Although parents frequently expect the sibling to help with the handicapped child in the home, they will probably be less likely to want the sibling to attend to the handicapped child's needs in the school setting.

The sibling who performs the duties regularly at home may feel responsible even though he/she is not asked to help. Since this seems like the simple solution, it seems natural for personnel in the school to assign a helping role to the sibling. Such a role may interfere with the parents' satisfaction with school services and may not be in the best interest of the development of independence in the handicapped child.

Even though families allow the handicapped child to be identified to secure other services for the child, the family and the siblings want to avoid also being labeled and appreciate being as normal a family as possible.

In a sense, as the public agency strives to serve the handicapped child without interfering with the rights of the normal child, it is trying to achieve the same difficult balance that the parents try to achieve in the home.

REFERENCES

Brazelton, T.B. *Infants and mothers: Differences in development.* New York: Dell, 1969.

Cranston, B. Personal communication, May, 1979.

Diekman, D. Personal communication, 1975.

Farber, B. Effects of a severely mentally retarded child on family integration. *Monographs of the Society for Research in Child Development,* 1959, *24* (2 Serial No. 71).

Freeman, K. Personal communication, March, 1979.

Fuller, M. Personal communication, 1976.

Grossman, F.K. *Brothers and sisters of retarded children.* Syracuse: Syracuse University Press, 1972.

Hayden, V. The other children. *The Exceptional Parent,* 1974, *4* (4), 26-29.

McGinley, P. Lament of the normal child. In O.J. Campbell, J. Van Gundy, & C. Shrodes (Eds.), *Patterns for living.* New York: Macmillan, 1949. Poem in book dated 1935.

Michaelis, B. Personal communication, May, 1970.

Michaelis, C.T. Personal experience, May, 1961.

Michaelis, C.T. Chip on my shoulder. *The Exceptional Parent,* 1974, *4*(1), 30-35.

Michaelis, C.T. *Early beginnings program.* Columbia, Md.: Howard County Association for Retarded Citizens, 1979. (a)

Michaelis, C.T. Mainstreaming: The readiness of the child and the school. *The Exceptional Parent,* 1979, *9* (5), R4-R5. (b)

Michaelis, N. Personal communication, 1964.

Peck, E. *The joy of the only child.* New York: Delacorte Press, 1977.

Reicharts, M. Personal communication, 1976.

Stone, L. My sister and I can never be strangers. *Ms,* August, 1976, 32-33.

Sutton-Smith, B., & Rosenberg, B.G. Modeling and reactive components of sibling interaction. In J.D. Hill (Ed.), *Minnesota symposia on child psychology.* (Vol. 3). St. Paul: University of Minnesota Press, 1969.

Taylor, P. Personal communication, March, 1979.

Chapter 7

Receiving and Understanding the Parent's Message

The personnel of one school district had repeatedly asked a mother for her permission to have her child evaluated for special services. After numerous contacts, the officials decided to visit the home and try again, since the child did need the additional services. The mother was asked again if her son could be evaluated. She replied, "No, I already told you. I will not let you cut off my son's leg." The word evaluation apparently sounded like amputation to her, and she had thought for two years that the school wanted to cut off her son's leg. No wonder she violently protested (Rabalias, 1979).

The school assumed that the mother was not interested in the son's progress when actually she was very interested in his progress. She thought that the school was trying to hurt rather than help her son. The mother was not expressing her concerns in a way that the school personnel understood. In order to understand parents' messages, it is necessary for the school personnel to be able to receive messages in any form.

SENDING AND RECEIVING MESSAGES

Infants learn language not to understand the content of the conversation about them, but to make their needs known. Adults usually enter a conversation not as a listener, but as a speaker. In order to be able to send messages effectively, it is necessary to understand thoroughly the messages that are sent. Some of the messages come in words, and some of the messages come in behavior.

Everyone sends messages all the time. Some messages are sent with a smile, some messages are sent with a slap, and some messages are sent with words, spoken and written. In order to understand the other person, the receiver must be able to receive all of the messages generated. Some of the "message" is directed toward the receiver, and some of the message is not really a message to anyone in particular; it is just an attitude.

It is usually assumed that all messages are sent in words, but there are language and nonlanguage messages.

Language Messages

An individual who wants to share an idea or a feeling with another person organizes the material into a code and sends the code to another person. The other person then takes the code, decodes the message, and receives the idea or feeling. If both the sender and the receiver have learned the same code and have had the same experiences using the code, the message received is the same message that was sent. This seldom happens. Since very few individuals have had exactly the same education and the same linguistic experiences, each person interprets the code in a different way.

Communication of ideas, thoughts, and even feelings by language has traditionally been the major goal of formal education. For educators, who have themselves been through the educational system, it is natural to assume that the language code used by the parent is as sophisticated as the code traditionally used in the school system. This may not be true. The parents of many children who have learning problems do not use standard English comfortably. Even those parents who communicate well about other subjects may find it difficult to express their deep feelings about the child to the school officials. To expect to be able to understand the parent's message by responding only to the language code of the parent is grossly inadequate.

Nonlanguage Messages

Some messages are not coded into words, but are sent in other ways. If someone is carrying a tennis racket and wearing shorts, it is not necessary to ask "Tennis anyone?" It is clear that the person is interested in tennis. The nonverbal message says, "I am a tennis player, and I am interested in playing right now." Other nonverbal messages may not be so easy to read. Some of the messages are sent by the facial expressions of the sender, some of the messages are sent by the way the person moves the body, some of the messages are sent by the appearance of the sender.

Facial Expressions

The face sends messages of surprise, fear, anger, disgust, sadness, and happiness by combinations of movements of the forehead, eyebrow, eyelids, cheeks, nose, lips, and chin (Ekman & Friesen, 1975). In order to know what the other person is feeling, it is necessary to look closely at the face. Some people telegraph messages in facial expressions easily; other people have learned to control or mask their facial expressions as part of their culture or family training (Argyle, 1975).

"Facial expressions may be controlled or uncontrolled. One expression may be voluntary, another involuntary. One may be truthful, another false. The problem is to tell which" (Ekman & Friesen, 1975, p. 19). Although one might study photographs to understand facial expressions better, the static photograph has not been a successful way to study expressions (Buck, Savin, Miller, & Caul, 1974). It is important to note the expression in the flow of the interaction rather than to choose one static expression and interpret feelings from it.

Surprise is demonstrated by raised eyebrows, eyes opened wide, and the jaw dropped. Fear is expressed by raised and straightened eyebrows, open eyes and the jaw dropped. Disgust is shown by raising the upper jaw and wrinkling the nose. Anger is expressed when the eyebrows are drawn down together, the eyes are tense and staring, and the lips pressed together or pulled inward. Sadness is shown when the inner corner of the eyebrow is drawn up, the inner corner of the upper eyelid is raised, and the corners of the lips are turned down. Happiness is shown by the corners of the lips drawn back and up, cheeks raised, lower eyelids showing wrinkles below, and crow's feet wrinkles going outward from the outer corner of the eyes (Ekman & Friesen, 1975).

Important messages can be sent by telephone and letter, but feelings are transmitted more effectively if the people can be face to face and reactions can be seen. The facial response of the other person helps the speaker to know how the other person is reacting to the message. "When someone is speaking he/she needs intermittent, but regular, feed-back on how others are responding, so that he can modify his utterances accordingly" (Argyle, 1972, p. 255).

Body Movement

Everyone knows people who can't talk without using their hands. The expression, "If they tied your hands, you couldn't talk," is a familiar one. There are no universal signals for the movement of the hand; different cultures and subcultures have different meanings for hand movement. In all societies, however, the movement of the hands adds meaning to the information communicated.

Movement of other parts of the body also indicates meaning. For example, a nod of the head is known to increase the frequency of the behavior of the other person at the time of the nod (Argyle, 1972).

The angle at which people sit or how close people stand to one another indicates the degree of interest the people have in one another and the level of communication. If one persons leans forward and touches the other, the space between them is eliminated (Weitz, 1974). In therapy situations, the body movements of the therapist and the client have been termed quasi-courtship, since the therapist and the client move their bodies toward one another and away from one another as their interest in the conversation increases or decreases (Scheflen, 1974).

Appearance

"The color, pattern and cut of a teacher's clothes affect the attitude, attention span, and conduct of the high school and junior high school students" (Molloy, 1977, p. 23). The teacher's clothes affect the parents also. People in middle class neighborhoods may accept clothing made of fabric with complicated patterns and bright colors, while people in the upper class suburban area may not. Young women in feminine clothes are not respected in the same way that women in their 40s and 50s who wear soft, feminine clothes are. Shoes and makeup also make a difference (Molloy, 1977).

For men, wearing a suit and tie expresses authority. Messages from authority figures may please some parents—and cause others to sit quietly withdrawn. In order for teachers and other school personnel to be able to receive messages from parents, it is necessary for them to look like they will listen.

TAKING TURNS IN CONVERSATION

It is not possible for the brain to process information for speaking and information for listening at the same time (Jaffe, 1978). In order for two individuals to communicate with one another, the roles of speaker and listener must be alternated so that both parties have equal time for creating and sending messages. The speaker who controls the conversation signals the listener to assume the role of speaker. The signal is given by dropping the pitch or volume of the voice, by breaking eye contact, or by stopping the speech and leaving a lengthy silence (Rosenfeld, 1978). Unless the speaker gives these cues, the listener cannot take the role of speaker without interrupting.

If the speaker is unwilling to switch roles, the other person does not have the opportunity to play the role of speaker. If the speaker is of higher status than the listener, it is much easier to indicate a desire not to relinquish the role of speaker. If the topic of conversation is potentially embarrassing to one of the parties, the flow of the communication is inhibited for that party (Siegman, 1978).

If the conversation is to be an exchange of information rather than a sending of information, the sender must be aware of the cues that the listener is giving in the conversation. The sender must look for more than the easily recognizable signs of yawning and clock watching. The speaker must attend to the cocking of the head, opening of the mouth, widening of the eyes, lifting of the hand, and clearing of the throat (Rosenfeld, 1978).

Structuring the Turns

Although the parent of an exceptional child may have status in other life situations, the role of parent of an exceptional child is not a status role (Spock,

1961). When the parent talks about the child to the teacher, who knows all about the child's weaknesses, it is potentially embarrassing for the parent. If the parent is to feel like taking the speaking role, the professional must be extremely sensitive to the responses that the parent is making to the information being sent by the professional. The nonverbal cues may be more representative of the parent's feelings than the verbal messages.

One way to make the parent feel free to talk about his or her concerns is to structure the conversation so that the role of speaker is given to the parent more frequently.

Receiving Parents' Messages

One master teacher was observed by a student teacher during parent conference time. The teacher was prepared with samples of each student's work and with a list of the things that he would like to tell each of the parents, but he didn't tell the parents anything. They told him. He ushered the parents into the room and started the conference by asking, "What does Johnny think about school?" Then he simply listened. The parents talked about the child and the strengths and weaknesses. The student teacher observing was amazed, because the parents told the teacher almost exactly what the teacher had planned to tell the parents. It was a lesson in the understanding that the teacher had of his students, that the parents had of their child, and that the teacher had of the parents (Patterson, 1969). (See Chapter 10.)

If parents are not talking about their children's needs, it may be because the professionals don't know how to relinquish the speaker role and become a listener.

Simple Listening

Listening may not be simple. Most people have a strong desire to structure for themselves the role of speaker as much as possible and pay little attention to the messages sent by the other. In the desire to leave the direction of the therapy with the client, Rogers does not take the role of speaker even during a silence. (See Chapter 9.) Some of the sessions were recorded so that interactions could be studied. Pauses of 12, 13, and 17 minutes are common in one of the sessions. The counselor left the role of speaker vacant so that the clients could easily express themselves (Meador & Rogers, 1973).

This type of turn-giving behavior may be helpful in encouraging the parent to talk about the concerns of the child. Unless the professional gives verbal and nonverbal cues that the parent may take a turn speaking, the parent will not be comfortable talking to the professional.

Active Listening

Rogers further expanded the listening role. In order to be sure that the message heard was the one that the speaker intended, Rogers suggested that counselors repeat what they heard, e.g., "You mean that you are tired of Joe not sleeping at night?"

Lichter (1976) describes how the process could be used with parents of handicapped children. The professional listens to the parent without giving any advice on how the parent should handle the child or run the home. The professional attends to the intent of the message sent by the parent and repeats to the parent what he or she understood, making sure that it does not become a "highly stylized way of responding which may become annoying to the speaker" (Lichter, 1976, p. 68).

Chinn, Winn, and Walters (1978) expand upon the concepts of transactional analysis and apply them to the face-to-face verbal interaction with parents of handicapped children. Suggestions and exercises are given to help professionals change their verbal communication style. Although the process can be learned and practiced, it is a weak substitute for genuine concern and interest in the parent's message.

Getting To Know You

For the professional to be able to receive messages from the parent it is necessary that the parent and the professional have contact with one another. If the only contact that professionals have with parents is the semiannual formal meeting, parents will probably not be comfortable enough to express feelings and concerns about the child. For the parents and professionals to meet, parents must come to the school or the professional must go to the home.

PARENTS IN THE SCHOOL

Helping the teacher is usually a privilege given to a student who continually does well in all school activities. Children who are having difficulty in school seldom have the opportunity to help the teacher, and neither do their parents. One of the best ways for the parent to feel comfortable in the school is to come to the school regularly. It is particularly important to the parents of exceptional children, since it helps them feel that they are accepted in the school.

Parents can do much more than furnish the punch and cookies for the Halloween, Christmas, and Valentine's Day parties. Parents can answer the telephone so the secretary can do other work. Parents can supervise the nurse's room when the nurse is not at school and call the parents when a child becomes sick. Parents can run off the eternal dittos. Parents can decorate the hallways for holidays, direct the Halloween parade, and make contacts for field trips. Parents can grade worksheets, teach enrichment classes, and take care of the plants and fish tank.

Although parents of exceptional children have more responsibilities in the home than they would if their children did not have additional needs, frequently they also are very interested in the child's schooling and many would be pleased to help at school regularly. If the parents were in the school at times other than conference times, the school personnel and the parents could come to know each other not just by their role designations, but also as individuals with skills, talents, and personalities.

Learning to communicate about mundane things is prerequisite to communicating about emotionally laden topics. The child's progress in the school might be mundane to school personnel, but it is an emotionally laden topic to the parents of exceptional children. The parents should be invited to school and made to feel welcome. (See Chapter 8.)

PROFESSIONALS IN THE HOME

One of the best ways to communicate with the parent is to restructure the setting so that the role of speaker is more comfortable for the parent. Parents will probably be more comfortable about speaking in their own home than in the school building. For example, just being in her own home made the mother comfortable enough to talk about the "amputation."

Educators could go into the home (a) to hold an Individual Education Program (IEP) conference, (b) to visit informally, (c) to gather a developmental history, and (d) to make a home observation.

An IEP Conference at Home

One teacher of severely handicapped children organizes and conducts the IEP conference in the child's home. The teacher makes an appointment with the family in the evening when the father can be home, takes her evaluation materials, and sits in the family's living room to discuss the child's needs (Williams, 1977).

Sometimes, when several professionals have examined the child, it may not be possible for the conference to be held in the home. If a conference cannot be conducted in the home, an informal visit by the teacher or another staff member could make it possible for the parent to explain feelings and concerns more comfortably. The person who visited in the home could then express those feelings for the parent at the IEP conference or help set the stage for the parent to explain them. (See Parent Liaison, Chapter 14.)

Informal Home Visit

Having an activity or an agenda can make the visit more comfortable for both the parents and the visiting professional, but a home visit can be made when there is no definite business to be conducted. After the family has become acquainted with the teacher, it is even possible for the teacher to drop by unexpectedly in some homes to talk about the child and ask about the child. Once the parents feel comfortable with the professional, it becomes natural for them to share their concerns with the professional who has become a friend and will simply listen.

Developmental History

Receiving the message and understanding the message are two different things. Even after repeating the message and the feeling that appears to accompany it, the listener may not understand what the information means in the life of the other person. In order to understand the message, it is necessary to know some of the events that have happened to the person in the past and it is necessary to know what events are happening to the person now. Only then can the listener construct meaning to the messages.

Earlier experiences of the child and the family can be gathered with a developmental history form. Present experiences can be gathered during a home observation.

Gathering developmental information helps the professional to understand the parents' attitudes and concerns for the child as well as the child's needs. Parents are concerned not only about the present circumstances of the child, but also about things that have happened to the child in the past. It is difficult for parents, especially mothers, to forget any trauma that may have occurred at the time of the child's birth and the early parenting difficulties. Although medical personnel frequently tell the family that the "crisis has passed" or that the child will "outgrow" the problem, parents cannot always put aside these early concerns for the child. Sometimes the present message can only be understood in relation to the past experience.

Since early disease or trauma to the child is frequently connected to later learning problems, information gathered about the child's earlier life is also important in planning the child's school program.

One of the most effective ways of getting information about the experiences that the parent has had with the child is to interview the parent and ask specific questions. Although a form can be sent to the parent and the parent asked to fill it out and return it to school, a personal interview has more advantages: (1) it is an important chance to listen to the parent talk about the child, (2) some important information about the child that is not related to the answers to the questions may surface during the discussion, and (3) many parents of exceptional children are not comfortable reading and writing standard English.

The developmental history form shown in Exhibit 7-1 has a broad variety of items. It is appropriate for use with the mildly handicapped as well as the severely handicapped, and it is designed to help the professionals understand the parent as well as the child. In addition to medical and developmental information, the parent is asked to describe such things as the child's favorite toys. One of the important features of the form is that it asks the parent to describe what he or she likes most about the child.

Some school districts may train parents to interview other parents. The parent interview form from the System of Multicultural Pluralistic Assessment (SOMPA) is to be given not only by another parent, but by a parent of the same cultural background. Items on the SOMPA form have been correlated to the child's ability to be successful in school (Mercer, 1979). The developmental history could be gathered by the teacher, principal, nurse, counselor, social worker, or other agency personnel. If the agency has a parent liaison person, it would be ideal for that person to gather the history. (See Chapter 14.)

Home Observation

In order to understand the parent's messages it is necessary to know something about how the child fits into the day-to-day life of the family. Parents could be asked to describe the situation, but it is almost impossible for them to describe accurately all the facets of a situation in which they are taking such an active part. A brief visit in the home helps the professional get a feeling of the interaction patterns, but family interaction during a visit is probably not typical. In order to understand the home setting well enough to discuss it with the family, the professional must make a structured home observation.

The observer goes into the home as an observer only and does not interact with the child or the family. The observation should be made over a 12-hour period if possible so that the family members will have time to go about their regular routines and learn to ignore the visitor. Although the purpose of the observation is primarily to gather data on the child's activities, responsibilities and concerns of the parents are also on display for the observer.

The home observation is perhaps a prerequisite for understanding by someone who has not been the parent of a handicapped child. Graduate students who have made observations in preservice training have usually completed the observation with the comment, "I don't know how they do it!" They usually develop a healthy respect for the chores and responsibilities of the parent of an exceptional child and find it difficult to suggest that the parents "do more" for the child. After the observer has walked behind the child for 12 hours, it is possible to understand when the parent explains that there is not time to practice phonics or the multiplication tables or to work on toilet training.

Exhibit 7-1 Home and History Information from the Parent

We would like to know your child better. Please help us by giving us
the following information. For some of the information you may need
to refer to medical records, the baby book, or your spouse. We
certainly appreciate your interest in your child and your help
with this information.

Date:_____

Form completed by:_____

Child

Name:_____ Nickname:_____ Sex:_____

Age:_____Birthdate:_____Race:_____

School:_____School address:_____

School phone:_____Principal:_____

Father:_____Mother:_____

Home address:_____Zip Code_____

Phone:_____

Referral

Referred by:_____

Reason for referral:_____
_____
_____
_____

Previous Evaluation of Child (When, Where, What, and By Whom)
_____
_____
_____
_____
_____

Specialists (Pediatrician, Eye or Ear Doctor, Neurologist, Psychiatrist,
            Psychologist, etc.)

  Name   Address   Phone
_____
_____
_____
_____
_____
_____

Exhibit 7-1 continued

Family History

Marital status of parents:_____Any previous marriages?_____
Which parent?_____Any children by previous marriage?_____
List parents and siblings, in order of birth, including deceased:

	Age	Sex	Educ./Grade	Occupation	Health	Birthplace

Father_____
Mother_____
_____
_____
_____
_____
_____
_____

Person with whom child lives now:_____

Special interests or hobbies of parents:

    Mother:_____

    Father:_____

Illnesses or other problems of other family members:

_____
_____

Child's attitudes toward other family members:_____
_____

Any language other than English spoken in the home:_____

Any relatives (living or dead) with handicaps or difficulty in reading:_____

    writing:_____spelling:_____speech:_____

    or other school-related tasks:_____

    foreign language learning:_____. Degree of relationship(father,

    brother, uncle, etc.):_____

Is child adopted?_____Age at adoption:_____

Has child been told he is adopted?_____

Any long separations:_____When?_____How long?_____

Child's Reaction:_____

Moves: How Many?_____When?_____

Child's Reaction:_____

Have any members of the family (parents, grandparents, aunts and uncles, siblings) had any of the following? If yes, state age of person, relationship
to the child, and when condition occurred:

Asthma_____
Bronchitis_____
Allergy (sinusitis, skin allergy, hay fever, "summer colds," etc.)_____
_____

Arthritis_____

Exhibit 7-1 continued

Deafness or impaired hearing_____
Epilepsy or convulsions_____
Nervous condition or mental illness_____
Heart disease_____
Lung disease (TB, etc.)_____
Diabetes_____
Low blood sugar (hypoglycemia)_____
Stammering or stuttering_____
Problem drinking_____
Cancer_____
Mental retardation_____
Cerebral palsy_____
Muscular problems_____
Impaired vision_____
Other conditions (blood, bone, etc.)_____

Medical and Developmental History of Child

Health of mother during pregnancy:_____

Is mother's blood RH negative?_____Child was born after_____ months of
    pregnancy. Child's birth weight was _____.

Delivery: Length of labor:_____Was labor induced?_____

    Forceps used?_____ Complications:_____

Condition of newborn:_____

    Jaundice?_____"Blue baby"?_____

    Adequate weight gain?_____Weight at 5 months:_____

Nursing and feeding: Breast?_____Bottle?_____Other:_____

    Weaned to cup at_____ months. Weaning my child was_____

    Early appetite & eating habits: (colicky, spitty, frequent feedings,
    other feeding problems, food allergies, etc.)___ _____

Elimination and toilet habits: Does the child keep dry for 2 hours?_____

    Does the child have bladder control?_____Bowel control?_____

    Is the child toilet trained?_____

Methods and problems:_____
_____

Current toilet habits:_____
_____

Method for handling child's elimination:_____
_____

Is the child diapered at night?_____ _____
Is he taken to the toilet during the night?_____
Is the child frequently constipated?_____
Does the child have medical problems related to elimination?_____

Exhibit 7-1 continued

Sleeping Habits: Restless sleeper?_____ Quiet sleeper?_____
Any special problems (nightmares, sleepwalking, etc.)_____
_____

Does the child bang head, suck thumb, etc., to go to sleep?_____
Current eating habits and appetite: Fussy eater?_____Frequent Snacks?_____
Food cravings, preferences:_____
Strong dislikes:_____
Any special mealtime problems?_____
_____

Can the child close his mouth?_____Can the child suck liquids in a straw?____
Can the child chew?_____Can the child swallow?_____
Does he choke easily?_____ Does he eat solid foods?_____
Semi-solid foods?_____Pureed food only?_____
Describe your feeding procedure:_____
_____
_____

Major illnesses	Date	Treatment
High fever		
Asthma		
Convulsions		
Measles		
Eczema		
Diabetes		
Chicken pox		
Mumps		
German measles		
Sore throats		
Ear infections		
Pneumonia		
Meningitis		
Hepatitis		
Encephalitis		
Venereal disease (specify)		
Fainting		
Tonsillitis		
Rheumatic fever		
Kidney or bladder diseases		
Mononucleosis		
Frequent headaches		
Frequent colds or viruses		
Influenza		
Ulcers		
Allergies (besides those listed)		
Prolonged medication		
Other		

Exhibit 7-1 continued

Accidents and head injuries (what and when): _____

_____

_____

Hospitalizations and/or operations (what and when): _____

_____

_____

Is child presently taking any medication? _____ What kind? _____

_____

When was his last physical examination? _____

Has he had his eyes tested by an opthalmologist or optometrist? _____

When? _____ Findings: _____

Does child wear glasses? _____ For what purpose? _____

Has child had his hearing tested? _____ When? _____

Findings: _____

Any symptoms of eye or ear trouble? (Burning, aching eyes, blurriness; draining, aching, or ringing ears, etc.) _____

Parent's Description of Child

_____

_____

_____

Hair color: _____ Eye color: _____

Complexion: _____ Body build: _____

Motor Development

This child could hold his head up at _____ months. Turn his body over at _____ months.

The child sat up at about _____ months, crawled at _____ months, and walked alone at _____ months.

Hand preference developed at about _____ months. Which hand does child use to eat with? _____ , draw or write with? _____ , throw with? _____

Fine motor and coordination skills: If your child can do the following tasks, please list the age at which he could do them: tie his shoes _____ , cut with scissors _____ , button his shirts _____ , hop _____ , skip _____ , jump rope _____ . Were (and are) any of these or similar tasks particularly difficult for your child? _____

Describe your child's general coordination? _____

_____

Describe his balance: _____

Describe your child's reaction to music: _____

_____

Does your child like to go for rides and trips? _____ Describe: _____

_____

How does your child respond to tension? _____

_____

Exhibit 7-1 continued

Language Development

Does the child babble and make cooing sounds?_____

Does the child say Mamma and Daddy?_____

This child's first words occurred at approximately _____ months. He began
speaking in sentences at about _____ months. Does he articulate clearly for
his age?_____ Does he often have to hunt for words with which to express
himself?_____Has he ever had speech therapy?_____If yes, describe briefly:

_____

_____

Sexual Behavior and Maturation

Has the child been interested in the sexual parts of his body?_____

Does he manipulate or rub the sex organs?_____

Has the child demonstrated curiosity about the facts of life?_____

Have they been explained?_____ If so, by whom?_____

Attitude toward other sex:_____

Has child reached age of puberty?_____Age at onset:_____

Any complications (excessive cramping, etc., for female; excessive self-
consciousness with voice "cracking," etc., for boy)?_____

Describe child's ability to handle information about sex:_____

_____

Social Behavior

The person(s) in the home with whom this child feels most comfortable and gets
along best is (are):_____

With what other person(s) in his family, if any, does this child share a bedroom?_____

Does he sleep with a toy or plaything?_____

My child seems to get upset most when_____

He is happiest when_____

Hoes does your child express fear or worry?_____

_____

With what group does child relate best? Adults____, Peers_____, Siblings_____

Does he prefer one playmate at a time_____, group play_____, or to play by
himself_____? Preferred age of playmates (older, younger, same age):_____

My child likes games that are rough_____, noisy_____, quiet_____, physically
active_____, have definite rules_____, require a great deal of make-believe
_____, other_____

Please describe favorite home play, recreation, preferred toys (puzzles, models,
building blocks, dolls, etc.):_____

_____

_____

Exhibit 7-1 continued

Does he avoid certain kinds of activities or games?_____

If so, describe:_____

Does your child get angry at other people?_____

Who does he get angry with?_____

How does he express it?_____

Fears:_____

In what situations is child confident?_____

In what situations is he uncomfortable?_____

How does he express discomfort?_____

Does your child have chores to do at home?_____

Does he do the chores or assigned tasks without being reminded?____

How much TV does your child watch?_____ List favorite shows:_____

Training Patterns

Who does most of the disciplining?_____

Method most frequently used:_____

Frequency of discipline:_____

Child's most common reaction to discipline (cries, sulks, laughs, repents, hits, withdraws, gets angry, sasses, places blame elsewhere, etc.):_____

_____

What kind of discipline is most effective?_____

What kind of discipline is least effective?_____

What rewards will your child respond to?_____

Is this child supervised at all times?_____If not, under what conditions is he allowed to stay alone?_____

If mother works, who takes care of child?_____

Behavioral Concerns

I am concerned about my child's:

1. _____

2. _____

3. _____

4. _____

5. _____

Exhibit 7-1 continued

Behavioral checklist:

Check which of the following items concern you about this child's behavior.

_____ nightmares	_____ profanity
_____ always tired	_____ rebellious
_____ poor sleeper	_____ bad temper
_____ complains of illness	_____ fights too much
_____ fussy eater	_____ bully
_____ doesn't dress self	_____ breath-holding
_____ nervousness	_____ bumps head
_____ moody	_____ hostile
_____ whines	_____ overly critical
_____ tattles	_____ irresponsible
_____ babyish	_____ runs away from home
_____ fearful	_____ difficult to discipline
_____ fear of dark	_____ excessive sex play
_____ thumb-sucking	_____ disturbs other children
_____ nail-biting	_____ shows off
_____ stuttering	_____ masturbation
_____ overly sensitive	_____ destructive
_____ shy	_____ lies
_____ complains of being picked on	_____ sex preoccupation
_____ confused	_____ takes things
_____ forgetful	_____ steals
_____ cries a lot	_____ disobedient
_____ has few friends	_____ hyperactive
_____ self-conscious	_____ jerking movements
_____ easily discouraged	_____ facial grimaces
_____ poor loser	_____ lacks self-control
_____ lacks motivation	_____ disorganized
_____ insecure	_____ demands too much attention
_____ overly passive	_____ excessively loud and noisy
_____ loner	_____ overly dependent
_____ depressed	_____ manipulative (works people to get
_____ daydreams	his own way)
_____ talks to self	_____ usually seeks approval
_____ inattentive	_____ hides things
_____ withdrawn	_____ too impulsive
_____ generally slow	_____ inflexible
_____ tantrums	
_____ hair-twisting	

Please describe what you most like about your child.

_____

_____

_____

_____

_____

_____

Exhibit 7-1 continued

Training and Therapy History

Preschool experience (nursery school, day care center, etc.):_____
_____
_____
_____

Public school experience:_____
_____
_____
_____

Postschool expectations for this child:_____
_____
_____

This child has been evaluated by:

    Person   Date   Location of Records

Physical therapist_____

Occupational therapist_____

Educational evaluator (psychologist, etc.)_____

Others_____
_____

Training and therapy programs have included:

_____Date:_____

_____Date:_____

_____Date:_____

_____Date:_____

He has received___ hours weekly by the _____therapist from

_____ to _____ (dates).

We have spent _____ hours daily in therapy at home.

Describe therapy and give dates of use:_____
_____
_____

Current home therapy program? Describe:_____
_____
_____

Are there factors that make this training/therapy difficult to give routinely?
Describe:_____
_____
_____

Exhibit 7-1 continued

Could you follow the home training/therapy program better if you had outside help? Describe:_____
_____

Have you ever received help from social services or other community agencies in connection with this child?_____ Describe:_____
_____
_____

For other reasons?___ Describe:_____
_____

Have you received family counseling? _____ Describe:_____
_____

What services could be given you that would help with this child?_____
Describe:_____
_____

Who cares for the child when you are ill or need to be away from home?_____
_____

Do grapdparents or other family members spend time with the child?_____
Who and how much? _____
Maternal grandfather_____Maternal grandmother_____
Paternal grandfather_____Paternal grandmother_____
Mother's sisters_____Mother's brothers_____
Mother's sisters-in-law_____Father's sisters_____
Father's brothers_____Father's sisters-in-law_____
Cousins_____Ages and sex:_____
_____
_____

Does this child associate with children in the neighborhood?_____
At church, etc.:_____If so, sex:_____age:_____
Amount of contact:_____
Does the family have any pets?_____Describe?_____
_____

Are there any other things about your child or your family that you feel might be helpful to us?_____
_____
_____

Thank you so much for your time. This information will help us know your child better.

Scheduling the Appointment

When the appointment for the visit is made, the family should be told that they do not need to change any of their regular activities. It should be explained that the observer will follow the child around and record what the child is doing so that an analysis of the child's activities can be made for the family. It is recommended that the 12-hour observation be made at one time. Perhaps the best time is on Saturday from 8:30 or 9:00 A.M. to 8:30 or 9:00 P.M. If it is not possible to make the observation in one day, two 6-hour observations can be substituted. If the observer comes for only short periods of time, the child and the family are distracted from regular routines and the data gathered are not typical of the child's activities. If the family or child is going somewhere during the observation, the observer goes along. Some observers have gone shopping, some have followed children on bicycles or watched them climb trees, and several have gone to church with the family.

The observation should be focused on the child's activities. Other things occurring in the household could be noted on the observation sheet, even though they are not directly related to the child. Since the parents will be receiving a copy of the observation, it is important that the observer describe the behavior objectively and in language that the parents can easily follow.

Making the Observation

The observation sheet (Exhibit 7-2) can be carried on a clipboard or on a piece of firm cardboard. Observations written in pencil are difficult to read, since the lead smears as the paper is handled. If the observer writes with a fine pen, it will be possible to make a detailed observation without carrying a large bulk of paper around. Since it will be necessary to make a copy of the observation for the family, observations should be recorded in black ink so the copy will be clear.

A sample of a completed observation sheet is shown in Exhibit 7-3. In the left-hand column of the observation sheet are markings for five-minute intervals; the observer writes the hour in the blank space at the left. During each five-minute interval, the observer writes what the child is doing, using key words and phrases with as much specific detail as possible. In the middle column, the observer writes who the child is with and whether the child is interacting with that person or just in the same physical surroundings. The column on the right is for the observer to record where the child is during that time. The location should be indicated as specifically as possible; the part of the room or the yard should be described.

For most children it is appropriate for the observer to say hello, show the child the observation sheet, and tell the child, ''I will be watching you and writing down what you are doing.'' The observer should not try to engage the child in conversation or play with the child, however, but should concentrate on the role of observer.

Exhibit 7-2 Sample Observation Sheet

Time	Activity	Who With	Where
__:.00			
05			
10			
15			
20			
25			
30			
35			
40			
45			
50			
55			
__:.00			
05			
10			
15			
20			
25			
30			
35			
40			
45			
50			
55			
.00			
05			
10			
15			
20			
25			
30			
35			
40			
45			
50			
55			

a.m p.m.

Date

Recorder

Name

Exhibit 7-3 Sample of a Completed Observation Sheet

		Activity	Who With	Where
	9:05	Helped w/garbage, Dad took it out-didn't have shoes	Mother, Dad	Kitchen, Porch
	9:10	Mom put on socks; put on tennis shoes; Mom tied shoes	Mother	Kitchen, hall
	9:15	Put an ashtray back in family room	Mother, brother	Kitchen, family room
	9:20	Writing in book, get paper from room	Self, Mother	Kitchen, own room
	9:25	Showed observer school papers, reading, math	Observer, Mother	Kitchen
	9:30	Same as above	Same as above	Same as above
	9:35	Take pill, put papers back in room, outside-see rabbits	Self, observer	Own room, outside, backyard
	9:40	Held rabbits, talked to rabbits	Brother, self	Backyard
	9:45	Brother asked her to watch rabbits, played on monkeybars	Brother, self, Mother	Backyard
	9:50	Played on monkeybars, swing set	Self	Backyard
	9:55	Talked to Observer about clipboard, played on swings	Self, observer	Backyard
	10:00	Talked about neighbors kids in trouble, changed swing	Self, observer	Backyard
	10:05	Talked to observer about lunch, dinner, and neighbors	Self, observer	Backyard

Left margin (rotated): p.m. (a.m.)   Time 9   Date 11/18/78   Recorder   J. Van Diek   Michele Hansen

Exhibit 7-3 continued

		Activity	Who With	Where
	10:10	Knocked leaves out of trees, fed the rabbits	Self, observer	Backyard
	10:15	Played tether ball	Self	Backyard
	10:20	Looked for strawberries, took inside	Self, Mother	Backyard, inside & back outside
	10:25	Asked to get seed pods from tree, played on swing set	Dad, self	Backyard
	10:30	Asked Dad what's for dinner, played on swing set	Dad, self	Inside back porch, back outside
	10:35	Climbed on tether to the monkeybars	Self	Backyard
	10:40	Demonstrated push-ups, j. jacks, situps, into get ball	Self	Backyard, back porch
	10:45	Asked brother to play ball, shared tangerine w/brother	Self, brother	Family room, upstairs, back outside
	10:50	Played ball w/brother, Mom got hit w/ball in stomach	Brother, Mother	Backyard
	10:55	Pushed lawn mower, Mom & brother played ball	Brother, Mother	Backyard
	11:00	Played ball w/brother, sat at picnic table	Brother	Backyard
	11:05	Ate apple, watched brother climb tree, sat on bike	Brother	Inside, back outside, backyard
	11:10	Moved bike for brother/inside to room, put on record	Brother/self	Backyard, inside, upstairs

Date 11/18/78 Time 10:10 (a.m) p.m.

Recorder J. Van Diek

Michele Hansen

Organizing the Data

The information is organized by the number of five-minute periods the child was engaged in various activities, with various people, and in various locations. A tally sheet is given for each category (Exhibits 7-4, 7-5, and 7-6). The most efficient way to categorize the data is to read through the appropriate column on the observation sheet and make a tally mark in the appropriate square on the tally sheet. A mark is made for each five-minute period that the child was engaged in that activity, with that person, or in that location. The activity tally sheet, for example, has 21 subcategories. If there are other activities that the child was engaged in, other categories can be made. Since some activities fit into more than one category, the tally does not show a percentage of time, but the number of five-minute periods that the child participated in that activity (Exhibit 7-7).

Summarizing the Data

After the data have been organized by categories and subcategories, the amount of time the child spends in various activities, with various people, and in various locations can be illustrated on graphs, either bar graphs or line graphs. The use of graph paper makes the task easier. Sample graphs are shown in Figures 7-1, 7-2, and 7-3.

A letter written to the parents could be used to summarize the data for both the parents and for the school's record (Exhibit 7-8).

Discussing the Observation with the Parent

One of the most effective ways of organizing and analyzing the data is for the observer and the parent to make the tally of the data together. Even though the parent has not participated in the organization of the information, however, it is important that the information be discussed with the parent. The discussion is an ideal time for the parent to express concerns about the child and the family's ability to meet the child's needs. The needs of the siblings of the exceptional child can also be duscussed (see Chapter 6, Working with Siblings in the School). It is an opportune time for the parent to ask questions about methods and procedures to enhance the child's development. If the professional listens carefully to each of the parent's questions or comments, the professional can understand the parent well enough to discover the information that the parent is ready to hear (see Chapter 3, Discussing More Than Grades: The Whole Child and Family).

Exhibit 7-4 Time Spent in Various Activities

Child's Name: _____ C.A.: _____ Recorder: _____

Analyzed By: _____ Date of Observation: _____ from _____ A.M. to _____ P.M.

Day of Week: _____

Bathing	Washing	Dressing	Grooming/personal hygiene	Toileting	Eating	Snacks
At doctor	At lesson/therapy	Church	At school	Recreation w/ family	Organized recreation	Ride in car
Watching TV	TV Educational	TV w/family	TV alone	TV adult show	TV child show	TV ballgame
Playing favorite toy (specify)	Playing toys	Playing household items	Trike/bike	Swing	Playing records	Specified task/chore
Nap	Sleep at night	Visiting/talking				

OTHER NOTES ON ACTIVITIES:

Exhibit 7-5 Time Spent with Various People

Child's Name:		C.A.:	Recorder:
Analyzed By:		Date of Observation:	from _____ A.M. to _____ P.M.
Day of Week:			

Alone	W/ Mother	W/ Father	W/ Both Parents	W/ Family
W/ Sibling (name)	W/ Sibling (name)	W/ Several Siblings	W/ Extended Family	W/ Friends
W/ Structured Group	W/ Strangers	In Public	W/ Neighbors	Talk to Self

OTHER NOTES ON INTERACTION:

Exhibit 7-6 Time Spent in Various Locations

TIME SPENT WITH VARIOUS LOCATIONS

Child's Name: _____   C.A.: _____   Recorder: _____

Analyzed By: _____   Date of Observation: _____   from _____ A.M. to _____ P.M.

Day of Week: _____

Own Room	Kitchen	Living Room	Family Room	Bathroom	Parent's Room
Front Yard	Back Yard	Relative's Home	Own Home	Public Restaurant	Park
Public Business	Doctor's Office	Driveway	Garage	In Car	

OTHER NOTES ON LOCATION:

Exhibit 7-7 Sample Tally Sheet Used for Time Spent in Various Activities

Child's name: Michele Hansen   C.A.: 9.2   Recorder: Van Diek

Analyzed by: Van Diek   Date of Observation: Nov. 18, 1978   from 9 ___ A.M. to 9 ___ P.M.

Day of week: Saturday

Bathing /// / 4	Washing /// 3	Dressing THL 5	Grooming/personal hygiene THL THL / 11	Toileting //// 4	Eating THL THL /// 13	Snacks // 2
Playing w/ rabbits /// / 4	Playing ball THL / 6	Walking THL // 7	Watching/talking to neighbors THL 5	Recreation w/ family	Organized recreation	Ride in car //// 4
Watching TV THL 5	TV Educational THL / 6	TV w/brother THL 5	TV alone	TV adult show	TV child show THL 5	TV ballgame
Sing/dance //// 4	Playing toys/games THL THL THL / 16	Reading THL THL THL // 17	Trike/bike // 2	Swing/monkey bars THL THL THL 15	Playing records THL / 6	Specified task/chore THL THL //// 14
Nap — Sleep at night		Walking/talking THL THL // 12	Other notes on activities:			

Figure 7-1 Sample Graph of Time Spent in Various Activities

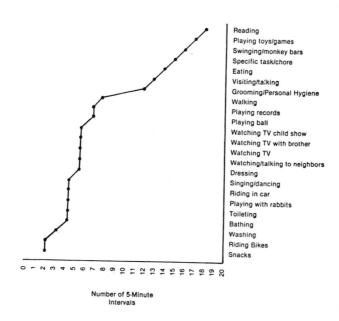

Reading
Playing toys/games
Swinging/monkey bars
Specific task/chore
Eating
Visiting/talking
Grooming/Personal Hygiene
Walking
Playing records
Playing ball
Watching TV child show
Watching TV with brother
Watching TV
Watching/talking to neighbors
Dressing
Singing/dancing
Riding in car
Playing with rabbits
Toileting
Bathing
Washing
Riding Bikes
Snacks

Number of 5-Minute
Intervals

Figure 7-2 Sample Graph of Time Spent with Various People

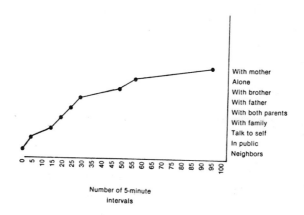

With mother
Alone
With brother
With father
With both parents
With family
Talk to self
In public
Neighbors

Number of 5-minute
intervals

Figure 7-3 Sample Graph of Time Spent in Various Locations

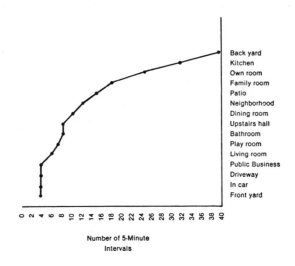

Back yard
Kitchen
Own room
Family room
Patio
Neighborhood
Dining room
Upstairs hall
Bathroom
Play room
Living room
Public Business
Driveway
In car
Front yard

Number of 5-Minute
Intervals

Personal Information Obtained from Home Visits

Concerns about the child and the family are very private, personal things. When the parent discloses this information to the public agency through the developmental history form or a home observation, the professional must treat the information as personal and private. Confidentiality for the messages sent by parents or observations made in the parent's home is as vital as the confidentiality of the written records of the child's progress at school. One supervisor of special education told the personnel at an in-service session; "If you talk about your students and their families to others, you can be sued. And if you do, I hope you are" (Jones, 1971).

In addition, the professional must treat the information from and about the parents and the household with respect, even when the professional's personal custom or religion differs from that of the family. Shock, surprise, doubt, and rejection expressed either verbally or nonverbally by the professional will inhibit the desire of the parent to communicate freely not only with that professional but also with others.

Exhibit 7-8 Sample Summary Letter

School Letterhead

Dear Mr. and Mrs. Hansen

   I would like to thank you again for welcoming me into your home to observe Michele. I would like to share my findings with you.

   Michele's day included a wide variety of activities. The activities that Michele spent most of her time doing included: reading, playing with toys and games, playing on swings and monkey bars, eating and talking. The activities that Michele spent the least amount of time doing included: singing and dancing, washing, riding in the car, playing with the rabbits, toileting, bathing and eating snacks.

   Michele's activities took place in all parts of the house, surrounding yard and neighborhood. She spent most of her time in the backyard, kitchen, her bedroom and the family room. The least amount of time was spent in the front yard, in the car, driveway and in public businesses.

   Michele interacted with all members of the family as a group and individually. She spent most of her time with her mother, alone with her brother and the least amount of time with neighbors and in public.

   It appeared that Michele's activities were productive and appropriate. Her activities took place in a variety of locations and her interactions with people varied. She did not play with her friends due to the fact that one was out of town and another was involved in an all day camping trip. However, she was able to initiate appropriate activities without being told to do so.

   An activity I enjoyed was seeing the family playing games together. Although Michele became upset and left the room when she was not winning, she did come back to finish the game. It would be good to include similar activities that involve the entire family.

   I would like to make a suggestion involving Michele's self-help skills. It would seem that Michele should be able to perform skills such as washing hands and face, brushing teeth, dressing and putting on shoes more independently. She is able to perform other tasks such as putting eggs in the egg tray, setting and clearing the table and taking care of her books and records independently.

   I hope you will find this information and these suggestions helpful. If there are other things that you would like to talk about please let me know.

Sincerely,

Mrs. Van Diek

UNDERSTANDING BY OBSERVATION

The Parent at School

School personnel can also listen to the parent by observing how the parent responds to the school. Does the parent visit the school? Does the parent send notes to school and call the school? Does the parent participate in meetings that the school organizes for parents? Does the parent participate in groups organized by parents? Is the parent willing to volunteer to help at school? If not, why not? Maybe the parent doesn't speak the language used at the school, or perhaps it is because no one at school really listens and understands the parents and the activities at home.

The Child at School

When parents do not come to school when they have been invited and do not seem interested in having the professionals come to the home, it is easy to assume that the parent is not interested in the child. Akert (1973) examines the relationships that family members have to one another by observing the way they stand, touch, and look at one another in family photographs. He observes energy, vitality, dominance, and sensitivity in postures, facial expressions, and dress.

It is possible to listen to the parent by observing the message that the parent sends to school every day: the child. Is the child at school on time with breakfast eaten and hair combed? Are the child's medical needs taken care of? Are the teeth clean and free from decay? Are the fingernails and hands clean? Does the child take baths regularly?

Sensitive teachers can hear messages in the way the parent dresses the child. Are the clothes clean, durable, and appropriate? Did the mother make the child's clothes? The parent sends messages by the way the parent plans the child's diet. Mothers who choose to place the child on a rigid diet express continuing concern for the child's well-being. If mother talks continuously about the diet, however, she may be overconcerned about the child.

Does the mother send a lunch with the child? One student in a commuter college carried a lunch obviously packed by a loving mother. Each day he appeared in his 8:00 A.M. class carrying a brown paper bag that had Charlie written on it in large red letters. Not only had his mother packed the lunch, but she had packed it especially for him. It was obvious that his mother was really concerned about her "little boy." Was she also unwilling to let him become Charles?

It is important that the messages gathered from observation of the child at school be understood in context. One professional complained because the children in one family did not bathe. He understood later when he found that the family of ten had no bathroom.

Receiving and Understanding the Parents' Messages

Receiving messages from parents and understanding those messages is prerequisite to being able to effectively send information to the parent. In order for the interaction to be effective, the parent must be comfortable during the flow of the conversation and feel free to take the role of speaker whenever the parent has a doubt or a question. If the parent's verbal and nonverbal responses are not sensitively monitored during the interaction, it is highly possible that the question or doubt may be unexpressed but continue to grow until the parent withdraws consent. Knowing how to relinquish the speaker role and how to listen to the nonverbal message sent by the parent is an important professional skill.

Communication with the parent in the home setting tends to reverse the dominant roles and gives the role of speaker more naturally to the parent. This setting can make it easier for the parent to express ideas or concerns. Gathering the history of the child's developmental experiences can give the parent an opportunity to tell about the child. It is also an efficient way to gather more assessment material about the child.

Observing in the home is a valuable experience because the professional learns through personal observation how the family's energies are spent on training the child at home. Knowing more about how the family faces these responsibilities makes it possible for the professional to hear how the parent feels more clearly, even during other conversations.

The professional has a responsibility for developing the skills to receive and understand messages from parents. A bonus for careful listening and understanding for the public agency is access to a greatly expanded body of knowledge about the child that can be used in program plans and instructional activities. And for the parent there is the sheer joy of having someone simply listen, understand, and perhaps even appreciate.

REFERENCES

Akert, R.U. *Photoanalysis: How to interpret the hidden psychological meaning of personal and public photographs.* New York: Peter H. Wyden, 1973.

Argyle, M. Non-verbal communication in human social interaction. In R.A. Hinde (Ed.), *Non verbal communication.* London: Cambridge University Press, 1972.

Argyle, M. *Bodily communication.* New York: International Universities Press, 1975.

Buck, R.W., Savin, V.J., Miller, R.E., & Caul, W.F. Communication of affect through facial expressions in humans. In S. Weitz (Ed.), *Nonverbal communication.* New York: Oxford University Press, 1974.

Chinn, P., Winn, J., & Walters, R.H. *Two-way talking with parents of special children: A process of positive communication.* St. Louis: C.V. Mosby, 1978.

Ekman, P., & Friesen, W.V. *Unmasking the face: A guide to recognizing emotions from facial clues* Englewood Cliffs, N.J.: Prentice-Hall, 1975.

Jaffe, J. Parliamentary procedure and the brain. In A.W. Seigman & S. Feldstein (Eds.), *Nonverbal behavior in communication.* Hillsdale, N.J.: Lawrence Erlbaum Associates, 1978.

Jones, H.B. Personal communication, May, 1971.

Lichter, P. Communicating with parents: It begins with listening. *Teaching Exceptional Children,* 1976, *8*(2), 67-71.

Meador, B.D., & Rogers, C.R. Client centered therapy. In R. Cosini (Ed.), *Current psychotherapies.* Itasca, Ill.: R.E. Peacock, 1973.

Mercer, J. *SOMPA: System of multicultural pluralistic assessment. Technical manual.* New York: The Psychological Corporation, 1979.

Molloy, J.T. *The woman's dress for success book.* New York: Warner Books, 1977.

Patterson, E. Personal communication, November, 1969.

Rabalias, K. Personal communication, September, 1979.

Rosenfeld, H.M. Conversational control functions of nonverbal behavior. In A.W. Seigman & S. Feldstein (Eds.), *Nonverbal behavior and communication.* Hillsdale, N.J.: Lawrence Erlbaum Associates, 1978.

Scheflen, A.E. "Quasi-courtship behavior in psychotherapy." In S. Weitz (Ed.), *Nonverbal Communication.* New York.: Oxford University Press, 1974.

Seigman, A.W. The telltale voice: Nonverbal messages of verbal communication. In A.W. Seigman & S. Feldstein (Eds.), *Nonverbal behavior and communication.* Hillsdale, N.J.: Lawrence Erlbaum Associates, 1978.

Spock, B. *On being the parent of a handicapped child.* Chicago: National Society of Crippled Children and Adults, 1961.

Weitz, S. (Ed.). *Nonverbal communication readings with commentary.* New York: Oxford University Press, 1974.

Williams, L. Personal communication, 1977.

Chapter 8

The Professional's Chance To Speak: How To Be Heard

MAKE IT PLEASANT

"A positive reinforcer can be anything that is desired or needed by the student. A positive reinforcer will strengthen the response it follows and make that response more likely to reoccur" (Hunter, 1967, p. 1). Everybody knows that! At least everybody who has studied education in the last 20 years knows that. And yet, there are many excellent educators who can apply the principle to the learning of children, but cannot apply it to their interaction with adults. Adults need positive reinforcement as much or more than children do.

Morgan (1973) suggests that every wife should "admire" her husband. James and Jongeward (1971) write that it is important to "appreciate the uniqueness of others." Harris (1969) indicated that without stroking, touching, and closeness a person will die. Somehow it seems easier to reinforce children than it does to reinforce adults. But in social learning, people teach each other (Sheppard, Shank, & Wilson, 1973), whether they are children or adults.

In the Walt Disney movie, *Bambi,* Bambi's friend Thumper gave an important message to Bambi. "If you can't say something good, don't say anything at all." Educators who can't say something good about a child with a learning problem shouldn't say anything at all, especially to the parents. If nothing positive is said about the child, the parents will not be ready to listen to anything at all. For some educators this might mean reprogramming. Most educators have been taught to assess the child to find the child's weaknesses. Most teachers do not mark things that are right on the paper, but the things that are wrong. Children are categorized and labeled not by what they know, but by what they don't know. Parents are told about their child's problems, not successes.

People see what they are looking for. Teachers who look for good things in a child will be able to find them. One cooperating teacher criticized her student teacher by saying, "I heard you compliment Rusty yesterday. You know that

Rusty can't do anything right!'' But the student teacher kept looking because she had seen Rusty do some things that were right, even though he did have trouble with reading, writing, and arithmetic.

For some children it is necessary to structure the setting so that they can do something successfully. Smith (1968), Gearheart and Litton (1979), Hewett (1968), and Alley and Deshler (1979) all stress that the teacher should structure the situation so that the child is able to be successful and feel the success. Teachers who cannot list the child's good qualities as well as the child's weaknesses have not listened to their own training.

One Individual Education Program (IEP) meeting centered around whether the child was emotionally disturbed or having an emotional reaction to not being able to do the work that she was asked to do, but the label to use was not relevant. What the child obviously needed was a teacher who knew how to give her some activities at which she could be successful. Teachers of exceptional children should be able to assess each child's ability well enough to design activities that the child, the parent, and even the teacher can enjoy. If the teacher can't genuinely enjoy the interaction with the child and find some good things about the child to tell the parent, then the teaching must be a tremendous emotional burden to the teacher.

COMMUNICATING THE POSITIVE TO THE PARENT

One of the best ways to get people to listen is to say what they want to hear. Parents of exceptional children desperately want *someone, anyone,* to like their child. Since almost all of the professionals, neighbors, and friends have made negative comments about the child, the parent is hungry to hear that someone thinks the child is valuable in some way. Parents are particularly anxious for the personnel of the school to ''like'' the child.

Sending positive messages sounds easy. Actually, it isn't. Many people have become so accustomed to hearing criticism that they do not know what to do when someone says something nice (Dyer, 1976). The standard response to ''That is a pretty dress'' is ''This old thing?''

Since most people tend to reject compliments, or overreact and see a compliment as an indication that everything is all right, stating a compliment in such a way that it is understood and accepted takes some practice. Learning to give compliments as a means of establishing lines of communication to the parents of a handicapped child when that communication must eventually include less positive information is not easy. Sometimes positive acceptance must be expressed for such a long time that the sender begins to wonder if enough rapport to discuss the child's real problems will ever be established. Telling the parent that the child has specific problems that need attention is a process that also must include plenty of positive things about the child.

Since parents are not used to hearing nice things about their handicapped child the parents may assume that the positive message is some kind of a mistake or even a joke. Some parents might even think that the professional is lying or trying to make fun of them. Some parents have become so accustomed to hearing negative things about their child that *they* cannot see any good things; these parents may have begun to identify themselves as "martyrs" and may cling to the "bad child" in order to qualify for the role of "wonderful parents" because they put up with so much.

At one young mothers' group the atmosphere was so heavy with the discussion of the problems of their severely handicapped children that the discussion leader changed the subject and insisted that the parents begin to describe the problems that they *wouldn't* have. After a few minutes, the mothers were laughing and crying as they listed such items as: "He will never run away" (the child did not walk), "He will never overdose on drugs" (the child could not feed himself), "He will not get a girl in trouble" (the child could not even toilet himself), "I can always get her dolls for Christmas." Parents of handicapped children have some real difficulties with their children, but most of them also get some real joy from their children (Michaelis, 1976). Educators can help parents feel some of that joy by conditioning themselves and the parents to notice good things about the child. (The Home History form, Exhibit 7-1, asks the parents to share this information.)

Creating Positive Messages

Rome wasn't built in a day and neither was a child. Most parents know that. They do not get their joy from hearing that the child will "live happily ever after" but from the little things that the child has learned. Parents would be happy to hear:

- Johnny drinks all of his milk.
- Johnny held his spoon and fed himself.
- Johnny sat up without his chair today.
- Johnny put on his coat alone today.
- Johnny opened the door for the principal.
- Johnny carried his own lunch tray.
- Johnny turned on the record player alone.
- Johnny erased the chalkboard as high as he could reach.
- Johnny helped Bob find the right bus.
- Johnny reminded Joe to take his jacket home.
- Johnny emptied the pencil sharpener without spilling the shavings.
- Johnny turned on the fountain and got his drink alone.
- Johnny came in quietly when the bell rang.
- Johnny sat still during math.
- Johnny told about the new kittens in show and tell.

- Johnny loaned Tom a dime when Tom lost a dime of his lunch money.
- Johnny shared his science book with Joe.
- Johnny led the class to lunch.
- Johnny took a note to the principal.
- Johnny helped Alice with the math assignment.
- Johnny helped the children in wheelchairs get outside during the fire drill.
- Johnny picked up papers on the school yard.
- Johnny always reminds us to turn off the lights.
- Johnny brings in the softball equipment when everyone else forgets.
- Johnny uses both sides of the paper so he won't waste paper.

The list may seem to have Johnny repeated too many times, but Johnny's parents wouldn't think so. The list could be endless. The key to generating items for the list is to think of small things that the child is performing well, even if it is only a small part of a larger activity. If education is to be a preparation for life, these personal and social skills are as important as reading, writing, and arithmetic skills.

The Ratio of Messages

Since educators have become accountable for their teaching, they have become number conscious. Records are kept on how many times various things occur. How frequently is a certain activity presented to the child, and how many times does the child make a correct response? The kinds of messages sent to parents could also be recorded. It might be appropriate to send messages to the parent in a ratio of one negative message to two positive messages. Therefore, the professionals must be keenly observant to be able to see many "good" things. It may even be necessary to alter teaching styles, the difficulty of goals, and the reinforcement pattern in order to create a situation in which the child can be said to be successful that much of the time.

Good News/Bad News Messages

Even when the message must be a negative message, it is possible to come up with a good news/bad news approach. Instead of saying, "Johnny didn't finish his math today because he was talking to the other boys," the teacher might say, "Johnny is getting along with the other boys very well, sometimes so well that it interferes with his work in math." If rapport has been established between the professional and the parent, and possibly even if it hasn't, the parent may be able to accept this message as if it came from an interested godparent. A godparent is someone who not only is a friend of the parent, but also can look at things from the child's perspective.

Other good news/bad news messages might be: (a) "Johnny is very careful about the way he copies his letters; sometimes he is so careful about the way he copies that he doesn't get finished." (b) "Johnny really enjoys going outside at recess; sometimes he enjoys it so much that he forgets to come in." (c) "Johnny enjoys eating; sometimes he enjoys it so much that he eats too fast." (d) "Johnny likes to look at the pictures in the reader; sometimes he looks at the pictures so much that he doesn't follow the words."

With the good news/bad news approach, Johnny is not accused of being mean, different, dumb, or evil. This approach only sets up a situation in which the parent can acknowledge that the child has problems without saying that the child has nothing but problems.

ORGANIZING THE PONY EXPRESS

There are many ways to send messages these days, especially to parents. The traditional note home is still the old stand-by, however. The local radio and TV stations are interested in an occasional human interest story, and the mail is a good way to send a novel message. Some messages can be sent by the teacher, some by the principal, and some by other administrators. It may be helpful to coordinate the messages sent to the parent through one individual, either the teacher or the parent liaison. (See Chapter 14.) Even though the public agency must be concerned about the official forms for notice of actions and decisions, it is the informal, personal messages that really reach the parents. Messages sent to parents can be categorized as: (a) routine, (b) now and then, (c) surprise, and (d) subtle.

Routine Messages to Parents

Children coming to school the first day show some hesitancy and uncertainty. The parents bringing the children to school show even more. Turning the child over to the teacher each fall is an experience of mixed emotions. Even mothers who are happy that the peanut butter and Kool-aid summer is over are a little reluctant to let another person have the care of the child. (See Chapter 5, Succeeding When Mothers Are Protective and Fathers Are Preoccupied.)

The teacher has the first opportunity to send a message by smiling, telling the parent about the all important lunch routine and what time the child is to come to school, and inviting the parent to school. A welcome handout might help (Exhibit 8-1).

Inviting the Parent to School

Inviting the parent to school at anytime probably won't produce as many distractions as it first appears, since few parents have the time to come to school frequently. Parents feel better about having the child come if they know that they

Exhibit 8-1 Welcome Handout

WELCOME

I am really looking forward to school this year.

I am pleased to have ___*Johnny*___ in my class.

If for some reason he/she will not be at school would you call the office
    so we won't worry that something happened on the way to school.
    The secretary gets here at 8:00. Phone Number 357-4169

School starts at 8:30 and the room is open at 8:15. We prefer to have
    the children play outside rather than to come into the room if the
    weather is not too bad. There is someone on the playground to supervise
    at 8:15 but not before. It would be a good idea to have your child
    arrive no sooner than 8:15 if he/she walks. The busses arrive between
    8:20 and 8:25.

Our class has recess at 10:00 to 10:15. We use the playground in the
    back of the school.

We rotate turns in the lunch room with the second and third grades. Our
    lunch time is from 11:30 to 12:15 but the exact time that we go changes
    from week to week.

Lunch tickets are $3.75 per week or may be purchased for the month for
    $15.00. We sell lunch tickets on mondays.   If you send a check please
    have it made to Lincoln School.

Our afternoon recess is at 1:45 to 2:00. We usually play group games in the
    afternoon on the playfield to the east of the school.

We would love to have you come to school at any time. If you come to visit
    stop by at the office so they will know that you are in the building
    then come on to the classroom. We will just go on doing whatever
    we are doing at the time that you come. If you want to visit call
    ahead of time and I will try to arrange to stay and visit with you
    after school.

Wednesdays are particularly good days to visit. The PTA keeps a pot of
    coffee in the teacher's room for anyone who would like it.
    We usually have a mini program on Wednesdays at 1:30 in our classroom.
    We have a brief sing time or show and tell or display of pictures or
    whatever else we have been working on.

I am happy to be able to spend my day with your child. Please let me know
    if there is anything that I can do to help your child or you.

Mrs. Smith

are free to come also, however. Children sometimes misbehave for the visiting parent, but learning not to do this may be one of the important skills that the child needs to learn. The parents should be told that regular activities will go on as usual and that it will not be possible to talk to the teacher during the school hours.

Having a special time listed as a time to come and see the children perform has a double advantage. Parents who want to see something other than the math lesson can be assured that they will see their child doing something and will not interrupt the schedule. In addition, it gives the teacher and the children a reason to practice and prepare to present something. Even if there is usually no audience, the occasional presence of a parent will be reinforcing enough to continue the practice. If there is an especially good program, parents can be sent special invitations for that afternoon. (See Chapter 13.)

The Notebook

Children with learning problems frequently have language problems that make it difficult for them to receive and send messages. Many exceptional children do not speak clearly. Parents of exceptional children frequently know less about the activities of the school than do the parents of children who ask more questions and repeat what the teacher said. In order to send routine messages to the parents a number of special educators use a notebook that the child carries back and forth to school. Each day the teacher writes a brief note in the notebook about the child's day at school, and the parent sends a note back. By reading the parent's reply the teacher knows if the parent received the message. A stenographer's notebook is a good size and is rather durable.

Instructions on the first page of the notebook might read:

> Almost every day there are some things that I would like to tell you. I will write a few sentences in this notebook and send it home with Johnny. Will you write a few sentences about the experiences at home? We will have Johnny take the notebook back and forth. I will remind him to take it home. Would you please remind him to bring it back to school?

The messages sent home could be about anything that happened at school. The messages that are sent depend upon the developmental needs of the child. For example, Jody was a teenaged retarded girl. Excerpts from her notebook:

> 1/22/74   We love having Jody in class! She is learning time now, but still needs to identify the hour hand. Perhaps you could help her with this at home. How is your foot now? [mother had surgery and a cast for six months]

My foot is doing fine, a little slow learning to walk. Time is all I need now. I have also noticed Jody's problem with the hour hand. I will try to help her. I told Jody that the big hand was long and the little hand was short. I hope that helps.

1/23/74   Good. Why don't we work on that first with only the hour hand being short so she won't get mixed up? If she can learn the hour hand first, the minute hand will come naturally. Thanks for the help!

Chuck is younger and has more serious problems. Excerpts from Chuck's notebook:

[School]   Sept. 30   Chuck sat in the new floor sitter while we fed him lunch. He seemed to enjoy it. I gave him the extra juice that you sent.

[Home]   Oct. 1   No BM last night. I hope he goes pretty soon or we'll be having troubles again. We'd like to see the floor sitter. Maybe we could use something like that at home. I didn't send the pictures back because I want to have some copies made.

[School]   Oct. 1   Go ahead and keep the pictures. We are still waiting for them to come to take our school pictures. We made video tapes today so it's been a very tiring day. No BM today.

It takes some parents a while before they feel comfortable about writing messages back to the school. Other parents don't write back because they are not confident about their ability to write. But if the parent can read, the teacher can still send messages home and expect the messages to get there.

Some parents don't read. In inner city Baltimore the "notebook" sent back and forth with messages was a tape recorder. The teacher recorded a brief message for the parents, showed the kindergarten child how to record on the machine, and sent the tape recorder home with the child. There was only one incident in which a tape recorder was damaged, and that happened at school. The project did not have enough tape recorders to send messages to each home each day, but the parents were pleased when they did get a message and were willing to record a message to go back to school. It was particularly important in that area, since many of the families had no telephone and there was no other convenient way to talk to the parents.

Medical-Physical Report Form

Everyone is concerned about a sick child. Children who have been "sickly" all of their lives cause intense, continuing concern for their parents, particularly their mothers. (See Chapter 5.) If the parents are to feel comfortable about the child's educational programming, they must also feel that the child's additional physical care needs are being met. Children with multiple handicaps that include physical involvement need daily monitoring of the biological routines of the day. A home-school activities form that shows the child's intimate physical activities of the day (Exhibit 8-2) could assist in monitoring these processes and make it unnecessary to restrict the child to a medical facility for education. The school nurse could assist with the form, although the ultimate daily responsibility for sending the form would, of course, be the teacher's.

A report of any seizure that a child who has uncontrolled seizures may have at school must be sent home to the parent that afternoon, and a copy should be placed in the child's record. Since medication for seizures is regulated partly on the frequency and intensity of the seizures, it is important that the parent have an immediate and accurate report. All school personnel should be trained to handle a seizure and a seizure report calmly, as a routine procedure (Exhibit 8-3).

The Telephone

Being able to have a private conversation with someone who is miles away has revolutionized business and personal lives. A simple, quick answer to a telephoned question can uncomplicate many activities. Educators who don't use the telephone to send quick, personal messages to parents are missing the most practical way to "keep in touch."

Since parents (and educators) are extremely busy, the conversations should be brief and to the point. Lengthy telephone discussions of needs and interests should be reserved for parents who are unable to visit or attend the conference. Then a time is set for a longer conversation. Even IEP conferences can be held by telephone if necessary. (See Chapter 2.)

One of the problems with using the telephone to call parents is that the school telephone is almost always in use. There may be a way to schedule a time for calls during the regular work time for a resource teacher, speech therapist, or psychologist. School officials who are aware of the importance of a telephone for parent contacts might find a way to budget another line just for this purpose. Ideally, there is a room or a booth without the sound of the ditto and Coke machine in the background. The best time to reach a parent is just before or just after school; unfortunately, those are the most difficult times to use the telephone at school.

It is not inappropriate to call the parent at a more "leisure time" from the telephone at home. The amount of time that the professional wishes to talk should be made clear in the beginning. Since parents have so many needs, some can ask questions for "hours." For this reason it is not recommended that the parent be given the home telephone number of the teacher, unless it is clear that it is to be used only for a specific purpose. Easy access to the professional at home encourages a type of dependence in the parent that may be difficult to modify.

Exhibit 8-2 Daily Activities Form

Daily Activities for_____ (Name) _____ (Date)

Morning	Afternoon	Activity	Evening	Nite	Morning
		Meals			
		Sleep			
		Snack			
		Liquid			
		Bowel Movement			
		Bath			
		Seizure			
		Medication Given			
		Teeth Brushed			
		Unusually Happy			
		Unusually Fussy			

Special Notice: (Change in Medication, Diarrhea, Special Activity, Amount Eaten, Unusual Amount of Sleep - etc)

Exhibit 8-3 Report of Seizure or Possible Seizure

Name of student_____Date of report_____

School_____Teacher_____

Report made by_____
      Reporter saw the situation? Yes ( ) No ( )
      Was told about the situation? Yes ( ) No ( )

Date of seizure_____Time of seizure_____

Location of student when seizure occurred_____

_____

People who were there at the time_____

_____

Activity of the class/student at the time_____

_____

Activity of the student just prior to the seizure_____

_____

Activity of the student earlier in the day_____

_____

1.   Did the student fall? Yes ( ) No ( )

2.   Did the arms go stiff? Yes ( ) No ( )

3.   Did the legs go stiff? Yes ( ) No ( )

4.   Did the arms jerk? Yes ( ) No ( )

5.   Did the legs jerk? Yes ( ) No ( )

6.   Did just one side go stiff or jerk? Yes ( ) No ( ) Which one?_____

7.   Did the head or eyes turn to one side? Yes ( ) No ( ) Which one?_____

8.   Did the student recover consciousness rapidly? Yes ( ) No ( ) How long__

9.   Describe the facial and hand movements during the seizure:_____

     _____

10. Did the student want to return to work after the seizure? Yes ( ) No ( )

11. Did the student sleep or rest after the seizure? Describe:_____

     _____

Other observations:_____

The Newsletter

Even though there is a pile of newspapers on the floor by the sofa, every time a new one comes into the house everyone in the house who can read takes a section of the paper and pores over it. Newspapers come in all sizes, from *The New York Times* to the local bimonthly gazette. Everyone wants to know what friends and acquaintances are doing and why. Newspapers about the school are just as important as newspapers about the town, and many schools print regular newsletters.

Oakridge School on Bailee Street in Vancouver, British Columbia, has been sending out newsletters written by the teachers to the parents for years. Perhaps even more important than the school newsletter printed by the administrators is a newsletter printed by the teachers, or even the children—not about the decisions of the school board, but about the success of the children, by name.

Although parents may enjoy seeing their names in print, they enjoy even more seeing their children's names in the paper. Parents of a child who is not succeeding at school particularly appreciate seeing something nice about their child in print, even if it is in bleeding ditto fluid. One retarded boy kept a camp newsletter describing his awards for the summer under his pillow until the paper deteriorated. His mother felt good about the camp each time she stripped the bed.

Parents are interested in the general activities and schedules of the class or the school, but they are far more interested in the children in the school. The newsletter should not just tell that the children went to the zoo, but that Johnny fed the giraffe, the ducks liked Alice's popcorn, and Bobby went to sleep in the bus on the way back. Since parents have usually become acquainted with the other children at school and the other parents, they will be interested in hearing what the other children are doing also (Exhibit 8-4).

If the children being described are able to read the newsletter, it should be written in language that they can read and with words that they have learned. An easy way to do this is to have the children dictate the descriptions. Children who have mastered more language skills could write their own newspaper. The collection of information and production of the newsletter could be the language arts curriculum.

Notes Every Monday

In some schools, the last few minutes of many school days are spent handing out one form or another for the child to take home to the parent. The next morning is spent collecting the signed and returned forms and getting them back to the office. In other schools, unless the information is required immediately, it is the practice to save all of the forms and notes for home, staple them together, and send them home at one time. Mondays were chosen by many schools since that allows a maximum amount of time for the child to remember to bring back those things that

Exhibit 8-4 Sample Newsletter

What's New?

NEIGHBORHOOD ELEMENTARY SCHOOL
November 1, 1979

SHOP WITH MISS ANDERSON

Miss Anderson's class went to the Piggley Wiggley Store. They pretended to go buy groceries. Two students worked together. They filled the carts. They added the money in their heads.   They added until they got $10.00 worth of groceries.   Then they checked out to see how much they got.

This is what each one got:

Jane Anderson & Bobbie Smith.....$9.96   Charlotte Bell & Joe Jones.....$8.98

Mary Jones & Art Wills...........$9.31   Joan Green & Nicky Norris.....$7.79

Beth Bills & Jerry Jayson.......$9.48   Jenny Pool & Mike Wert........$9.01

It is hard to add in your head!

FALL WEATHER

It is still warm outside. That is nice. We can still play outside. Alice Smith and Janet Jones jump rope outside. Bob West plays marbles. Sophie picks up the trash. Joe Green and Alice Anderson like to jog. Tommy Tens plays on the jungle gym.

CERAMICS

We make ceramics. Some are for Christmas. Jane Welch painted a flower plate. It is blue. Bob North painted a brown horse . It has a white mane. Sonya Black and Alice Jones painted red apples.   Would you like some ceramics for Christmas?

need to come back before Friday. Papers left in the home over the weekend are seldom returned to school. When the papers that are of little personal interest to the parent, such as the note about the school pictures, insurance, and field trips, come at one time, the parent can handle those mundane things with a minimum amount of energy. The parent can plan to sit down on Monday and get the notes out of the way for awhile.

Mini-Report Card

Some teachers have found it helpful to give the parent regular feedback about how the child is doing at school by sending home a mini-report card, sometimes daily, sometimes weekly. Although the teacher could write in a notebook, a printed form may be quicker to mark and may seem more official to the parent and the mildly handicapped child. The mini-report card has on it the items that the child is currently learning (Exhibit 8-5), and the teacher can mark quickly how the student is progressing. This method makes it possible for the parent to assist in reinforcement of the desired behavior at home when it needs to be reinforced rather than at report card time when the behavior may have been forgotten. Some cultural groups are particularly respectful of a report card.

Now and Then Messages

Anything that is repeated often is not noticed nearly as much as something that only happens now and then. In addition to the routine messages to the parent, there should be some now and then contacts. One of the most effective is a notice that looks like a combination between a cartoon and a diploma. This is given to the child for some achievement.

The awards can be planned so that the child knows that awards are given for finishing workbooks or following the playground rules, or the teacher can surprise the students with a Friday afternoon awards ceremony for good behaviors that have occurred during the week. There may be some awards that the child earns and some awards that the child wins. If the awards are given for almost anything, they will end up in the wastebasket rather than on the bulletin board. If the awards are not given frequently enough, they will not be an effective motivator. The teacher should make sure that each child has earned at least one award. Children with learning problems need to feel success in order to keep trying.

The teacher can either make the awards or purchase beautifully colored ones for almost nothing from a school supply house. TREND Enterprises, Inc. (P.O. Box 43073, St. Paul, Minnesota 55165) has some nice ones (Figure 8-1). TREND Enterprises also makes interesting Scratch and Sniff bookmark awards. Although these awards seem to be given to the child, any recognition given to the child is a soft warm puppy to the parent.

Exhibit 8-5 Sample Mini-Report Card

```
_____Name  _____Date


Work in _____was_____today.


*******************************************************************


_____Name  _____Date


Remembered to:    ( ) Wipe Nose
                  ( ) Wash Hands
                  ( ) Wash Face
                  ( ) Clean Fingernails
                  ( ) Comb Hair
                  ( ) Go to lavatory
                  ( ) Sit at table to eat
                  ( ) Use Napkin
                  ( ) Use spoon
                  ( ) Drink carefully
                  ( ) Eat slowly
                  ( ) Eat with Mouth Closed
                  ( ) Eat from own plate
                  ( ) Brush teeth
*******************************************************************


_____Name  _____Date


Remembered to:    ( ) Say Thank You
                  ( ) Say Please
                  ( ) Say excuse me
                  ( ) Say I'm sorry
                  ( ) knock at the door
                  ( ) Shake hands
                  ( ) Say goodby
                  ( ) Listen
                  ( ) Stand in Line
                  ( ) Be quiet inside
                  ( ) Answer when called
                  ( ) Look at speaker
                  ( ) Take turns
                  ( ) Share


*******************************************************************


_____Name  _____Date


Worked well today   ( )yes      ( ) no      ( ) only in the morning

Finished assignments ( )all    ( ) math   ( ) language ( )reading

Remembered school rules  ( ) yes    ( )no   ( ) except_____
```

Figure 8-1 Sample Award

Source: TREND Enterprises, Inc. Reprinted by permission.

One first grader came home and announced that he was a "cinnamon." In answer to all the questioning, he could only say that he was a cinnamon. Later the mother found that each class in the school chose a "Citizen of the Month." Blaine didn't know what he had won, or why, but he knew that it was nice. And so did his mother. It seemed to say to her, "Mother, we think that you are doing a good job."

The Invitation

Everytime there is any excuse, a special invitation to visit the school can be sent to the parent. Parents can be invited to come and see the pictures of the fall pumpkins, the Christmas decorations, the snow sculpture, and the fort of leaves. Parents can be invited to come and hear the Christmas carols, the multiplication tables, the new record, or the reading of poems. The children should make the invitations, of course. (See Chapter 13.)

Extra, Extra

Whenever the class or some of the students do something special, a report can be made and sent home (Exhibit 8-6). Although it can be included in the routine newsletter, it could be a reason to create another contact. Also, including it in the regular newsletter may crowd out some of the daily things. The report of the field trip can be of double value if it is generated as an experience story. Then the report can be read to the parent by the student, and no school has a better town crier than the parent's own child.

About the New Unit

The fact that the class is starting a new unit of study would be interesting to the parents. Children who do not have language difficulties go home and tell parents almost everything that has happened and what was studied. Parents of exceptional children can get those messages only if they are sent by the teachers. If the parents know what is happening at school, they can reinforce those skills at home.

Surprise!

No one outgrows the joy of pleasant surprises. Parents especially can be warmed by a pleasant surprise about their child, since most unexpected events of parenting turn out to be a cold or the measles.

Most local TV stations are interested in human events stories. Even to people who are not parents, children are charming. Depending on the pressure of other news, the TV stations may be interested in things as slight as making butter in a Mason jar. Sometimes the material is taped and saved until there is time to use it. Parents are sure to feel approval for any sponsor, even the public school, that shines a warm spotlight on their child.

Because radio stations tend to be smaller than TV stations and serve a more local audience, they may be even more interested in the children's activities. They enjoy a change in the programming from time to time. The local newspaper will print stories about things as small as a child's birthday party at school. Black and white glossy pictures are not difficult to take. Even good Polaroid shots will print well. The parents will treasure the yellowing page with the child's picture.

When a nice note about the child and a copy of some work that was well done arrives in the mail, the parent may not mind the bills that are also in the mailbox. A birthday card that arrives for the child in the mail is treasured by the parent as well as the child. It might be treasured even more if the teacher came by in person to deliver it.

Exhibit 8-6 Sample Report on a Special Student Activity

Extra Extra

We had a ball. We went to the shopping center on Friday. We saw all of the Christmas decorations. We heard the Christmas carols. And, of course, we saw Santa Claus.

Each one of us did some shopping. We won't tell what we bought. We had lunch. These are the things that we could buy:

Hamburger	55¢
French Fries	30¢
Coke	30¢
Root Beer	30¢
Pizza Slice	50¢
Fishburger	70¢
Ice Cream	35¢

We walked around the mall. We saw the stores. Some stores had shoes. Some stores had books. Some stores had clothes for ladies. Some stores had clothes for men. Some stores had clothes for children. Some stores had good things to eat.

There was a big water fountain in the mall. We watched the water fall down. We saw other people at the mall. There were some children from another school. We waved at them.

These are the people who went: Joe Anderson, Sally Smith, Alice Brown, Jennifer Tanner, Barbara Black, Duaine Thompson, Tommy Tune, Jake Hones, Tamera Brown, Ann Brown, Clif Drake, Susan South.

Subtle Messages

Underneath all of the notes and papers and letters and cards is the real message to the parents. The real message is "I like you and respect you, even if you have a handicapped child" or "No wonder your child is having troubles; look at you!"

Some parents, like some children, are harder to like. Some parents may be hostile, poorly groomed, and unable to understand very well. It is easy to send the subtle message to these parents that the child can be expected to have learning problems; like father, like son. And in some cases that might be true. Some parents not only do not read to their children, but also do not feed their children. Some parents abuse their children, even sexually. Learning to understand some of the parents' backgrounds can help professionals to understand why. The only way to break the chain of that kind of family interaction is to assist the parents in becoming better parents.

Ask for Help

Only the best friend is asked to stand up with the groom or be a bridesmaid. Only the most capable matrons are asked to help serve at the tea. It is an honor to have a part in some things. Parents feel that way about school. The faculty meeting might include some brainstorming time to try to think of different things that parents might be asked to do for or at the school. Asking for help can be a subtle message of respect for the parent.

One mother, no longer young, remembers when her children were in elementary school and they went with friends to cut a 12-foot piñon pine for the school's Christmas tree. It was so big and fluffy that, when the PTA ladies decorated it, the tree looked beautiful in the hall of the school. In the history book of the PTA there is a picture of the mother and her youngest child standing by the decorated tree. It made the mother feel part of the school. It made her feel that the school was partly hers. The PTA group also had a luncheon for the teachers just before school started, and they had a tea later in the year. Some mothers were chosen as room mothers, and from time to time they brought treats to the children.

Parents of exceptional children are seldom asked to help. One of the sweetest messages anywhere is "We need you and want the pleasure of your company." Parents might be asked to:

- send pictures of the child as a baby
- send the recipe for German pancakes
- get a white shirt for Johnny to wear in the program
- send some dressing for the salad we are making to study vegetables
- send some scraps of bright cloth
- send some scraps of wood
- come and play the piano for us to sing along
- build some shelves to hold our puzzles

It must be remembered that the best man, the bridesmaids, and the ladies who pour at the tea are asked to help way ahead of time. The parents should be given time to find what is needed, to arrange to be there, or just to think it over. Fathers also like to be needed. Some fathers have old catalogues, scratch paper, boxes, and other useful teaching objects.

Have the Child Make Things To Take Home

One mother of an institutionalized ''girl'' of about 50 cried when she was given a plaster of Paris brooch that the daughter had painted for her. No mother ever had too many crayoned pictures or notes of ''I love you,'' and no father ever had too many painted pencil holders. Although parents appreciate any little gift that is made for them, the message of acceptance can be stronger if the gift that the child brings home is personalized.

A shadow silhouette in black construction paper is treasured by the parents if it looks like Johnny. It can be mounted on a burlap wall hanging that has been fringed by the child and attached to a dowel. Simple Polaroid pictures make any scene personalized. One teacher put the picture in the center of a yellow construction paper daisy and folded the petals over the picture.

For a gift that is made at school, the parent thanks not only the child but also the teacher. The teacher expresses a personal feeling toward the parent when the project that is to go home is carefully personalized.

Sending Messages That Parents Will Want To Hear

Parents of exceptional children are anxious about the child's progress. Messages from the educational agency can easily increase the anxiety. If the only time the parent hears from the agency is to be told that the child is having trouble, the parent will be conditioned to respond by shutting out the message.

Parents need messages of acceptance as a person and plenty of positive news to go with the bad news messages. If you want parents to hear you, somehow you will have to say what you want to say in the way they want to hear it.

REFERENCES

Alley, G., & Deshler, D. *Teaching the learning disabled adolescent: Strategies and methods.* Denver: Love, 1979.

Dyer, W.W. *Your erroneous zones.* New York: Avon, 1976.

Gearheart, B.R., & Litton, F.W. *The trainable retarded: A foundations approach.* St. Louis: C.V. Mosby, 1979.

Harris, T.A. *I'm OK—You're OK: A practical guide to transactional analysis.* New York: Harper & Row, 1967.

Hewett, F.M. *The emotionally disturbed child in the classroom.* Boston: Allyn and Bacon, 1968.

Hunter, M. *Reinforcement theory for teachers.* El Segundo, Calif.: TIP, 1967.

James, M., & Jongeward, D. *Born to win: Transactional analysis with Gestalt experiments.* Reading, Mass.: Addison-Wesley, 1971.

Michaelis, C.T. Merry Christmas, Jim, and happy birthday! *The Exceptional Parent,* 1976, *6*(6), 6-8.

Morgan, M. *The total woman.* New York: Pocket Books, 1973.

Sheppard, W.C., Shank, S.B., & Wilson, D. *Teaching social behavior to young children.* Champaign, Ill.: Research Press, 1973.

Smith, R.M. *Clinical teaching: Methods of instruction for the retarded.* New York: McGraw-Hill, 1968.

Chapter 9

Using Counseling Techniques

COUNSELING DURING CONFERENCES

It is not unusual for school personnel to find themselves being told about the family's marital, financial, or interpersonal problems at a conference with a parent about a child who is having difficulties at school. School personnel may at times think that they are answering the "help" hotline.

The needs of the handicapped children and the family create problems, and the parents frequently have no one with whom they can discuss them. The problems may be so intertwined within the family structure that the people who are close to the parents are part of the problem. Parents of handicapped children may not have friends who are willing to listen to all of the problems in the home. Parents may turn then to the public agency, the training institution, or the school. Since the school personnel know the child and the child's capabilities better than other professionals, it is natural for the family to go there for help, especially when the parents feel that the child's additional needs may have intensified or even created the problem.

Even when parents don't come spontaneously for help, problems more complicated than the learning of multiplication tables may surface during the conferences about the child's school progress. Communication with the parents about the concerns of the school may open a Pandora's box of other concerns that the parents have. Families facing the task of training a handicapped child find that the stress involves not only the child's progress at school, but also other areas of family life.

Just as volunteers who answer hotline telephones need a thumbnail understanding of counseling techniques to work with people under stress, personnel of the public agency can benefit from an understanding of counseling techniques. Knowing when and how to listen and how to respond can make the discussion run more smoothly and be less stressful for both the parents and the professionals.

COUNSELING THEORIES

A variety of counseling theories and techniques have proved to be successful for professional counselors (Corsini, 1973). Even though training and supervised practice is necessary in order to practice psychotherapy professionally, an understanding of the concepts can assist public agency personnel in working with families that are experiencing stress. "Teachers and administrators can also profit from learning how to manage conflicts effectively" (Moracco, 1979, p. 119). Three theories that present different approaches to understanding and problem solving are represented by the work of (1) Freud (psychoanalysis), (2) Rogers (client-centered therapy), and (3) Wolpe (behavior therapy).

Psychoanalytic Approach

The difference between a disordered person and a normal person was seen by Freud as a difference in ability to handle the anxiety aroused by being unable to satisfy individual needs (Fine, 1973). Methods of dealing with anxiety are the same for normal and disordered individuals, but disordered individuals are less successful in using these methods. Psychotic patients are so seriously disturbed that they may be dangerous to themselves or others. Neurotic individuals are not dangerous to themselves or others and can usually be treated largely with "talking therapy" (Sloane, Staples, Cristol, Yorkston, & Whipple, 1975).

The purpose of the talking is to help the individual become aware of the "unconscious mental processes that exist" in each individual (Sloane, Staples, Cristol, Yorkston, & Whipple, 1975, p. 8). In each individual there is a body of thoughts and feelings that the individual is not able to recall at will. In his book, *The Psychopathology of Everyday Life,* Freud describes how forgetfulness and false recollection indicate a desire to alter the events of the individual's unconscious memory (Freud, 1951). The goal of psychotherapy is to bring to the surface the memory so that the experience, or feelings, can be examined rationally. It is believed that the more perfect a person's self-knowledge, the more likely it is that he or she will function rationally (Fine, 1973).

The Theory of Personality

Freud described the personality as having three parts: (1) the id, or biological part of the person; (2) the ego, or psychological part of the person; and (3) the superego, or social part of the person. The id is the source of all drives and the reservoir of energy for the individual. Drives such as hunger, thirst, and sex were seen by Freud as making it necessary for the individual to act in order to fill biological needs. The ego works to regulate the id and channel the energy toward appropriate persons, objects, and activities. The ego also wards off the anxiety associated with "forbidden" impulses through the use of defense mechanisms. External dangers can be handled by the ego by directing the individual to flee. It is more difficult to reduce the anxiety from internal dangers (Fine, 1973). The superego serves as a mediator between the individual and the environment. It causes the individual to strive for perfection and conform to moral and social values. The superego is idealistic and strives to help the normal person work with and love others (Fine, 1973).

The Use of Energy

There is a limited amount of energy available to each individual, and the energy must be used both for the maintenance of the body (breathing and digesting) and for the psychic activity of the body (thinking and remembering). If energy is used in one way, it cannot be used in another way. Young and undeveloped personalities use more energy in the original form, the id, for immediate physical pleasure. Stiff and rigid personalities have been organized with much of the energy in the superego and this energy is used for moralistic rather than realistic goals and purposes. The goal of psychoanalytic therapy is to develop mental and emotional stability by the balanced use of energies (Fine, 1973).

Anxiety

Anxiety is produced when individuals use the energy to interact with the environment, but are unable to satisfy their needs. In order to avoid the anxiety, they defend themselves from the situation by denying that the situation really has occurred. They do not plan to put aside the uncomfortable knowledge, but do so "unconsciously."

Defense mechanisms include (1) repression, the forcing of disturbing information or memory into the unconsciousness; (2) projection, the assigning of responsibility to another person; (3) reaction formation, an extravagant show of interest when in reality there is no interest; and (4) fixation and regression, clinging to or returning to the behaviors of early childhood (Hall, 1954).

Stages of Development

Freud saw the development of children as learning to handle the sexuality of their body and to use the energies of that body to relate effectively to others. The well-adjusted man or woman has been able to learn to handle the instincts.

> The ultimate goal of sexual development. . . is achieved by a union of
> the tender and sexual feelings toward a person of the opposite sex. Thus
> the capacity for maturity involves the capacity for love, and not merely
> the capacity for orgasm. (Fine, 1973, p. 14)

In order to develop the capacity for orgasm, children grow through various stages of understanding of their own sexuality in relation to the sex of the parents.

Methods of Treatment

The therapist should be a warm, accepting, nonjudgmental individual who listens and encourages the patient to talk, but does not give advice or direction, except in extreme cases. In therapy patients learn to understand the relationship that they have had with their parents in the light of their relationship with the therapist. Freud thought that this was only possible through a profound study of each individual (Fine, 1973). The purpose of the study is to foster more self-understanding for the patient so that more information becomes available to the consciousness. Individuals who can rationally understand their own behavior are better able to regulate the energies of their id and use the defense mechanisms of the ego in healthy ways (Freud, 1917).

Psychoanalytic Theory and Parents of Exceptional Children

Parents of handicapped children are no more or less psychotic or neurotic than parents of normal children. (See Chapter 4.) In fact, many parents of handicapped children are also the parents of normal children. (See Chapter 6.)

Parents have varying degrees of self-awareness. Some parents may be able to see themselves and their activities clearly enough to keep significant information in the consciousness and use defense mechanisms appropriately to cope with the additional stress of dealing with a handicapped child. Other parents may not. To suggest that an educator should diagnose and deal with the parents' emotional support system is unrealistic.

Educators do, however, meet with the parent in a setting that is similar to a counseling session when they meet for a parent conference or an Individual Education Program (IEP) conference. The parent's expectation that the public agency personnel and the teacher will have special information to convey is similar to the client's expectation of a counseling session. The parent is likely to expect the professional to convey information that is significant for decision making.

It is highly possible that in this setting the parent may use defense mechanisms as the progress of the child is discussed. Parents may not want to deal consciously with the knowledge that the child is not able to progress in learning as other children can. Such information is extremely painful.

The Use of Defense Mechanisms

Since the progress of the child is so vital to the parent, the parent might need to forget about the child's difficulties whenever possible. The parent is likely to force the disturbing information about the child's problems into the unconscious (repression). The parent may also want to be relieved of a feeling of responsibility for the child's problems and may blame the school or teacher for the difficulties that the child is having at school (projection). It would be interesting to know how many first grade teachers are thought to have "caused" a child's learning problems. In a desire to conceal the pain and disappointment, a parent might become very interested in the child's problems and become the classic overprotective parent. (See Chapters 4 and 5.) The parent may make an extravagant show of interest when, in reality, the parent is not at all interested (reaction formation).

Other parents may be so overwhelmed by the problems that the child poses that they return to the dependent, clinging behaviors of their own early development and become a nuisance to the teacher and other agency personnel by asking for advice about every little concern of the child's life (fixation and regression).

It is important to remember that the use of defense mechanisms in dealing with the anxiety and stress is entirely appropriate, even necessary for the survival of the individual. Since parents of handicapped children have more than the usual amount of stress in their lives, it would be natural for the parents to use defense mechanisms more frequently than parents of children who are progressing according to developmental norms.

Sexual Identity and Self-Confidence

One of the measuring points in developing an adult identity is the ability to reproduce. Freud saw identifying with the parent of the same sex and learning an appropriate adult sex role as the goal of the developing personality. Producing a faulty product with the sexual part of the body can inhibit the individual's confidence in performing the adult sexual role. Since many parents of handicapped children are concerned about the possibility of having another handicapped child, their sexual expression may be inhibited. This may lead to additional frustrations.

Results of Defense

Although a discussion of the child's needs might be the goal and purpose of a conference with parents, the professional must realize that the parent may have had to force a large amount of information into the unconsciousness in order to avoid being consumed by the reality of the problem. Since forcing undesirable information into the consciousness is a painful experience, the parent may postpone a conference and miss conference appointments even after they are made.

All parents are prone to compare their children to other people's children, and it is naive to assume that the parents of a handicapped child have not noticed their child's deficiencies. The parents do not want that information to immobilize their entire life, however, and unconsciously avoid thinking about it whenever possible.

Freud expected the therapist to be warm, accepting, and nonjudgmental. Perhaps these traits would be helpful in the conference when the public agency representative is directing an agenda that causes an abundant flow of anxiety. If the anxiety level is higher than necessary, the parents will need to use more defense mechanisms and the conference will be more difficult to conduct. (See Chapter 10.)

Client-Centered Therapy

Rogers developed a type of counseling in which the counselor does not "give professional guidance" but assists clients in developing the confidence to guide themselves. The focus of the counseling session is not the knowledge of the therapist but the fundamental American frontier belief that people can learn to do whatever is necessary. Rogers describes the therapy as client centered to indicate the emphasis on the growth-producing factors for the individual client (Meador & Rogers, 1973).

Unconditional Positive Regard

The major emphasis in the therapy is making the client feel the warmth of a deeply sensitive, personal interaction. A feeling of personal worth, according to Rogers, is something that an individual can develop only after having been totally accepted by another person. The therapist does not participate in problem solving or tell the "student" what the solution should be, but strives to listen and understand how the client feels and thinks. The focus of the therapy is not the problem of the client, but the relationship that is developed (Rogers, 1942).

Rogers maintains that as clients learn to trust and share themselves, they begin to be able to solve their own problems rather than to look outside for "magic formulas." Rogers describes his theories by quoting Emerson, "leave us to be what we only were" (Meador & Rogers, 1973, p. 120). Clients learn to look at themselves and "accept the responsibility of being different from others" (Meador & Rogers, 1973, p. 136). Clients learn that they have unique needs and should arrange to fill those needs. They learn that life is good and that they can expect to find not only the caring of the therapist, but also the caring and concern of others.

Anxiety from Self-Evaluation

When people find that their ideal self and their real self are incongruent, there is tension and confusion; they become defensive. The goal of client-centered therapy is for clients to learn to accept themselves even though they may not be "perfect" and to live comfortably with the reality of whatever is happening to them. Clients gain confidence that they can find ways to handle whatever is happening to them.

The Counseling Interaction

With the permission of the clients, Rogers tape-recorded many therapy sessions, and the tapes can be studied by those desiring to learn the methods that Rogers developed. Although most of the sessions were specific appointments, there is no attempt to "cover" a certain amount of ground in the session or to induce the clients to talk about whàt the therapist was thinking. Many of the tapes have long silences in which the therapist and client just sat in the room together. Comments made to clients were not questions or probes for more information, but acknowledgments of the clients' expression. Client-centered therapy as practiced by Rogers is directed by the client and the client's desire to disclose rather than by the therapist and the carefully worded questions that the therapist asks. The therapist mostly listens as the client chooses what to say and the speed at which to say it.

As the clients "mature," they begin to be able to look at what is happening when it is happening and to talk about their problems. At first, the conversation in the therapy session is about external, unimportant things, such as the weather. Gradually, the clients begin to describe their past feelings and to express the fears that accompanied the feelings. Later, they begin to describe their feelings as the feelings occur, and they learn to check with other people or external events to see if their perceptions are accurate. The nonjudgmental responses of the therapist make it possible for the clients to begin to share the perceptions.

Rogers sees this nonthreatening atmosphere as appropriate in the educational setting. In a nonthreatening atmosphere, the student has an opportunity to learn more from a teacher than if the teacher is an authority figure. Real learning does not come from outside the person but from the inside; learning takes place when individuals choose to enhance themselves with new experiences.

Client-Centered Therapy and Parents of Exceptional Children

Sometimes in the delivery room and usually many more times before the child entered school, the parents have been told that the child needs special care and attention. The family may have taken the child from one doctor to another or from one educational setting to another to find someone to help them with the child's problems.

It has been assumed that parents of handicapped children needed training, and groups have been formed to train parents in the "correct" way to handle the child. In other situations, parents have asked for specific assistance in training the child to eat, in toilet training, or in improving the child's academic skills. The parents may begin to believe that the child's needs are so great that, indeed, they are not able to be good parents for this child.

In order to determine the factors that contributed to the birth of a handicapped child, genetic researchers may ask questions about the history of the pregnancy and the problems that other members of the family may have. Discussing and rediscussing the problems, along with the extra attention that the child needs, can lead the parents to wonder if they can organize emotional and financial resources to meet this child's need. The focus of most interaction with parents of handicapped children is not how capable they are, but where the inadequacies are.

Acceptance

Conveying sincere acceptance of the parents may be difficult at times. Most public agency personnel and teachers share a middle class value system in which couples marry before they have children, the father and often the mother work, the family keeps daily routines, and problems are solved by "talking things out." Many children identified as handicapped do not come from such a culture. The parents of some handicapped children have never been married, had regular employment, or eaten meals around the dinner table. It may be difficult for the agency personnel to understand and accept those parents, parents who do not provide food and clothing for their children or parents who abuse the children. Some parents may need more assistance than can be given through the school, but it is important that the parents do not feel that the school personnel see them as inadequate. Interacting with the families with genuine empathetic understanding takes professional training, practice, and commitment.

Encouragement

Perhaps the most important thing that a public agency could do for a child who is having difficulty is to help that child's parents feel that they can help the child grow and mature. After all, the school does not have total responsibility for the child; the parent usually spends more hours with the child than the school does. It is not the role of the school to take the complete responsibility for the child, and it is important that the school help the parent feel able to fill the child's life needs. Talking as if the methods and procedures used by the school are "magic" and can produce changes that cannot be produced by the parents is irresponsible and untrue. In the Marshalltown project for early childhood education, it is assumed that the parent is the child's best teacher, and teaching in the home is encouraged and supported (Marshalltown Project, 1973). Although the school may have some hardware that helps to make teaching and learning easier, exceptional children learn most from the interaction and feedback from people in the school. The methods of interaction and feedback used in the school can be used in the home if the parent understands them.

The client-centered approach can help the parents gain confidence to make the big and little decisions about the child's care and training. Although parents who lack confidence are easier to deal with, the purpose of the interaction with parents is to create a learning environment for the child that will enhance the child's development. To act as if the parent is a problem to be avoided is to ignore some of the most important variables in the child's development and to stifle the greatest support available to the school. (See Chapter 2.)

Parents who are genuinely listened to and see the situation clearly can become a school system's greatest asset. The parents are the patrons of the school. The parents are the employers. They deserve to be appreciated.

Behavioral Approaches

Behavior therapy and behavior modification stem from the influence of behavior in therapy. Behavior modification is a familiar technique in institutional and school settings; it is used to change the overt behavior of children and adults. Behavior therapy is an outpatient technique in which the emphasis is placed on emotional learning. Although both behavior modification and behavior therapy treat behavior, the concepts and treatment plans are not the same.

Behavior Modification

In behavior modification it is assumed that the individual progresses along a developmental sequence according to a defined heirarchy of tasks. The individual is taught to do each task when the trainer organizes the environment to include rewards when the learner performs each identified task under specified circumstances. Emphasis is placed on observed behavior, which is "modified" by external rewards identified and skillfully applied by the trainer.

Behavior Therapy

In behavior therapy, the clients take an active part. They choose to participate in the therapy and actively assist in defining their problems. The therapist and client design together the details of the "treatment." The reinforcement in behavioral therapy is not an external reward but the internal satisfaction of the participant. Since a sequence of emotional development has not been standardized, emotional learning does not respond to a prior sequencing. Although behavior modification has been used to teach developmental skills to more severely handicapped children and children with behavioral disorders, it is not suggested as a tool for counseling with parents of handicapped children. Behavior therapy or emotional learning could be beneficial, however.

Behavior therapy as a treatment for neurosis was developed primarily by Wolpe (1958, 1964, 1969). Behavior can be understood, according to Maher (1966), by knowing the combination of: (1) past learning in relation to similar circumstances, (2) current motivation states, and (3) individual biological differences.

A History

In the initial meetings, the therapist and patient create a history of the situations that have been stressful for the client. The therapist does not suggest which behaviors may be inappropriate, nor does the therapist suggest a means of treating the problem. During the process of gathering information about what the patient sees, feels, and does, the therapist and the patient develop a working relationship. The therapist expresses understanding and acceptance by his or her behavior and helps the patient to feel both that the two of them are working together and that the therapist has skills and resources that can be of help.

The goal of therapy is to weaken the bond between the stimulus and the anxiety that the stimulus produces. In order to do this, the therapist does not push the patient into further situations that provoke anxiety. The therapist uses clinical judgment and allows the patient to discuss problems at a rate that is comfortable for the patient. If a patient decides to drop out of therapy, the therapist is considered responsible, since he or she did not create an atmosphere in which the patient was comfortable (Goldstein, 1973).

Identifying the Specific Behavior

Behavior therapy is designed to deal with specific behavior that the client helps identify and describe. Sometimes the client has already identified the behavior and comes seeking treatment. Other times the behavior is identified as the client and therapist interact. If several problems are identified, priorities are set and unrelated problems are met in turn.

The client is taught to keep a record of the situation that is uncomfortable or undesirable. Sometimes the frequency of the target behavior is graphed. Since the memory of the feelings associated with the behavior is strong, the client may avoid activities that are associated with or reminiscent of the earlier experience. The therapist and the client work to desensitize the client to these irrational feelings. The client is taught a systematic desensitization process that involves imagining the scene and learning to relax while thinking about the situation.

Learning a New Behavior

It is assumed that the client learned the maladaptive behavior through the normal learning processes, and the therapist may use these processes by rehearsing the new behavior with the client until it becomes natural. The client's right to be assertive about personal needs and feelings, as long as no one else is hurt by the process, is stressed.

Behavioral therapy is intended not to reorganize the total personality, but to assist the client in learning to do some specific thing. The therapist helps the client examine closely the conditions surrounding the behavior that the client does not like. Then the therapist assists the client in learning behaviors that are more comfortable.

Behavior Therapy and Parents of Exceptional Children

One of the reasons that it is easier for the teacher to work with a handicapped child than it is for the parent is that the teacher does not have the intense emotional relationship with the child that the parent does. (See Chapter 5.) Of course, it would not be appropriate for the child or the parents to have the parent learn not to "care" about the child, but frequently the parent cares so much about the child that the surplus "caring" makes it difficult to interact with the child. Since the parent has had more time with the child (the first few years totally and 138 of the 168 hours each week), it is likely that the parent already is acutely aware of the child's difficulty and must avoid the surplus feelings and fears.

The situations in which the feelings are especially strong are likely to be the areas in which the child is having difficulties. The parent is so anxious for the child to do well that the anxiety immobilizes the parent. When the child needs additional help at home, the parent is commonly asked to spend "just 10 minutes each evening listening to Johnny read" or "please let Johnny dress himself" or "could you get Bobby up earlier so he would have time to get ready for school?" These suggestions may trigger so much anxiety that the parent will need to avoid interacting altogether.

Taking a History

If the educator approaches the parent as a therapist would approach a client, the first step would be to build rapport while taking a history. The child's early medical, developmental, and educational experiences are pertinent to any assessment. (See Chapter 7.) The factual information given by the parent is of value in the IEP planning. If a form (see Exhibit 7-1) is used in a personal conference, it is likely that the parent will make statements that will give cues to the family's concerns. If the child has two parents, it is important to listen to each of them, since they may have different areas of concern.

Identifying the Areas of Concern

The IEP planning process in which meetings are arranged to discuss the child's needs is similar to the process of behavior therapy in which areas of concern are selected for treatment. If a parent is allowed an active part in the data-gathering process (home history, informal and formal evaluation, etc.) and a working relationship is established, it should not be too difficult to decide which areas are of concern to the parent. If the discussion is allowed to deviate to cover topics as they come up, the initial conversation will take longer. Since educators usually have a long-term relationship with the child and the parents, however, developing that relationship by going slowly in the initial stage of the relationship will increase the long-term satisfaction with the goals.

The public agency could assist the parent in the identification of behaviors that the parent wants to improve. If the parent learns specific activities to enhance the child's development rather than the vague "listen to him read" or "help her with math," the parent could be successful in at least that part of parenting. The more successful the parent feels, the more successful the parent will become.

WHAT THE PUBLIC AGENCY CAN DO

By understanding the techniques used by counselors, personnel in the public agency can create the best circumstances possible for communicating information to the parent that is likely to make the parent uncomfortable. Perhaps one of the priorities of the agency could be in-service sessions on the techniques of counseling. Role-playing situations could enhance the personnel's ability to use the counseling techniques. (See Chapter 14.)

The Educator As a Counselor

Even the school counselor has been trained only to assist with school-related matters, not in-depth personal counseling. As educators interact with parents about the educational needs of their child, it is sometimes evident that the family has other problems. Although the total family atmosphere affects the child's developmental experiences, it is not appropriate for the school personnel to attempt to help the family with all of their problems. It is important to be able to limit the "helping" relationship only to the child's educational needs. Since it is difficult to ignore other problems that may surface, school personnel should be able to assist the parents in securing more counseling through a public agency when it appears appropriate.

Referral to Counseling

Someone in the school system should have complete knowledge of mental health and social services that are available in the community. Since this information is seldom advertised, many families may not be aware of such services and may need help in order to apply and participate. Because most people are not comfortable about receiving counseling, the information about counseling should be given to the family by someone who has already built rapport with the family. It may be that only the principal or the school counselor has the details of the services, but the discussions about professional counseling should be initiated by someone who has already made the parent feel accepted. In order that the "other parent" not feel that he or she has been left out, it would be wise to make the suggestion to both of the parents at the same time.

The information given to the parents should be complete. The cost of the services and whether it will be paid for by social services or private insurance should be discussed. The parents will want to know if the counseling will be in the day or evening or if it is available on the weekend. The location of the counseling center and how the counseling sessions will be structured will also be important to the family. If the family will participate in group therapy, the family will want to know who else will be in the group.

In addition to knowing the services available, it is important for the agency to be able to assist the family with the referral. Some parents may need assistance in securing the forms and filling them out; others may need emotional assistance. For some families transportation to and from the clinic may be a problem. If the family does need this type of direct assistance, it may be possible to arrange for help through the PTA or other parent organization. For many families the knowledge that others have participated in therapy successfully is a source of inspiration and comfort. Names of other parents would be given to parents only after the other parents had given permission, of course.

Sometimes parents see the problem as only the child's problem and want to have the child treated, but do not wish to participate themselves. In some situations this may be appropriate, but most counseling for children includes at least some contact with the child's parents. Frequently one parent is willing to receive counseling, but the other parent is not interested in talking about it (see Chapter 5).

Parent Groups

In addition to the professional counseling that is available in virtually all communities, the parents of exceptional children can support one another. The National PTA has an exceptional child chairman in each of the local organizations. United Cerebral Palsy, Easter Seal, National Association for Retarded Citizens, and LD parents have local organizations in most communities. (See Chapter 13.) Sometimes it is difficult at first for parents to associate themselves with the parent group, since it is a public acknowledgment that their child is handicapped and labels the parents as well as the child. Instead of suggesting that the parents join, school personnel might suggest that they simply go to a meeting. Most of the organizations advertise their meetings and would be pleased to send someone to stop by and bring a "guest" to the meeting. Most parents who are active in the parent organizations have themselves had to learn to be comfortable about participation in the group, and they will usually treat the new parent with tact.

Parent-to-Parent Counseling

A concept that began with an Association for Retarded Citizens in Omaha and has now spread to a variety of places is that the parent who has "been there" can assist another parent perhaps even better than a professional counselor can. "Pilot parents'' are armed with some training, and then "old parents" are assigned to "new parents." An effort is made to match families, children, and ages. As the families interact socially and the new parents are accepted by the old parents, the families share their problems. As they talk, the new parents are better able to understand their feelings consciously (Freudian psychotherapy), develop confidence in their ability to run the household and assist the child (Rogerian counseling), and learn to devise ways to face specific child-rearing and home management tasks (behavior therapy).

If there is no such organization locally, it may be to the advantage of the public agency to assist in the organization of parent-to-parent counseling. (See Chapter 13.)

Building Rapport with Parents

Just as the beginning sessions of counseling focus on the development of trust and rapport between the client and the counselor, the informal interaction between the public agency and the parent sets the tone of the relationship. Treating parents with respect in the manner in which lunch money is collected, room assignments are made, and telephone calls are answered helps the parent to feel an important part of the child's school. Policies that "expel" or "suspend" the child as a way to control behavior tend to make parents feel unaccepted and incompetent.

Giving parents a list of scheduled events well in advance is important. (See Chapter 13.) Allowing parents to help decide whether snowballs will be thrown on the playground or the door will be open before 8:30 is also important. Elementary schools frequently have PTA volunteers invited to all faculty meetings.

One elementary school purchased several rubber stamps that said "PTA tonight." On the proper day, PTA volunteers went into each classroom just before the close of school and stamped the hands of the children so the parents might be reminded of the scheduled meeting and feel personally invited. One of the best ways to make the parents feel invited to the school is to have the parents welcomed as visitors and volunteers. (See Chapter 13.)

Many parents need assistance in securing transportation to school for conferences and other events. Preplanning for this service to be provided when needed could help some families feel more comfortable with the school. Other parents could provide the transportation. (See Chapter 13.)

The Role of Other Professionals

Although all personnel of the agency contact parents at some time (see Chapter 14), only certain professionals contact parents at the critical time of evaluation and placement. The school nurse can discuss the child's medical needs and tell parents how to have their child seen in one of the public clinics for special needs. The school nurse may also know about assistance that may be available to purchase glasses or hearing aids.

The school psychologist has a key role to play in describing the evaluation studies that may be made and in discussing the results. The words chosen to describe the child's needs are the key to the building of rapport with the parents. (See Chapter 11 for suggested descriptions of some widely used examination materials.)

The school psychologist could also be a resource to the teacher and the family in other ways. The teacher and/or principal may need to clarify the child's needs as seen by the psychologist. The psychologist could play a major role in the organization of parent-to-parent counseling or perhaps groups for the siblings of handicapped children. (See Chapter 6.) The psychologist could also organize counseling groups for the children themselves and help them understand why it is more difficult for them to learn than for the other children.

WHAT THE TEACHER CAN DO

Listen

Since the teacher has the most intense, sustained relationship with the child, the teacher has the most opportunity to use counseling techniques. Lichter (1976) titles his article "Communicating With Parents: It Begins with Listening." Chinn, Winn, and Walters (1978) describe a technique of active listening in which the teacher takes time to repeat the parent's message to make sure that the message was heard correctly. Each of these techniques is suggested by the client-centered therapy approach in which clients describe problems as they see them and the counselor just listens. (See Chapter 10.)

Send Messages of Acceptance to the Home

The teacher has the opportunity to respond positively to the parent by sending home newsletters and happy grams describing the skills of their child that are admired by the other children and the teacher. (See Chapter 8.)

It is important that the teacher notify the parent of the curriculum plans well in advance when special items are needed. Frequently, exceptional children learn from concrete activities, and most parents do not mind sending items to be used at school. Time must be adequate for the mother to find an old shirt or a white elephant, however. One mother was asked to send a ripe avocado the next day for the special salad which was part of the study of Mexico. She hurried to three stores and a produce house. There were only green avocados, and overnight was not enough time for them to ripen.

Discuss Management Strategies

The teacher should discuss with the parent any significant change that is planned in the behavior management system to be used at school. It is a well-known phenomenon that when the requirements and rewards change in one setting, there is overflow behavior in other settings. Therefore, when management procedures are changed at school, the child's behavior often improves in school and becomes worse at home. If the teacher wants to maintain rapport with the parent, it is important that changes be planned together.

The teacher can give the parent specific "recipes" on how to assist with the development of a desired skill. A home visit may also be appropriate. (See Chapter 7.)

CONCLUSION

Being a parent of an exceptional child does not automatically label the parent as disturbed or distraught. It does, however, indicate that the parent has more than the usual amount of strain in the parenting role. The additional needs of the child in the home and school setting cause additional strain on the parent. Counseling techniques were developed to help work with individuals experiencing stress. Since the stress of the parent and the family centers on the difficulties that the child has in becoming independent, the school setting is the focus of most of the parent's strain and disorder.

The school is also the focus of the parent's greatest hope that something will be done to assist the child in development. This almost always causes some conflict between how the parent sees the situation and how the public agency sees the situation. "Conflicts in and of themselves are not harmful; rather, the way they are handled can be devastating" (Moracco, 1979, p. 113). By understanding and applying counseling techniques, personnel in the public agency can set a constructive tone for the interaction with the parent.

REFERENCES

Chinn, P.C., Winn, J., & Walters, R.H. *Two-way talking with parents of special children: A process of positive communication.* St. Louis: C.V. Mosby, 1978.

Corsini, R. (Ed.). *Current psychotherapies.* Itasca, Ill.: R.E. Peacock, 1973.

Fine, R. Psychoanalysis. In R. Corsini (Ed.), *Current psychotherapies.* Itasca, Ill.: R.E. Peacock, 1973.

Freud, S. [*The history of the psychoanalytic movement*] (A.A. Brill, Trans.). New York: Nervous and Mental Disease, 1917.

Freud, S. [*Psychopathology of everyday life*] (A.A. Brill, Trans.). New York: Metor Books, 1951.

Goldstein, A. Behavior therapy. In R. Corsini (Ed.), *Current psychotherapies.* Itasca, Ill.: R.E. Peacock, 1973.

Hall, C.S. *A primer of Freudian psychology.* New York: New American Library, 1954.

Lichter, P. Communicating with parents: It begins with listening. *Teaching Exceptional Children,* 1976, *8*(2), 67-71.

Maher, B.A. *Principles of psychopathology.* New York: McGraw-Hill, 1966.

The Marshalltown Project. 507 East Anson Street. Marshalltown, Iowa 50158, 1973.

Meador, B.D., & Rogers, C.R. Client centered therapy. In R. Corsini (Ed.), *Current psychotherapies.* Itasca, Ill.: R.E. Peacock, 1973.

Moracco, J.C. Counselor's role in conflict resolution. *Counseling and Values,* 1979, *23*(2), 113-121.

Rogers, C.R. *Counseling and psychotherapy.* Boston: Houghton Mifflin, 1942.

Sloane, R.B., Staples, F.R., Cristol, A.H., Yorkston, N.J., & Whipple, K. *Psychotherapy versus behavior therapy.* Cambridge, Mass.: Harvard University Press, 1975.

Wolpe, J. *Psychotherapy by reciprocal inhibition.* Stanford, Calif.: Stanford University Press, 1958.

Wolpe, J., Salter, A., & Reyna, L.J. *The conditioning therapies.* New York: Holt Rinehart and Winston, 1964.

Wolpe, J. *The practice of behavior therapy.* New York: Pergamon Press, 1969.

Chapter 10

Having a Conference without Conflict: The Ultimate Goal

THE PROFESSIONAL'S PERSPECTIVE OF A CONFERENCE

Just the thought of sitting down to talk to one set of parents after another is exhausting. After two days of conferences with parents, one prim teacher of about 60 surprised a new teacher who was just finishing her first sessions of conferences by saying, "I don't know about you, but after conferences I go home and have a glass of wine." Conferences are even more exhausting if they must be directed toward the special needs of the exceptional student.

Anyone who has worked with children knows that it is not possible to be exact in anything about them. Sometimes a child behaves well for one teacher and not for another. Some teachers are almost like the Pied Piper of Learning; others seem to have problems with most of the children. Some principals can solve behavior problems with just a look; others can be annihilated by the sixth grade boys. Once a teacher has dealt with several children who don't seem to respond, it is easy to wonder, "Do all these children have learning problems, or do I have teaching problems?" To have to go to the conference and say, "I have not been able to help this child learn," is almost like saying, "I am not a very good teacher." At least, that is what it will probably feel like to the teacher and sound like to the parent.

Psychologists, speech therapists, occupational and physical therapists, and others who have tested the child are painfully aware of the inadequacies of testing procedures and the subjectiveness of the recommendations. Being required to defend the evaluations and reports feels like professional competence is being questioned.

THE PARENT'S PERSPECTIVE OF A CONFERENCE

It is not possible for the parent of an exceptional child to feel comfortable at a conference about the child. The bonding that begins even before the child is born helps the mother see the child's problems as her own. Fathers, too, are uncomfortable at conferences. The only reason that the conference is called is that the child is not doing as well as other children of the same age. For father part of the joy of parenthood is gone, because he plans that each child is going to be "my brain surgeon." (See Chapter 5.)

In order to deal with the child's problems, the parent spends as much time as possible in settings where the child doesn't appear to be different, and it is possible to forget the differences. The conference is not one of those times.

Even seeing the child's teacher in the grocery store can be uncomfortable, because the parent knows that the teacher knows. The school building is a reminder, too. Having everyone know that the child is "behind" implies that the child is not valued as much as those children who are keeping pace in development and are "on grade level," or even ahead.

The parent is also concerned about the conference. One mother said that she wanted to ask another question toward the end of the conference, but she decided that, if she did, she might cry, so she didn't ask (Whitney, 1975). Other parents have felt similarly uncomfortable talking about personal and private things to people who are not close friends. It takes a great deal of courage for a parent to come to the public agency to talk about "nature's mistake." For some the "mistake" is even considered to be a "sin." (See Chapter 4.)

TENSION IN THE AIR

With the parent trying to prove that the child might still be a brain surgeon and the public agency trying to prove that the child has identified learning problems, the conference room could have the atmosphere of a Sunday afternoon football game. Each team tries to make points and prevent the advances of the other.

With both parents and professionals uncomfortable, it is no wonder that conferences often produce tears and anger. It may be appropriate for the conference room to be routinely supplied with a box of Kleenex, since the mother may cry. Montague (1952) suggests that one of the strengths of women is that they cry and receive the physical as well as psychological benefits from shedding tears. If mother cries, pass the Kleenex box and go on with the conference. If the conference is delayed until she finishes her tears, the child may be over school age (Michaelis, 1974). The father may get angry, but he is not really angry at the school. There is simply no other concrete object on which he can focus the anger. (See Chapter 4.)

Although the parents may display the emotion that they feel, it is not appropriate for the professional to do so. If the professionals get paid for attending the conference (no matter how little), they lose amateur status and can no longer behave as they feel and must modify their own feelings by their cognitive understanding for the good of the "team" that hired them.

FORMAL PARENT CONFERENCES

Getting Ready for the Conference

Perhaps the most important thing that a professional can do to get ready for a conference is to get a good night's sleep, which means that the personal world of the professional must be in order. If the professional is struggling with almost insurmountable personal problems, it is an overwhelming burden to sit calmly and talk about the difficulties of working with the child in the school setting. Emotional responses generated by one set of circumstances permeate the entire system, and the professional who has serious personal concerns will have little patience with the pain and discomfort the conference will unavoidably inflict upon the parents.

Other things that the professional can do are mundane but nonetheless important, such as wearing clothes that are comfortable and appropriate. One teacher signaled her discomfort in the conference by wearing an orange lace party dress to the conference. Male teachers may choose between wearing a tie and wearing the shirt collar open by knowing the life style of the parents. Female teachers could weigh the choice of pants or skirt by the clothing that would seem more natural to the parents. (See Chapter 7.) One teacher got a new girdle for the conference. Although she might have looked better, she felt worse.

Professional Preparation

Samples of the child's work in strong as well as weak areas should be collected. Anecdotal records of the child's behaviors, both those identified as needing improvement and those that are adequate or even exemplary, should be prepared. Evaluations should be completed, and written copies should be available for the parents and others who will be participating in the conference.

Legal Preparation

When the parents are contacted about the need for a meeting, a time convenient for them should be arranged. The signed form concerning the organization of the meeting should be in the child's folder. The parents should receive a copy of the agenda (Exhibit 10-1).

The employees of the public agency that need to be at the meeting must be contacted. It should be kept in mind that the intent of the conference is not to overwhelm the parents with a variety of input from a variety of people, however; the group must be small enough to permit open discussion. Arrangements must be made for the classes of the teachers to be covered by a qualified substitute if the conference is held during the time that the school is in session.

Exhibit 10-1 Agenda for Parent Conference

                                                                    Child's Name

Date _____

Place _____Room _____

From _____to _____(time)

Team Leader _____

Discussion Leader _____

    I. Introduction.
       Purpose of the meeting
       Introduction of those present, including a statement of how each worked with child
   II. Review materials.
       Content of referral form
       Reading of any previous Individual Education Programs
  III. Report on evaluations.
       Formal evaluations made
       Informal evaluations
       Progress made by the child since last conference
  IV. Parents make statement of the child's progress.
   V. Complete the developmental checklist for the child.
  VI. Discuss needs as shown by the checklist.
 VII. Decide which are priority needs.
VIII. Write goal statements for these needs.
  IX. List related services needed for the child.
   X. Discuss appropriate setting to deliver needed educational services.
  XI. Sign forms, if agreement—set another meeting time if necessary.

Meeting will adjourn at_____.

Practical Preparation

The availability of a room for the conference must be confirmed before a definite time is set. A regular conference room with a table and large, comfortable chairs is most appropriate. Coffee and juice should be available. Someone should be there to take notes or tape-record the interaction. If the session is to be recorded, the equipment must be checked and plenty of blank tapes supplied. Copies of the checklist for parent conferences should be prepared. It is also appropriate for the conference to be held at the home of the parent (see Chapter 7, Receiving and Understanding the Parent's Message).

Conducting the Conference

The conference should begin at the time that was planned, even if all the participants are not there—except the parents, of course. If the parents are late, the professional should wait a reasonable amount of time, about the same as for a college professor, and then call to see if there is some problem. They may have been delayed by work and home responsibilities, or they may have been delayed in traffic. It is not only polite but wise to wait for them. If the parents are late, it is likely that they will be even more nervous about the meeting when they do arrive. If the meeting started without them, tears or anger are even more likely.

A few comments about the weather may be appropriate, but it is important that the meeting not seem like a casual conversation. A discussion leader should be appointed if the team leader does not want to take that role. (See Chapter 14.) The discussion leader might say, "We are pleased to meet here today to plan the program for Johnny. I am Mr. Jones, the principal. I would like each of you to introduce yourself and tell how you have met or worked with Johnny." The participants could respond with "I am Mrs. Anderson. I worked with Johnny last year." "I am Mrs. Black. I teach children who learn in a way similar to the way Johnny learns." "I am Barbara Smith. I came to keep notes for Mr. Jones."

The team leader would then make a statement about the purpose of the discussion, for example, to design an appropriate educational program for Johnny or to review last year's educational program. The discussion could begin by having the referral form read if it is a first conference or by having the old Individual Education Program (IEP) read if it is an update conference. A brief report of all the formal and informal evaluations that have been made would then be given. The reports would include the progress that Johnny has made since the last conference if previous conferences have been held.

As part of the reports of progress or evaluation, the parents should be asked to make comments or state concerns. The professionals should listen to the parents' concerns even though they may not seem pertinent to the child's needs at school. If the concerns indicate that another evaluation is necessary or that more information is needed in order to plan the program, the meeting should be discontinued at this time so that the other information can be gathered. Any questions that the parents have should be answered.

Since the evaluation by each of the professionals describes the child's needs in a different way, the information must be organized so that the parents can see the child's needs as a whole. This organization may also be helpful to the professionals, who can then see the child's needs from another professional viewpoint. One of the ways to direct the discussion toward the child's programming needs is to use a checklist to direct the discussion.

The parents and each of the participants could be given a copy of a blank checklist. The discussion could proceed from item to item, and the group could decide together what the child's skills are in each area. Although preparing the checklist for the parents in advance may seem easier, it may be more complicated in the long run. If the parents do not understand the needs and agree with the evaluation process that determined the needs indicated on the checklist, it will be necessary for the professionals to take time later to discover and respond to the parents' questions.

CHECKLISTS FOR PARENT CONFERENCES

The area of need for children with developmental problems differs by the handicapping condition and the severity of the handicap. It is easier to show deficiency areas if a checklist is used to help organize the discussion around the skills that are pertinent to this child. Checklists have been developed that can be used in either a formal conference or an informal discussion with parents (Exhibits 10-2 through 10-8). The checklist forms could also be used in early parent contacts to help show the parent the need for the child's capabilities to be evaluated.

The greatest strength of the checklist is that it is impersonal. Using a printed checklist, the professional can direct the discussion to topics that would be awkward for the professional to introduce. Each item on the list is taken in turn and becomes part of the discussion. Many professionals have difficulty discussing the child's personal hygiene, social skills, or preacademic skills. The use of a checklist makes it possible to bring the topic up without the parents feeling personally attacked.

Creating Individualized Checklists

Since each child needs a checklist that fits the child's areas of need, it might be appropriate to create an individualized checklist by combining parts from several of the lists. It might disturb the parents to know that the list was created just for their child, however. Most schools have access to copying machines that produce high quality copies. By cutting and pasting, the individualized checklist could be made with the school letterhead on the top.

Exhibit 10-2 Language Skills Checklist for Parent Conference

Achieved	Developing		Comments
		Child's Name	
		Date	
		Watches an object that moves in front of face	
		Moves to get desired object	
		Waves bye-bye/shakes hands/plays patty cake	
		Attempts to operate toy	
		Looks toward sound/speaker	
		Watches object fall	
		Can tear, crumble, stretch, or slide toy	
		Hugs doll/pushes truck, etc.	
		Responds to name or no no	
		Repeats name of object/person	
		Uses name of object/person	
		Can answer wh- questions	
		Can form questions	
		Tries to sing along	
		Can recite nursery rhymes/finger plays	
		Can tell full name	
		Takes turn in conversation	
		Can tell simple story	
		Contributes to class discussions	
		Can prepare and make presentations to class	

Exhibit 10-3 Arithmetic/Number Skills Checklist for Parent Conference

Child's Name

Date

Achieved	Developing		Comments
		Knows own age	
		Understands one-to-one correspondence	
		Understands grouping	
		Can count by rote	
		Recognizes symbols	
		Can do simple addition	
		Can do simple subtraction	
		Recognizes coin value	
		Counts money	
		Tells time	
		Can do story problems	
		Understands addition/carrying	
		Understands subtraction/carrying	
		Can do multiplication	
		Can do division	
		Understands fractions	

Exhibit 10-4 Mobility Skills Checklist for Parent Conference

Achieved	Developing	Child's Name / Date	Comments
		Controls head	
		Sits supported	
		Side lying	
		Rolls over	
		Sits alone	
		Crawls	
		Creeps	
		Stands supported	
		Stands alone	
		Walks	
		Rides tricycle	
		Pushes wagon	
		Runs	
		Plays in playground	
		Chases others	
		Plays tag	
		Plays alone in playground	
		Rides bicycle	
		Walks in hall with group	
		Walks in hall alone	
		Crosses street with adult	
		Crosses street alone	
		Delivers messages in school	
		Plays hopscotch/marbles/jump rope	
		Plays teacher-directed circle games	
		Plays teacher-directed group games	
		Walks to school alone or waits for bus alone	
		Goes to lavatory alone	
		Carries lunch tray	
		Plays student-directed group games.	
		Plays teacher-directed team sports	
		Plays student-directed team sports	

Exhibit 10-5 Writing Skills Checklist for Parent Conference

_____
Child's Name

_____
Date

Achieved	Developing		Comments
		Copies shapes from desk copy	
		Copies shapes from chalkboard copy	
		Copies alphabet from desk copy	
		Copies alphabet from chalkboard copy	
		Writes alphabet from memory	
		Copies words from desk copy	
		Copies words from chalkboard copy	
		Writes familiar words from memory	
		Copies sentences from desk copy	
		Copies sentences from chalkboard copy	
		Writes familiar sentences from memory	
		Copies poems/stories from desk copy	
		Copies poems/stories from chalkboard copy	
		Writes familiar words when given out orally	
		Writes own name and address	
		Spells simple words after study	
		Writes short stories	
		Writes letters	
		Writes answers to questions	
		Spells simple daily words	
		Finds spelling of words in dictionary	
		Outlines ideas for writing	
		Finds information in reference books/pamphlets	
		Writes original reference paper	

Exhibit 10-6 Self-Care Checklist for Parent Conference

Achieved	Developing		Comments
		Child's Name	
		Date	
		Uses toilet	
		Wipes nose	
		Washes face	
		Washes hands	
		Cleans fingernails	
		Combs hair	
		Takes bath	
		Washes hair	
		Wears clean clothes	
		Undresses self	
		Dresses self	
		Brushes teeth	
		Uses napkin when eating	
		Uses spoon/fork for eating	
		Drinks from cup	
		Eats slowly	
		Eats with mouth closed	
		Eats from own plate	
		Does not eat before others are ready to begin	

Exhibit 10-7 Social Skills Checklist for Parent Conference

Achieved	Developing	Child's Name / Date	Comments
		Smiles when spoken to	
		Says thank you	
		Says please	
		Says I'm sorry	
		Says excuse me	
		Knocks before entering	
		Answers door	
		Answers telephone	
		Shakes hands	
		Says good-bye	
		Listens	
		Stands in line	
		Is quiet when asked	
		Answers to name	
		Looks at speaker	
		Takes turns	
		Shares	
		Works cooperatively in groups	
		Works quietly alone	
		Does not distract others when they work	
		Completes task	
		Puts materials away	
		Uses free time as planned	

Exhibit 10-8 Reading Checklist for Parent Conference

Achieved	Developing		Comments
		Child's Name	
		Date	
		Discriminates like/different objects	
		Discriminates like/different pictures	
		Discriminates like/different symbols	
		Identifies primary colors	
		Segregates shapes	
		Recognizes name when written	
		Recognizes names of significant others	
		Reads signs in school building	
		Reads household labels	
		Knows alphabet sounds	
		Knows alphabet order	
		Recognizes whole words	
		Understands word attack skills	
		Understands story	
		Can repeat story	
		Can answer questions about story	
		Can sequence story	
		Can make conclusions about story	

Checklists for Mildly Handicapped Students

The lists shown in Exhibits 10-2 through 10-8 would be appropriate for mildly handicapped children. Although there are many skills listed that the students have probably already achieved, it is not inappropriate to leave them on the list so that the parent can see that the child has acquired some skills. Since a handicapping condition may cause the child to be low in one specific area, skills in some areas that are usually acquired at younger developmental levels may be listed.

Developmental Checklists for Severely Handicapped Students

For severely and profoundly handicapped children, another checklist that emphasizes infant and early childhood development could be used (Exhibit 10-9). Since there are many skills that must be acquired before the child is ready to begin the traditional reading and writing skills, it might confuse the parents of severely handicapped children if those skills were listed on the checklist.

It is, of course, appropriate to mix and match the various lists in order to have a list that is tailor-made for the individual child's needs. Some children may have severe physical problems, but high cognitive skills. Other children may be proficient at mobility skills, but have difficulty with language skills.

Discussing the Checklist

The discussion leader can direct the discussion to the items on the list. If the child does some of them well, the parents should be told. If some of the items don't apply, this can be mentioned. The parents should be told that there are some "potential problems" that have been avoided. When a problem area is noted, it might be wise for the discussion leader to say, "That might be something we want in the IEP" or "That might be something we need to talk more about," and ask that a note be made of the item.

As the group discusses the items on the checklist, each item can be marked as achieved or developing. The items that will make the most appropriate goals for the child's educational program will not be the items that the child has not attempted, but the items that the child is beginning to be interested in and has some skill already developing. As the group finishes the discussion of the items on the checklist, they have also identified the areas of concern for the IEP.

"Let's see now, are there some things that you are concerned about, Mr. and Mrs. Jones?" (Mom and Dad sounds personal and condescending.) Then the discussion leader directs the question to the others at the conference. If either the parents or others at the conference suggest things, they are added to the "possible" list.

Exhibit 10-9 Developmental Checklist for Parent Conference

Child's Name _____
Date _____

Regressed	Progressed	Met Objective		
			EATING	
			Sucking	Objectives: _____
			Swallowing	_____
			Chewing	_____
			Finger feeding	Comments: _____
			Self-feeding	_____
				_____
			DRESSING	
			Passive cooperating	Objectives: _____
			Active cooperating	_____
			Undressing	_____
			Dressing	Comments: _____
				_____
				_____
			TOILETING	
			Diapered	Objectives: _____
			Scheduled	_____
			Trained	_____
				Comments: _____
				_____
				_____

Exhibit 10-9 continued

Regressed	Progressed	Met Objective	

GROOMING

Nasal hygiene	Objectives: _____
Washing	_____
Dental hygiene	_____
Hair care	Comments: _____
Personal hygiene during menstruation	_____
	_____
	_____

COMMUNICATION

Responds	Objectives: _____
Attends	_____
Vocalizes	_____
Understands gestures	_____
Understands 2-word statement	Comments: _____
Understands 4-word statement	_____
	_____
Attempts verbalization	_____
Communicates needs	_____

SOCIALIZATION

Responds one to one	Objectives: _____
Responds small group with adult	_____
Peer interaction	Comments: _____
	_____
	_____

Exhibit 10-9 continued

Regressed	Progressed	Met Objective	
			MOTOR DEVELOPMENT
			Gross Motor: Objectives: _____
			Controls head _____
			Sits supported _____
			Side lying _____
			Rolls over _____
			Sits alone _____
			Crawls _____
			Creeps _____
			Stands supported Comments: _____
			Stands alone _____
			Walks _____
			Prosthetic aids _____
			Fine Motor: _____
			Grasps _____
			Releases _____
			Eye-hand _____
			coordination _____
			CLASSROOM SERVICES
			Speech Objectives: _____
			O.T. _____
			P.T. _____
			Psychologist _____
			Doctor Comments: _____
			Nurse _____
			_____
			_____

The discussion leader may have copies of the "things we want to help Johnny with" made for everyone to refer to during the rest of the conference, if the parents are comfortable with the reading and writing of standard English, or these things may be written on a chalkboard. If the parents are not comfortable with standard English, it may be wise to set priorities for the goals and carefully word them before they are written for the parents.

Formulating Goals

"Now which of these things are most important to Johnny?" As the areas are chosen, someone in the group might word the goals in the jargon of evaluation. In almost every group, there is someone who has a "gift" for writing goals with the simple format: (1) What behavior do you want to improve?, (2) How do you plan to measure it?, and (3) Under what conditions will you measure the skill?

As the goals are formulated, the recorder writes them down and reads them back to the group. After all of the priority areas have been selected, a second discussion of priorities may be necessary. It is not unusual for parents to be anxious for the child to "catch up" and learn the more advanced skills, particularly the academic skills, before the child is developmentally or socially ready to learn these tasks. Since the checklist is written in developmental order, it can be used to explain to the parents that the more basic skill must be mastered before the child is ready to start on the more advanced skill. It might be necessary to remind the parents that the goals will be changed when the child achieves them, but that goals must be written for the first things first.

The exact wording for the year's goals should be repeated for the tape recorder or the person who is taking notes of the discussion. It would be appropriate for the goals to be transferred to the IEP sheet and to have the IEP sheet signed by the parents if they feel comfortable about the goals. The IEP Summary Sheet could also be filled out at this time. (See Chapter 12.) It is not appropriate to have the parents sign blank forms and later type the information onto the form.

Considering Placement

If this is the first conference for a child, and even if it isn't, the conference should include a discussion of what setting would be most appropriate for the child to receive the necessary help to achieve the goals that have been established and what services the child needs. A variety of placements should be considered, but only after it has been determined that the "program requires some other arrangement." If the program does not require another setting, "the child is educated in the school which he or she would attend if not handicapped" (*Federal Register*, 1977, p. 42497).

The decision on placement may not be made in the meeting. It may be necessary for the parents to visit the proposed setting before they can be satisfied with the arrangement. Chapter 11 describes various placement options in nontechnical language. Although waiting to have the parent visit the proposed setting may seem like an unnecessary delay in the procedure, in the long run it may make it easier for the parents to accept and be comfortable with the placement. Since all decisions about the child's placement are dependent upon the consent of the parents, and the parent's consent can be revoked at any time, it is important that the parent feels good about the decision after "thinking it over."

Setting Another Meeting

If the meeting is running longer than expected, another meeting can be arranged to close the discussion. It is important for the parents and for the professionals that the meeting not run beyond the scheduled time. Important decisions cannot be made when people are concerned about other appointments. If a second meeting is held, the professionals should be cordial and avoid making remarks about the amount of time that the process is taking.

When a decision is made about another meeting time, the parents and other participants should sign a Notification of a Meeting form, which is then placed in the child's folder.

After the Meeting

Copies of the records made at the meeting should be sent to the parents and put into the child's folder. If the forms are not ready for the parents to sign at the conference, they must be taken to the parents or the parents must be asked to come in to sign the papers.

A letter sent to the parents after the conference thanking them for being there and a copy of the materials that will be put into the child's file could help establish more good will for the next conference. The letter could ask the parents to check the accuracy of the materials. (Exhibit 10-10). If they find some problem with the materials, it is important to know at the outset.

INFORMAL PARENT CONFERENCES

There may be times when a smaller conference, one between just the teacher, the therapist, or the psychologist and the parent, would be appropriate. Usually, these conferences are called for some specific purpose. Since the setting will be less formal, it is especially important that the conference is well organized.

Exhibit 10-10 Sample Letter to Parents after the Conference

LETTERHEAD

Date

Mr. and Mrs. Jones
At home
Our Town, USA

Dear Mr. and Mrs. Jones:

We do appreciate the time that you spent with us on August 29th. We enjoyed hearing about the things that Johnny has been doing at home and the things that you are interested in having him learn.

Enclosed is a copy of the plan that we discussed that day. Please look at it to see if it is written correctly.

We are pleased to work with parents who have as much interest in their children as you do.

Thank you,

The Team Leader
Our School

The time and place should be mutually arranged. If the professional specifies an ending time for the conference, it will be easier to conclude. Even though a large conference room may not be necessary, a place for the conference must be planned and arranged. Conferences held while standing in the hall or in the corner of the faculty room do not produce satisfactory results. Even the classroom is not as good a place as a more "neutral" location.

Preparing for an Informal Conference

The professional's personal preparation for an informal conference is perhaps even more important than that for a formal conference; there will be only one professional to give input and yet direct the discussion. Since it is likely that the room will be small and the parent will be closer to the professional, clothes and personal grooming of the professional will be more noticeable.

In a smaller group, particularly if the conference is between two women, it is more likely that Kleenex will be needed, so a good night's sleep may be even more important. Even though conferences may be billed as something else, copies of the checklist may be helpful in explaining things to the parent. Parents may ask more "whys" in an informal conference. Materials in Chapter 11 about handicapping conditions may also be helpful in describing the needs of the child.

Conducting an Informal Conference

An informal conference requires even more sophisticated skills to make sure that the role of speaker is "given" to the parent. (See Chapter 7.) The parent's nonverbal messages as well as the verbal ones should be read and responded to.

Many things that the parent would like to discuss are difficult to say to a large group of people, and it is far more likely that the parent will ask for advice or information in an informal conference with one professional. It is important to keep within the time agreed upon, but another conference can be scheduled if the parent is "just getting started" when the time is up. The new legislation requires that parents be allowed as many conferences as they need.

Follow-Up on an Informal Conference

Follow-up for an informal conference need not be a formal letter, but a note or a telephone call would be appropriate. In most instances, the discussion makes it necessary to find more information for the parent or to make some contact and report back to the parent. The follow-up note can indicate that the contact has been made, or the note can accompany a copy of the additional information (Exhibit 10-11). Information in Chapter 11 may answer some of the questions. Printed note paper helps give an air of authority to the note, but still keeps the interaction informal.

A SUCCESSFUL CONFERENCE

In order for the conference to seem successful to the parent, the parent must feel that the school personnel and the teacher "understand" and are concerned about the child. This can happen only if the professionals understand the parent's position, describe everything in "language understandable to the general public," and listen to the nonverbal as well as the verbal messages of the parent at the same time being well versed on the child's needs. A conference is successful when the parent understands the school's message and is comfortable with those who send the message. This means that the professional must direct the conference to include not only the football scrimmage, but also the half-time entertainment, and that takes training and practice.

Exhibit 10-11 Sample Follow-Up Note after Informal Conference

---

REFERENCES

Federal Register, Vol. 42, No. 136. Aug. 23, 1977.

Michaelis, C.T. Chip on my shoulder. *The Exceptional Parent,* 1974, *4*(1), 30-35.

Montague, A. *The natural superiority of women.* New York: Collier Books, 1952.

Whitney, C. Personal communication, 1975.

Chapter 11

Parents Must Understand: Technical Concepts in Nontechnical Language

Professional conferences have a pattern. The day is spent listening to formal presentations of research, projects, and curriculum design. There are slides, graphs, overheads, video tapes, and handouts. The speakers stand in front of a seated group and use a microphone or pretend that others can hear them without "this thing." The listeners sit and take notes. If there is time, at the end maybe one will raise a hand and be called upon to ask a specific question related directly to what was presented. The presentation lasts a specific length of time and is in a specific place. The speaker does not touch the listener and the only way he knows if the speaker has heard or not is if the speaker leaves. And leaving the room is not an insult, it may even mean that the listener agrees totally.

When the magic hour arrives, conference goers get a glass (no telling how many of them are full of gingerale) and walk around close to one another, frequently touching on the arm or with an arm around the shoulder or waist. There is laughing, there are questions, there are answers, and no one raises a hand, unless it is to wave to someone across the room. No one worries about the time, and talking and touching can go late into the evening before small groups start heading off toward the restaurant across town or the bar in the lobby.

Not only is the behavior different after the magic hour begins, but so is the language. "Hell, no!" and "You old son of a gun" are seldom heard in the meeting room, but they are familiar phrases in the ballroom during the magic hour. Yet the people are all the same. Some of them have not even changed their clothes. One physician described his professional conference as a chance to hear each of the speakers briefly so that he would know which ones he wanted to talk to about their ideas and work. Then at the cocktail hour he found them and talked to them. The cocktail conversation is the reason he went to the conference. Parents of exceptional children may understand "cocktail hour conversation" better than formal presentation, just as the professionals do.

219

THE COMMUNICATION SETTING WITH THE PARENT

Everyone is used to communicating in a variety of settings and with a variety of styles. Conversation in the faculty room is quite different from conversation in the classroom. Educators are quite used to switching from formal to informal and from child language to adult language—except with parents. It is very difficult for most educators to be informal and friendly with parents. Anyway, would the school board approve of a happy hour in the multi-purpose room?

Prepackaged, prepared information that can be disseminated to parents has become the accepted solution to this problem. The material has been prepared at the "parent level." Although this is better than handing parents the textbooks of the master's degree program, it is effective for only one type of parent: the curious, well-educated parent who has time to study and who is not threatened by discussing the child's needs with people that are not personally well known. Usually this parent is the middle class, full-time mother. This parent is the only one who has the prerequisite skills to benefit from the program or who wants that much information. (See Chapter 3.)

Parents, like children, come with different needs, backgrounds, and experiences. They are not all ready for the same thing. Parents of children with more severe problems do not necessarily have more severe problems. There are several variables to be considered; e.g., formal education, life experience, emotional health, and physical health. Experience with children, especially with handicapped children, makes a difference. Even though the father might be a brilliant radiologist, he does not necessarily understand the language of education. (Educators wouldn't understand the language of his profession either.)

LANGUAGE UNDERSTANDABLE TO THE GENERAL PUBLIC

Formal notice to parents about the needs of the child is to be in "language understandable to the general public." There are several types of information that professionals are required to disseminate to parents: (a) description of current special education terms/concepts, (b) evaluation procedures and materials, (c) explanations of handicapping conditions, and (d) explanations of teaching/learning strategies.

Since parents are ready to learn only what pertains to their child and their own life situation, it would *not* be appropriate to gather all the information in a booklet for parental dissemination. Materials must be mixed and matched for an Individual Education Program. Some of the following materials could be used directly as written for some parents; for others it is necessary to explain the information through a verbal question/answer session.

Description of Current Special Education Terms/Concepts

Summary of Public Law 94-142

The 94th Congress of the United States passed a bill (#142) that requires the states to accept all children in the public education system. Parents should be active participants in planning ways to meet the needs of children who may have difficulty learning (participation in state plans). Public Law (P.L.) 94-142 provides that:

1. All children are entitled to go to the public school closest to their home that serves children of the child's chronological age (least restrictive).
2. If there is some reason that the child might have difficulty doing the things that children in that school are doing, the school should arrange to have help for the child so he or she can do as many things with the children in that school as possible (related services).
3. In order to arrange for the other help for the child, the school must discuss with the parents what they think the child needs (notice).
4. The parents and the school should talk about what other things they need to know to help the child develop (evaluation, parent understanding of content).
5. The parents and the school should decide together what people should help them learn about the child's needs (consent).
6. All of the records and reports that the school writes about the child are for the parent to read, and permission must be granted for anyone else to read them (free access and confidentiality).
7. After the parents and the school have collected all the information they can about the child, they should plan together what things the child is ready to learn and how long it will probably take the child to learn those things (IEP meeting).
8. The school and the parents should "keep in touch" to see how the plan is working (documentation of contacts).
9. At least once a year the parents and the school should look at the plan together to see if it is still helping the child learn (review IEP).
10. At any time that the plans do not seem to be working, the parents and the school should get together and determine what can be done to help the child learn better (consent is voluntary).
11. If the parents and the school do not seem to be able to decide together, another person who has no personal or professional interest in the child can be called in to help determine what seems to be a good plan to help the child learn (due process hearing).

12. Education for all children should be "free," except for incidental expenses. The extra things that the child needs should be paid for by school funds, even if those things are things to help the child at home or help the family understand the child better (free public education at no expense to the parent—including counseling services).

Adapted Physical Education

Moving is part of learning, especially for young children. All children need to run and play and learn to cooperate through playing games together. Some children are not able to keep up with the other children and need help in learning how to play and move. For them, physical education must be adapted to their individual abilities to understand instructions and move their bodies.

Career Education

Children are sent to school to prepare them for life. Career education is the concept that preparation for life comes through learning how to deal with the practical problems of life. It stresses educational experiences that help children to develop daily living skills and personal-social skills as well as those that provide occupational guidance and preparation. Under this concept, parents and the community are involved in the attempt to make the education relevant to daily life and give children actual experience in the community and on the job site. Reading, writing, and arithmetic are taught in relation to the way they will be used in life rather than from a textbook.

Consent

Whenever the school wants to do something with one child that they are not doing with all the children in the school, the school must show that (a) the action has been explained to the parents, (b) the parents understand it, and (c) the parent agrees that it is all right for the school to do that. If the parent decides later that he/she does not want the action taken or that it is not working well, permission may be withdrawn.

Due Process Hearing

(Description for Parents)

If you do not feel that your child has an educational handicap, or do not agree with the evaluation, or do not like the placement of your child, you may request that a meeting be held to look at the child's records and listen to statements about your child's needs. The meeting is conducted by someone who is trained in educational law and policy and who is not connected with the local school agency. The person conducting the meeting would be called a hearing officer.

You could have anyone that you want help you get ready for the meeting and go with you to the meeting. You could request that certain other people also attend the meeting as witnesses. You could have your child's abilities evaluated by an independent evaluator and have that information placed in your child's records and considered at the meeting.

All information that would be used at the meeting would be sent to the qualified hearing officer five days before the meeting. You could talk about the material that was sent to the hearing officer during the meeting. Before 45 days have passed since you made the request for the hearing, the hearing officer will have arranged the meeting, held the meeting, and written a report of the findings.

If you do not agree with the report of the hearing officer you may appeal the decision. Your child will remain in the current educational setting until the process is completed or, if not in school, he/she will be placed in the school attended by other children of the same age in the neighborhood.

If you decide to request a hearing, you may ask the school agency to supply you with information about any free or low cost legal services that may be available and also information about where independent educational evaluations may be obtained.

Free Appropriate Public Education (FAPE)

It is the responsibility of the public agency to see that children who need special help in order to learn have an individual plan made for their education. The parent is not to pay for what the plan says the child needs, even if the child needs therapy or has to go to a special school. Transportation is also to be provided without cost to the parent. Parents will be expected, however, to pay for what parents of other children pay for, such as book, laboratory, or towel fees.

Individual Education Program

Schools plan to teach all children of the same age the same thing. When a child is not ready to learn what the other children of the same age are learning, it is necessary to teach that child something else. By watching how the child does some things, it is possible to find how the child learns and what he or she is ready to learn. Then a program can be designed that shows (1) the child's present educational performance, (2) what the child is ready to learn this year and goals along the way, (3) when the teaching will start and how long it is expected to be needed, and (4) how the child's progress will be measured.

In order to be sure that everything about the child is known, the school is not to plan the program without the parent. The school people and the parent are to meet together to talk about what the child needs to learn, how to help the child learn, and where is the best place for the child to go to school. A new plan is to be made at least once a year.

Institutions

Children who have been tested and found to be severely handicapped or children whose families cannot care for them may live away from their family's home and be cared for by paid staff. These students are to be educated with nonhandicapped children whenever possible. Since many of the children have been placed in institutions not because of the severity of the learning problem, but because families did not have the resources to care for the child, there are many children living at home that are more severely handicapped than those living in institutions.

Itinerant Teacher

The teacher with special training is assigned to see children in several schools. The teacher keeps a regular schedule and may spend time helping the child or helping the child's teacher prepare to work with the child.

Least Restrictive Environment

The school system provides the special help that a child needs without taking the child away from other children any more than necessary. Even if it is necessary to be away from other children some of the time, the child should be in the same school as the neighborhood children, if possible. If that is not possible, the child should be in a school as close to the family home as possible. Children in public or private institutions are also to be in schools with nonhandicapped children whenever possible.

Each child is considered individually. At least once a year the child's progress is measured to decide which school and class is the best place for the child to learn.

Normalization

One of the ways of dealing with someone who is different is to treat that person differently. Sometimes the handicapped person is put into a place where someone provides more help than the person really needs. Normalization means that the handicapped person should make as many decisions as possible and live as much like the normal person as possible.

Noncategorical or Generic

Children have learning problems for a variety of reasons. If children are grouped for teaching not by the reason for the problem, but by the severity or the type of learning problem, the class or school is called noncategorical or generic and the teacher is called a noncategorical or generic teacher.

Physical and Occupational Therapists

The occupational and physical therapists have learned how the body moves and how to help the body move better. They may specialize in the movement of different parts of the body, but, since the movements overlap, the therapists work together. Most of the things that children do in life require movement, and a therapist at school can help a child learn by helping the child to move better. The therapist can show teachers and parents how to help the child move correctly. Sometimes the therapist designs some equipment to make it easier for the child to move or be more comfortable when sitting.

Psychologist

A psychologist has studied how to measure the way people think and behave. A school psychologist measures children's behavior by observing and testing them and then makes recommendations about how to help the children develop in school. Sometimes the psychologist works with one child or a small group of children by talking with them about their problems.

Resource Room

A classroom in a regular school where a teacher with special training works with children who have learning problems is called a resource room. The children spend part of the day in the regular classroom and part of the day in the resource room. The regular teacher and the special teacher work together on each child's program.

Self-Contained Class

When students are assigned to work with one teacher and the teacher stays with the one group of children all day and directs all lessons and activities for the children, the class is said to be self-contained. The class could be in a regular school building, but it is more likely to be in a special school building.

Self-Help Skills

Throughout life there are certain things that are part of everyone's day-to-day life: eating, bathing, grooming, etc. When children are young, these things must be done by someone else. As the children grow, they become able to help themselves. Most children are still learning how to do these things in kindergarten and first grade. Handicapped children may take even longer to learn, but these personal skills must be learned before others can be developed.

Sheltered Workshop/Group Home

Growing up means being able to do as much as possible for oneself. Some children with learning problems can become relatively independent adults. They may work in a plant that has specially trained supervisors and be paid for the amount of work that they actually complete. Sometimes they can learn to handle their personal needs better if they live in a home with other adults who also need some help and support to live without their parents. The group home is supervised by house parents.

Socialization Skills

Young children do not see the needs of others and plan only for their own needs. Part of the learning at school involves how to get along with other people. Children who have learning problems frequently need help to understand the needs of others and to follow the routines of school. Without the ability to cooperate, the child is not able to learn and is also disruptive to the learning of others.

Special Education

Learning is easy for most children. The teacher just tells them what to do and they do it. Some children don't learn that easily, however. They need to watch things being done or work with the materials themselves. A teacher who is busy with a class full of children does not have time to help the child with learning problems. If the child needs more help, another teacher, one who has studied more about children with learning problems, may help the child. Sometimes this happens in the regular classroom; sometimes, in another room of the school. Since the child has a specially trained teacher, his teaching is called special education.

Special School

Some schools have been built with more lavatories, wider halls, or other things that children with learning problems sometimes need. Other schools have been remodeled to have some of these things. All of the students in the school have learning problems, and all the teachers and other personnel in the school have special training. Usually, most of the students are bussed from other neighborhoods to the school so it will have enough students to be able to finance the building and staff.

Speech Therapist

A speech therapist has studied how language sounds are made and how children develop the ability to listen and talk to other people. The therapist may work with one child or a small group of children to teach them how to make speech sounds or how to choose words to say what they are thinking. Learning to use the mouth and tongue well for eating helps in learning how to talk. Some therapists help children learn to close their lips when they are eating and to move the tongue so that it does not push outward when they swallow.

Evaluation Procedures and Materials

Testing

Asking a person to answer questions or do certain activities helps understand how much that person knows or can do. Without the test it would be possible only to guess. If the exact skills are known, it is possible to plan more appropriate activities for learning.

Screening

Giving a group of students a test to see which ones need special help is called screening. Those scoring low on the test are given more specific tests to see exactly what they have trouble doing.

Placement Evaluation

Students who score low in some of the screening are given individual tests that measure learning potential, learning style, and emotional stability.

Standardized Test

When a test has been given to children of various ages and backgrounds in exactly the same way and the scores have been kept, the test becomes a standard. The scores of a child who takes the same test later can be compared to the other children's scores.

In order to find out more about what most children could do at various ages, many children were watched. Lists were made of the things that they did. After the list was made, more children were asked to do the things. The age or grade at which each child could do each task was recorded. Then more children were asked to do the tasks, and what they did was compared to what the first children had done. Special care was taken to be sure that the children from different sections of the country and different size communities were included.

Directions were written for those people who were going to ask the questions. To be allowed to use some tests the person giving the test must practice while someone else watches to see how carefully he/she gives the test. Some tests must be given by someone who has completed this training (a psychologist). The psychologist not only gives the test, but also records the child's answers and writes a report. Since the test has been given to so many children and the answers recorded, averages could be figured. The score that a child gets can be compared to the average score that other children got. The psychologist can also compare the way the child acted while taking the test (sat still, walked around, seemed nervous) to how other children have acted.

Tests that are given to just one child at a time are called individual tests. Some tests are given to groups of children. These are sometimes given by teachers. If the test has been given to many other children, a child's score on a group test can be compared to the average score of other children the same age or in the same grade. Scores on standard tests are seldom told to the child, but the score and the report is put in the child's educational record, which is always open to the parent. Copies of reports and scores are also available for parents (or the child if he or she is over 18).

The purpose of a standard test is not to find how fast or slow a child is but how much the child can do and how much the child understands. From this information the school can plan activities that are neither too hard nor too easy, but exactly at the level that the child is ready to learn. A teacher can use the scores on standard tests to write goals, choose materials, and plan lessons.

Explanation and Permission for WISC

(Always type a fresh copy with the child's name included.)

We would like to know more about how Mary follows directions and answers questions about the things around her. It would help us to plan activities for her at school. There is a list of questions that have been asked many children. Some of the questions are about facts like how many boxes would be needed to carry 50 books if 6 books can go into each box? Others require her to do things like finish a drawing or repeat a list of numbers. We would like to ask Mary these questions so we can tell how Mary reacts compared to how other children react.

Some people have practiced giving the test and can ask the questions the same way each time. Mr. Jones does this for our school. We would like to ask Mary these questions at 1:30 P.M., May 1st, 1981, in the school library. It usually takes about two hours.

After he finishes, Mr. Jones will make a written report of what happened. It will take about two weeks for him to have a copy typed for you. When the copy is ready, Mr. Jones will call you and set up a time to visit with you about what he found. If you would like to visit with me or Mr. Jones to find out more about what is included, please let us know. Mr. Jones can be reached at 388-4123; my telephone number is 388-4321.

The test we would like to give Mary is usually called the WISC. It stands for Wechsler Intelligence Scale for Children. All intelligence means is how easily Mary can understand the things that she is asked to do.

I am sending two copies of this letter to you. If you could sign one and send it back, we will keep it in Mary's file.

I give my permission for Mr. Jones to give my daughter Mary the WISC.

_____	_____
Parent	Date
_____	_____
Parent	Date

Achievement Tests

Questions or activities to test how much the child has learned in school in specific skill areas are called achievement tests. An achievement test can be used to help screen the child for further testing. Some achievement tests are:

- California Achievement Test (CAT), which tests (a) vocabulary, (b) comprehension, (c) mathematics (computation, concepts, and problems), and (d) language (mechanics, usage, structure, and spelling)

- Iowa Tests of Basic Skills (ITBS), which test (a) vocabulary, (b) reading, (c) language, (d) word study, and (e) mathematics

- Metropolitan Achievement Test (MAT), which tests (a) word knowledge, (b) word analysis, (c) reading, (d) language, (e) spelling, (f) mathematics (computation, concepts, and problem solving), and (g) science

- Stanford Achievement Test (SAT) which tests (a) vocabulary, (b) reading comprehension, (c) word study skills, (d) mathematics (concepts, computation, and application), (e) spelling, (f) language, (g) social science, (h) science, and (i) listening comprehension

- Gates-Mac Ginitie Reading Test, which tests (a) vocabulary, (b) comprehension, and (c) speed and accuracy

- Peabody Individual Achievement Test (PIAT), which tests (a) mathematics, (b) reading recognition and comprehension, (c) spelling, and (d) general information

- Wide Range Achievement Test (WRAT), which tests (a) reading, (b) spelling, and (c) arithmetic

Group Intelligence Tests

In order to identify those students that may need further testing, group intelligence tests are routinely administered to all students. Most tests have several sections; some are timed, and some are not. Some tests have subparts given at different sittings. They require the student to perform tasks that have been performed by other children; then the scores are compared. Some group intelligence tests are:

- Cultural Fair Intelligence Tests, which measure (a) substitutions, (b) mazes, (c) selecting named objects, (d) similarities, (e) series, (f) classification, (g) matrices, and (h) conditions/typology

- Cognitive Abilities Test (CAT), which measures (a) vocabulary, (b) sentence completion, (c) verbal classification analogies, (d) quantitative relations, (e) number series, (f) equation building, and (g) figure analogies, classification, and synthesis

- Goodenough-Harris Drawing Test, which measures child's ability to see and remember. Student makes three drawings, one of self, one of man, and one of woman, and they are scored according to the amount of detail.

- Henmon-Nelson Tests of Mental Ability, which measure (a) listening, (b) vocabulary, (c) size and number, (d) sentence completion, (e) opposites, (f) general information, (g) verbal analogies (classification and inference), (h) number series, (i) arithmetic reasoning, and (j) figure analogies

- Kuhlmann-Anderson Intelligence Tests (KA), which measure learning aptitude

- Otis-Lennon Mental Ability Test, which measures general mental ability

- Primary Mental Abilities Test (PMA), which measures (a) verbal meaning, (b) number facility, (c) perceptual speed, and (d) spatial relationships

- Short Form Test of Academic Aptitude (SFTAA), which measures (a) language, vocabulary, and memory, (b) nonlanguage, analogies, and sequencing

Individual Intelligence Tests

When a child has low scores on a group test, it may be because of the situation. The child should then be given a test with only the child and the examiner present. The examiner is well trained and knows the questions and activities of the test very well and has practiced giving it to many children. The test has been given to many children, and their scores have been recorded (standardized). The score of any child who takes the test can be compared to the other children's scores. The examiner also writes a report of how the child reacted to the testing situation. The tests are usually given by a psychologist rather than a teacher. Some individual intelligence tests are:

- Stanford-Binet Intelligence Scale, which measures verbal and motor skills

- The Wechsler Scales (WISC-R, WPPSI, WAIS), which measure: (a) information, (b) comprehension, (c) similarities, (d) arithmetic, (e) vocabulary, (f) digit span, (g) sentences, (h) picture completion, (i) picture arrangement, (j) block design, (k) object assembly, (l) coding, (m) mazes, and (n) geometric design

- Slosson Intelligence Test, which measures general mental ability

- McCarthy Scales of Children's Abilities (MSCA) for children ages 2½ to 8½, which measure (a) verbal, (b) perceptual performance, (c) quantitative, (d) memory, (e) motor, and (f) general cognitive ability

- Full-Range Picture Vocabulary which measures verbal intelligence

- Quick Test, which measures verbal intelligence through a brief screening, can be given by a teacher

- Peabody Picture Vocabulary Test (PPVT), which measures verbal intelligence

Explanations of Handicapping Conditions

Learning Problems—Hearing

What the child does:

- does not look at the person talking

- does not finish activity or school assignment

- daydreams

- does not speak clearly and is not easy to understand

- asks "wh-" questions frequently

- does not join groups or spend time with others easily

What will help:

Mild . . .
- have child sit close to teacher in school

- write as well as say directions

- have large rather than small group discussions

- provide auditory training to discriminate sounds
- provide training in lip reading
- provide speech training for accurate sounds
- train child in hearing aid care and use (if conductive loss)

Severe . . .
- use creative dramatics for communication
- use nonverbal communication/sign language/language board
- emphasize speech and language curriculum

How these problems are measured:

- screening/identification with a whisper test
- hearing test with an audiometer
- examination for presence of infection
- examination for severe emotional shock or strain
- examination for type of loss
- hearing aid if loss is conductive

Terms to describe the problem:

- deaf: little or no hearing at birth or before language was developed
- deafened: acquired language and later lost hearing
- hard of hearing: reduced hearing since birth, or lost some hearing at any time in life

Learning Problems—Understanding
What the child does:

- plays with younger children
- does not finish activities
- gives up easily
- does not ask for help, just quits

- does not understand complex game rules

- does not follow instructions for assignments

- does not understand directions

- does not work alone

- does not know what to do in an emergency

- is uncomfortable if routine changes

- does not seem to understand meaning of ABCs and numbers

- sometimes walks around just looking at things rather than doing things

- does not ask questions

- does not know how to meet people, may hide or hug

- may be careless in grooming and appearance

- appears awkward and is frequently clumsy

- does not know what to do in a new situation

What will help:

Mild . . .
- design activities that are not too hard for the child

- have study time short

- demonstrate or model the skill/activity for the child

- have all work related to child's life experiences

- tell the child immediately if the work is right or wrong

Severe . . .
- have learning experiences that take place in the community

- have on-the-job training

- develop personal rapport with the child

- provide instruction and feedback during routine activities of the day

- describe the activity while it is happening

- teach child to use objects rather than paper and pencil

- design situations where child can practice interacting with other people

How these problems are measured:

- group intelligence test for screening
- individual intelligence test for diagnosis
- achievement test of learning
- measurement of self-help skills (adaptive behavior)
- measurement of socialization skills (adaptive behavior)
- observation of interaction with other children

Terms to describe the problem:

- slow learner: IQ score 80-100, follows along with other children but does not keep up in reading and math skills
- educable mentally retarded: IQ score 60-80, usually plays with children who are younger, needs someone to demonstrate each part of reading or math lesson
- trainable mentally retarded: IQ score 40-55, does not talk so that everyone can understand, has not learned to play with others or go around community independently
- profoundly mentally retarded: IQ below 40, says only a few words, is dependent upon others for daily routines

Learning Problems—Perceptual Difficulties

What the child does:

- has trouble standing or sitting in one place
- has difficulty copying from the board or from a paper
- uses one hand for some things, the other for other things
- has difficulty putting one thing away and starting another
- has difficulty concentrating on one thing at a time
- is bothered by sudden noises and bright lights
- cannot see the whole picture or reason
- must touch and feel things instead of just looking

- has trouble finding the words to say what he wants to say
- has trouble making friends
- hears only part of what is said to him
- has trouble cutting, doing fine work
- is clumsy
- unable to distinguish the important from the detail
- gets feelings hurt easily, gives up easily

What will help:

Mild . . .
- give directions in short simple sentences
- give directions for one thing at a time
- write as well as say the directions
- allow the child to touch and feel objects
- have the child sit where he/she will not be distracted by sights, sounds, and people
- have routine ways to do things and put things away
- have lessons about anger, friendship, interpersonal relations

Severe . . .
- have child sit in study carrell for work
- have child walk down hall after or before other children
- allow the child to schedule work and decide when it is finished
- have child eat lunch in classroom or before or after other children in lunchroom
- role play interaction and friendship roles
- teach child to tape-record lectures and instructions

How these problems are measured:

- group intelligence test for screening
- individual intelligence test to determine understanding

- achievement test to determine what has been learned
- Illinois Test of Psycholinguistic Abilities for perceptual organization
- neurological examination by neurologist
- general physical to include hearing and vision testing

Terms to describe the problem:

- learning disabilities or specific learning disabilities: child has IQ of 100 or above and does not have physical, hearing, vision, or emotional problems yet has trouble in organizing thoughts, speech, and interaction with others

Learning Problems—Behavior Difficulties

What the child does:

- breaks crayons, scissors, rulers, and sometimes windows on purpose
- teases, restrains, kicks, spits on children or adults
- uses abusive language without apparent cause
- torments and abuses animals
- withdraws and chooses to interact with others as little as possible
- daydreams and is inattentive
- is irritable, uncooperative, and self-conscious
- has extreme fear of unknown
- becomes sick when upset

What will help:

Mild . . .
- discuss problems with child and offer rewards for good behavior
- assign child to work with other children in supervised setting
- have child take care of animal in supervised setting
- have lessons about appropriate social behavior
- compliment the child for appropriate social behavior

Severe . . .

- observe child carefully to see what happens before and after the child misbehaves

- pay no attention to the inappropriate behaviors

- observe the child carefully to see what the child likes

- offer what the child likes if he behaves appropriately

- remove the child from others when the behavior is not appropriate

- plan simple, short activities in which the child can be successful

How these problems are measured:

- group intelligence test for screening

- individual intelligence test to observe behavior in testing setting

- achievement test to determine what has been learned

- physical examination to determine vision, hearing, and general health

- record of child behavior in the classroom and at school

- observations of the psychologist during testing and interview

Terms to describe the problem:

- emotional disturbance, behavioral disorders: child has not learned how to cope with the day-to-day problems of life and interaction with others

Learning Problems—Visual Difficulties

What the child does:

- rubs eyes

- tilts head

- squints

- rolls eyes

- is sensitive to light

- does not attend to visual tasks

- is awkward in eye-hand activities

- avoids close work

- prefers tasks that require distant vision

- complains about inability to see

- lacks normal curiosity of visual objects

- does not enjoy walking around an unfamiliar place

- does not smile back in greeting

- does not express feelings in facial expressions

What will help:

Mild . . .
- have child sit close to teacher/chalkboard

- have working area well lighted

- make sure printed material is clear

- do not use old ditto masters

- tell child what you would like him/her to look at

- present the information by telling as well as showing

- use large print books, if needed

- fit with glasses, if needed

Severe . . .
- use large print books

- teach Braille

- teach to type on Braille typewriter and regular typewriter

- teach to use magnifying equipment

- train other senses

- teach how to get around buildings and community

- teach personal grooming/facial expressions

- work with the child on posture

- assist child in learning how to make friends

How these problems are measured:

- examination by ophthalmologist
- individual intelligence test to determine understanding
- achievement test to determine what has been learned
- general physical to include hearing testing

Terms to describe the problem:

- blind: vision 20/200, or able to see at 20 feet what a normal person sees at 200 feet
- partially seeing: vision better than 20/200 but not better than 20/70 or what a normal person sees at 70 feet, in the better eye with correction

Learning Problems—Speech/Talking

What the child does:

- does not talk
- talks but can be understood only by family
- does not take part in conversation
- points and gestures to show what he wants
- repeats words and parts of words when talking
- uses one sound when another one is appropriate
- does not participate in discussions
- does not talk to friends
- talks to self when others are present

What will help:

Mild . . .
- create situations in which the child can interact with toys
- create experiences in which the child can talk to an adult
- create games of sound recognition
- talk to the child about what is happening

- refrain from telling the child what to say

- accept what the child says and repeat it back correctly even if there is an error

- demonstrate what you want the child to do rather than just tell him

Severe . . .
- speak to the child in short, simple sentences

- allow ample time for the child to respond

- design a method for the child to express ideas with pictures or other symbols

- talk to the child about what is currently happening

How these problems are measured:

- group intelligence test for screening

- verbal intelligence tests/Peabody/Full Range

- sample of natural interaction

- measure of articulation difficulties

Terms to describe the problem:

- language delayed: child is learning language, but language is similar to language of children who are younger

- speech impaired: child does not speak clearly, repeats words or phrases, voice does not sound natural

Learning Problems—Movement/coordination
What the child does:

- cannot move body when and where desired

- cannot pick up small objects

- cannot use eyes and hands together to do something

- has trouble making speech sounds

- has trouble chewing and swallowing

- has trouble keeping eyes focused

- cries or laughs without apparent reason

- has difficulty understanding speech sounds

- may have seizures

What will help:

Mild . . .
- have treatment plan for child designed and monitored by a physical therapist

- have treatment plan for child designed and monitored by an occupational therapist

- adapt physical education

- train in auditory and visual perception

- assist in learning self-help skills

- train in socialization skills

- allow more time for the child to do things

- use a board with words for communication

Severe . . .
- have direct treatment by a physical therapist

- have direct treatment by an occupational therapist

- provide equipment to help the child sit in normal position

- provide equipment to help child move or stand in normal position

- assist with self-care routines

- train how to interact with others

- design individual feeding utensils

- provide developmental speech and communication therapy

How these problems are measured:

- screening by a physician or pediatrician

- individual physical therapy evaluation

- individual occupational therapy evaluation

- individual speech therapy evaluation

- individual psychological test given by person experienced with motor problems
- perceptual evaluation
- neurological examination

Terms to describe the problem:

- cerebral palsy: central nervous system problems that cause movement messages to be blocked or distorted
- neurologically impaired: unable to organize feeling, vision, and hearing
- orthopedically impaired: limited strength or movement
- other health impaired: acute health problems
- severe specific learning disabilities: difficulty with fine motor activities, difficulty sitting still and attending, difficulty seeing, hearing, and understanding

Down's Syndrome

The term *syndrome* means a group of signs and symptoms that occur together. The medical profession frequently labels the group of symptoms with the name of the doctor who wrote the first description of them, and Dr. Landon Down first described the group of symptoms that he recognized occurring in some children over 100 years ago. The term *Mongoloid* probably originated because the child's eyes slope upward and outward and appear to be like the eyes of individuals of the Asian races. Actually, the shape and slant of the eyes are not like those of Asians, but the label continues to be used by individuals who have not studied the development of the children.

Down's syndrome babies are born in all races. Mothers who are older than 40 have more chance of giving birth to a Down's syndrome child, but since more women have babies when they are younger, many of the children are born to younger mothers. Down's syndrome children have small heads, ears, and mouth. The long bones of the body are shorter, making the fingers and toes shorter. The face is round and the skin usually dry. Many of the children have vision difficulties and usually have awkward coordination. It was discovered in the 1960s that Down's syndrome children have an extra chromosome in their body cells. Although the condition is being studied and diagnosis of the condition can be made while the child is still in the uterus, the cause remains a mystery.

Down's syndrome babies, children, and adults have learning problems and can not usually "keep up" with the children their own age. How far behind a Down's syndrome child is depends largely on what kind of experiences the child is exposed to. Even Down's 100-year-old description notes that the children imitate the adults (and children) that they see. Down's syndrome children are most anxious to be like the people that they are around and learn best from having the experience modeled for them rather than to have the situation described. They learn by participation, not by lecture or verbal direction; they learn to "do" more than they learn to "say." One of the reasons that Down's syndrome children living in the community function higher than those living in institutions is that children in the community can participate in the routines of daily life with normal people who make good models.

With the advanced medical care available now, Down's syndrome babies grow to adulthood. It is important that they are given warm acceptance and lifelong training experiences. "Look alikes," as one retarded boy labeled them, are reputed not only to look alike but also to behave alike. They are usually lovable and easy to manage, unless, of course, the caretakers abuse the accepting child and are harsh and demanding. When their more than the usual amount of patience is exhausted, Down's syndrome individuals can defend themselves strongly. When Down's syndrome children and adults are given warm, accepting care, they almost always express devoted concern for those in their immediate world.

Epilepsy

Epilepsy can be defined as excess electrical energy in the brain that causes a functional disturbance of groups of brain cells. There are four types of seizures:

1. grand mal. This type of seizure is sometimes preceded by an aura, or unusual odors or sights, that may be brief or long lasting. The person stiffens (tonic stage) then jerks (clonic stage). After two or three minutes, the person relaxes and usually is tired and may sleep.
2. petit mal. The person has momentary loss of consciousness and may nod the head or blink the eyes, have vacant stare, or drop an object in the hands. It may last only a few seconds.
3. Jacksonian. This type of seizure usually starts with jerking movements in the foot, hand, or one side of the face. It progresses until it involves one side of the body. Sometimes it can be prevented by the individual using a large amount of physical energy.
4. psychomotor. This is less common in children. The person appears to be in a trance and repeats what may be purposeful behavior but does not attend when spoken to.

Treatment:

Can usually be controlled by medication.

If sitting or standing at the time of a seizure, the individual should be gently directed to a safe place for movement (usually the floor). It may be necessary to move furniture so the individual does not bump sharp edges. The tongue should not be held. A record should be kept of the exact movement made during the seizure (i.e., left arm began to move, head dropped, etc.) and of the frequency and length of the seizure movement. The individual should rest after a major seizure.

Seizures do not cause learning and medical problems, but an individual who has seizures may have other problems that require treatment. To educators the greatest problem caused by seizures is that the individual is not attending to stimuli during the seizure and therefore misses part of the lesson or other interaction.

Cerebral Palsy

Cerebral palsy is any alteration of movement or motor function arising from a defect, injury, or disease of the nervous tissues contained in the cranial cavity. Problems include motor development (movement) difficulties, perception difficulties (hearing, vision acuity, and discrimination), learning problems (memory, transfer, etc.), emotional problems (low tolerance to stress), speech problems (articulation and language difficulties). Diagnosis is made by skilled practitioners after a careful observation of the child's general condition, body parts affected, degree of involvement, and associated disabilities (vision, hearing, intelligence, speech, and learning).

Several types of movement are associated with cerebral palsy.

a. Spasticity, which occurs in 40 to 60 percent of individuals, results from a lack of balanced tension on muscles. The child is rigid, movement is difficult, and relaxation is difficult.

b. Athetosis occurs in 15 to 20 percent of individuals. Movements are uncontrollable and jerky. Movement is not rhythmical, and more tension causes more movements.

c. Ataxia is unsteady movement. It becomes apparent when grasping and walking begin. In a tremor, the whole body shows irregular involuntary vibrating movements.

d. Rigidity results from diminished rather than abnormal motion. Posture and movements are stiff.

Early and continued treatment can help the child keep as much movement as possible. Special needs include:

- more space to move in

- regular physical and occupational therapy

- individually designed positioning equipment

- special equipment for eating

- team approach in which each specialist prescribes and the team decides on appropriate, individual programming

Explanations of Teaching/Learning Strategies

Learning Style (To Explain Need To Evaluate)

People learn in different ways. Some people can read directions and do the task immediately. Others need to watch someone else do it before they will even try. Some are uncomfortable trying when other people are around.

In school, directions are given, and children are required to do the task after it has been explained to them. For many children, this is not a good way for them to learn. They need to touch and hold objects and watch other people doing the task in order to learn to do it themselves. When the teacher tells all the children to do a certain task, these children do not understand. They must be shown what to do and the teacher must work with them individually.

By observing a child who is having some trouble doing the tasks the teacher is explaining, it is possible to find a better way to teach the child. Sometimes in the observation the child is asked to do certain things from lists of things that other children have been observed doing. By watching the child the professional can determine if the child learns better by watching someone rather than just listening. The child may need the help of a teacher who has learned how to teach this way and has time to stop and work with each child when help is needed.

Learning Centers

Children learn better when they can touch and use the materials on their own. This can be done, even in a classroom of many children, if the materials are set up and ready to be used in various parts of the room. After learning how to take care of the materials, the children take turns using them. The place where the materials are kept is called a learning center. Learning centers can be set up for science, reading or creative writing, or even for more specific topics, such as the weather, foods, or Christmas in many lands.

Perception

Sights, sounds, and smells are everywhere. We see or hear or feel them when they come close enough to be picked up and organized and the messages sent to the central nervous system. The system then organizes the messages so the individual knows how to react to the feeling. For some children the process of organization of sights, sounds, and smells is awkward, slow, and inaccurate.

Visual Learning and Auditory Learning

When something happens over and over again, the child begins to know how it will happen the next time. The thing that happens can be something that the child sees or something that the child hears. For some children it is easier to remember things that are seen over and over again. For other children it is easier to remember things that are heard over and over again.

Kinesthetic Learning

Young children do not learn by having someone explain what they need to know. Young children learn by having someone show them and then by doing the activity themselves. Children with learning problems continue to need kinesthetic (touch and move) experiences to learn, even after they reach school age.

Multisensory

Having the child practice the skill or idea by hearing the materials, seeing the materials, and touching the materials is a multisensory approach to learning.

Incidental Learning

Lessons are planned to teach a child a certain skill. Sometimes the child learns some things besides what the teacher planned for the child to learn. Children with learning problems do not learn as well without specific instruction as other children do. Most children learn how to get along with other children and solve new problems without a specific lesson, but children with learning problems frequently need to have lessons planned to teach them these things.

Acting Out Behavior

Everyone needs to be noticed and recognized. If a child does not know how to do something that would earn a compliment from the teacher, the child may do something that he/she is sure will be noticed. Acting out behavior may be anything from throwing spit wads to having temper tantrums.

Mobility Training

In order for the child to be as independent as possible, it is often helpful to have someone assist the child in learning how to move about safely. For children with hearing problems, it might be training in how to use the public transit safely. For children who have problems understanding, it might be how to recognize danger. For children who have trouble seeing, it might be learning to get around the school. Depending on the child's age and ability, the training might be done in the building, on the playground, or in the city streets.

Montessori Method

Montessori was a woman physician who, in the early 1900s, was hired by the Italian government to provide programs for preschool children of mothers who were working in the factories. She designed motor and daily living experiences as well as language experiences for the children. She taught the children personal care and gymnastic exercises; she taught them to put puzzles together, to sort items by color, and to march to music. She thought that children should be guided without feeling the presence of the adult.

The children are taught how to use the materials and then allowed to choose what they want to do. They are free to come to the teacher, and the teacher is to answer the children's questions as they are asked. Montessori felt that it was necessary for children to participate in activities. She summarized her reasons by stating, "I hear and I forget, I see and I remember, I do and I understand."

Encoding and Decoding or Expressing and Receiving

In order to exchange ideas and feelings with others, it is necessary to be able to put ideas into words (code) and understand the words (code) of others. Sending the code to others is called encoding or expression. Receiving the code from others is called decoding or reception. It is possible to have good ideas, but have trouble with the coding process.

Preacademic

Learning to use symbols is called academics. Skills that must be well developed before symbols have any meaning are called preacademic skills. Usually, children must learn to care for their body (self-help) and to get along with others (socialization) before they are ready to use symbols to describe activities. Before children are ready to use written symbols for ideas, it is necessary that they be able to observe how one thing is different from the other things. Then they must learn how one symbol is different from another symbol. They must also have had experience with the ideas or activities that the symbol represents. Children are ready for academics (symbols) at different times, depending on their individual experiences and abilities. Children with learning problems need more experience with activities and objects before they are ready for symbols.

Behavior Modification

Children (or even adults) will do something again, if others paid attention to what they did. If adults have been scolding the child, the child will tend to do those same things again. The child will stop doing something if no one pays attention to it. Behavior modification is a careful plan to have everyone pay attention to the good things that the child does and to ignore entirely the inappropriate things that the child does.

Task Analysis

Some things must be learned before other things. For example when a coat is put on, it is necessary to put the arm in the sleeve before pulling up the zipper. By analyzing the task, it is possible to tell which things should be learned first and teach the things in the order that they can be used.

Hyperactivity

All children move to learn. Young children especially look at things by touching them. As children grow older, they can remember what it was like to move and touch, and they do not need to move and touch again and again. When a child moves and touches all the time, it is said that the child is hyperactive (more active) than other children of the same age. Children who are labeled hyperactive usually move and touch like children who are younger than they are. To someone who is not used to being around children or who does not enjoy being around children, all children seem "hyper" active.

Rote Learning

It is possible to be able to repeat something over and over again and not be able to understand what it means. If the ideas are repeated often enough, the child will be able to repeat it, but the child may not be able to apply it to any real life situation.

Overachiever

Children who are overachievers do well in the work that is given to them but they must work harder than most children to do the work well.

Underachiever

When a child's work is not nearly as good as the child is capable of doing, the child is an underachiever.

Sign Language

For some children saying words is difficult. It is possible to send the message another way, by moving the hand (wave) or by pointing to a picture. Some of the hand movements have been written down and are used by many people. They are called sign language systems.

CONCLUSION

Most parents have not had the opportunity to learn the professional jargon that was created to describe the learning problems of children. If the jargon accurately describes the child, however, the parent should be able to understand it easily— when it is translated to the parent's language. After all, the parent is with the child more than the professionals: before school, after school, weekends, and all summer. The parent sees the child as the child tries to learn everything! In order for the parent to understand the language of the education system, educators will have to learn the language of the parent and recode the information into cocktail conversation.

Chapter 12

Complying with Legal Requirements

"When I grow up, I'm going to do what *I* want to do!" is just another fairy tale. There are perhaps more rules and regulations for adults than there are for children, and people who work for the public are subjected to even more regulations than are other adults. Most regulations carry penalties if they are not obeyed.

Parents and advocacy organizations are undoubtedly pleased with the requirements that "assure that the rights of handicapped children and their parents are protected" (*Federal Register,* 1977, p. 42474), but the public agency personnel may not be excited about the extra effort required by the regulations. It may sometimes seem difficult to find time both to meet the requirements and to work with the children. It is no wonder that the additional responsibilities are not as welcome to the educators as they are to the parents.

In order to protect the parents' rights, methods of exchanging information between the parent and the educational system must follow specified formal procedures. These procedures fall into three categories: (1) informed consent, (2) prior notice, and (3) confidentiality.

INFORMED CONSENT

Consent as a legal concept implies three things: (1) capacity for the individual to understand, (2) information about the topic, (3) voluntary approval that may be withdrawn at any time.

A person who is of majority age (usually 18) and possesses intellectual capacity is generally considered capable of making decisions. If a person has the ability to manage his or her own affairs and demonstrates a rational understanding of life situations, it is assumed that this person has the capacity for decision making (Turnbull, 1977).

"Consent is ineffective unless the person has information about the matter (e.g., medical treatment) for which consent is sought. 'Information' as a prerequisite of consent consists of two elements: (1) the substance of the information, and (2) the manner in which the information is communicated" (Turnbull, 1977, p. 8). Because it is the responsibility of the professional to communicate the information to the individual, the professional must organize the information so that a person who has not been trained in that field can understand it. The facts, risks, benefits, and alternatives must be stated. The information must be sent at an "appropriate communication level" for the person receiving the information (Turnbull, 1977, p. 10).

A free choice must be made without "fraud, deceit, duress or coercion." The person should have sufficient autonomy to make the choice and not be obligated to act against his own free will. "Consent, once given, is almost never permanent" (Turnbull, 1977, p. 11).

Consent in the School System

Before the public agency can give a child any formal or informal evaluation tests or suggest that any special services not given to all of the children in the grade or class are needed, the agency must have the consent of the parent. This means that the professionals must communicate information about the procedures and conditions that require the procedures to the parent at an "appropriate comprehension level" or "language understandable to the general public." The public agency must provide evidence that the communication has taken place and that the parent was able to understand clearly and approved.

Since understanding is more of a cognitive experience and parenting is more of an emotional experience (see Chapters 4 and 5), meeting the three requirements of consent takes some careful effort on the part of the school agency personnel.

Meeting the Capacity Requirement

The law assumes that the parents of the child are responsible for that child. If a parent has refused to have the child evaluated or placed in special education and the public agency still feels that the child should be evaluated, the agency may use the hearing procedures to "determine if the child may be evaluated or initially placed in special education" (*Federal Register*, 1977, p. 42495). However, it is necessary to follow the notification procedures and show that the parent was informed appropriately before alternate steps can be taken.

Either parent has the legal authority and capacity to act for the child unless the agency has been advised to the contrary due to such matters as guardianship, separation or divorce.

Surrogate Parent

The parent is defined as the natural parent, the child's guardian, or anyone acting as a parent, including a grandparent or stepparent. In the event that the parent cannot be identified, the parent cannot be located, or the child is a ward of the state, a surrogate is appointed for the parent. The person selected as a surrogate should (a) have no interest that would conflict with the interests of the child, (b) possess the knowledge and skills to represent the child, and (c) not be an employee of the public agency that educates or cares for the child. The surrogate parent may represent the child in matters of identification, placement, and free appropriate public education. The state plan is required to show that training is provided for surrogate parents and certify that an individual is qualified to serve in that role.

A surrogate parent cannot be appointed by the agency if the natural parent is available and able to manage his or her own affairs. Although the public agency may want to appoint a surrogate for parents who do not appear to be adequate parents, it is not the prerogative of the educational agency to make that determination. The school agency might, however, gather information that could be used by the proper agency to make such a determination.

Although the responsibility of parenting may ultimately be taken from the natural parent, the public agency's responsibility toward the natural parent is clear and simple. The interaction requirements are not changed even if it seems obvious that the parent does not have the capacity to make adequate decisions for the child. The public agency can only assist in the determination of that capacity in one way: to show that adequate attempts have been made to inform the natural parent. The contacts and information exchange must be documented.

Meeting the Information Requirement

Sending information is the business of the school. Students are given information about a variety of subjects through books, films, and discussions. Schools also evaluate the amount of information that students have received by testing them to see how much they have retained and can display in the testing situation. The school then assigns a grade to each student's work and indicates how well that student was able to assimilate the information in the form that the school chose to give it.

In order to give information to parents that will meet the requirements of consent, a new concept of information sending must be devised. In this case, the responsibility for understanding of the information is not the responsibility of the receiver (the student) but of the sender (the professional). A failure of the receiver (parent) to understand the information is the "fault" of the sender of the information (the professional).

This concept is foreign to many traditional educators, who have been trained to expect the student to do the studying. If the sender is to be responsible for the understanding, then the sender must not only know the information well, but also study the receiver and find how best to give the information so that it will be understandable to the receiver. In this situation, it is not the "student" who studies the information as organized by the teacher, but the "teacher" who studies how the student is organized in order to decide how best to send the information to that student. It is not the parent's responsibility to understand what is told to him/her, but the professional's responsibility to know the parent well enough to organize the information so that the parent will be able to understand.

This process requires continued contact over time between the school agency and the parents. It also requires that a variety of methods be used to transmit information to the parents. Some parents can read the technical information of a monograph; others cannot. Some parents are ready to know the full story when the child is first evaluated; others are not. Some parents understand standard English; others do not. Some parents find it comfortable to come to group meetings; others do not. One of the child's parents may be comfortable with a means of information exchange that causes the other discomfort. Mother may enjoy group meetings; fathers may want to avoid talking about the child to others. A parent may be able to understand one concept in written form, but need to have someone to talk to in order to understand another concept. It is not possible to predict what information the parent is ready to receive by the parent's chronological age. Life experiences differ, and so do the feelings about life experiences.

When the amount of knowledge about a topic or situation is limited, it is not possible to repeat that information except in the form that it was learned. In order to organize and reorganize the information for the understanding of a particular parent, the professional must thoroughly understand the concept or procedure. Consent is necessary for identification, evaluation, and educational placement of a child. These procedures are complicated and require an understanding of many concepts.

One graduate student confided to her seminar group that she started to explain visual perception to a parent and found herself saying, "Well, visual perception is . . . well, *visual perception*" (Overgaard, 1978). To understand this explanation of visual perception, the parent would need a master's degree in special education, preferably in learning disabilities. Some explanations of a variety of procedures are given in Chapter 11, Parents Must Understand: Technical Concepts in Non-technical Language. These explanations can be given to some parents as handouts, but for other parents it will be necessary to dissect the material and regroup the ideas perhaps again and again.

Procedures and Consent Form

The procedure of consent requires that the parent be given notice of the proposal to initiate change or the refusal to initiate change. In order to prepare information about the intent of the agency, the professional must understand the referral process clearly. There are a variety of ways that referrals can be made, and it is important that all of the professionals in the school know both the formal and informal processes for that school.

Although the forms and signatures may be the same for all schools within a district, various schools may implement the process differently. Some schools expect the teacher to get the form from the secretary; others, from the psychologist. Some principals keep the materials in their office. If the parent is to feel comfortable about the process, the professionals must know the process well and be comfortable with it before they explain the procedures to the parent. The form (Exhibit 12-1) is to be signed by the parent to indicate that consent has been given. The professional should understand the procedures completely before requesting that the parent sign the papers.

The regulations require that the parent is given a full explanation of procedural safeguards, a description of the action proposed or refused by the agency, and an explanation of the reasons for the agency's decision. Some parents need more "why" than others. Each one's needs must be met individually.

PRIOR NOTICE

The regulations specify definite things that must be included in the information communicated to the parent about evaluation and placement. The information is to include (1) a complete explanation of the procedural safeguards (due process hearings), (2) a description of the action proposed or refused, (3) a description of each evaluation test, and (4) a description of any other factors relevant to the proposal or refusal.

Explanation of Procedural Safeguards

The due process hearing is a legal procedure to ensure that all the information is considered fairly. It is an established part of the democratic system. Handicapped children and their parents are protected in the development and implementation of a free appropriate public education for the children by due process, which has already been used in civil and criminal cases. Although parent advocacy organizations disseminate information about the hearing process to their members, many parents are not active members of these groups. For these parents, the only source of information about the hearing process is the public agency. The agency is required to give proof that this process has been explained to the parent.

A description of the hearing process is included in Chapter 11. Although the information could be used in this format for some parents, other parents will not be able to abstract information from the written language and must have the concept and procedures explained to them in their own linguistic patterns. For some parents, this will mean an interpreter from a similar background.

Exhibit 12-1 Sample Consent Form

Child _____ DOB _____

Parent _____ Address _____ Phone _____

Date _____ Location _____

_____ from _____

Name of Individual   Name of Agency

talked with me about _____

_____

_____

_____

_____

I understand that _____

I was told that I can change my mind at any time   Yes (   )   No (   )

I agree to have _____ done for/with/to my child.

_____   _____   _____
Signature of Agency Personnel   Title   Signature of Parent

_____
Date

Description of the Action Planned or Refused

Since the emotional impact of the conference is high for the parent (see Chapter 4), it is possible for the parent to sit through the conference and make comments without understanding exactly what is being planned for the child. It is important for the professional to know the exact plans for this child's program; a general understanding of programming options is not sufficient. If a clear and concise description of the plan for this particular child can be given, the parent may find it easier to agree.

The description must also include a reason why the plan is appropriate or a reason why the plan cannot be implemented. Frequently, these reasons are related to school and agency regulations. Therefore, the professionals must be aware of the regulations so that the reasons for certain actions can be explained convincingly.

Description of Each Evaluation

Only a masochist (or perhaps a psychologist) enjoys the testing situation. Parents are concerned about having their children tested. One psychologist in training gave tests as practice to the children in a comfortable suburb. Although all of the children tested were doing well, both in school and in life, each of the parents was anxious to know "How did my child do?" (Michaelis, 1974). Parents are even more anxious if the child has some learning problems.

Psychological reports are written (1) for the needs of the immediate mission, (2) in anticipation of questions and future needs, and (3) for the creation of a record (Tallent, 1976). They are not written so that parents can understand the child better. They do not always help other professionals to understand the child better either, since many educators do not understand the standardized testing process.

There is a mystique about evaluation procedures, even for educators, if they are not involved in giving standardized tests. Teachers who thoroughly understand the routine standardized achievement and intelligence tests given to groups of students can be more helpful to parents. It would be appropriate for the faculty to have some in-service training tests that are administered to the children individually by the school psychologist. If the teacher is familiar with the evaluation procedures, the teacher may be able to communicate that information to the parents more clearly than the psychologist. The teacher, who has already established rapport with the parents, might be able to discuss more openly what can be discovered about the child's learning processes through a psychological examination.

A by-product of having all the professionals understand the testing situation better is that the information uncovered by the psychologist becomes more accessible to the other professionals.

Description of Other Relevant Factors

There may be any number of administrative reasons that prevent the public agency from offering the services to the child that the parent wants. Reasons might include problems with building structure, inability to budget money for another lift bus, or the lack of a physical therapist, occupational therapist or a teacher trained to work with children who have that type of disability. Since the parents are usually intent on the needs of the child, the routine problems of implementation may not seem significant to them.

The size and population concentration of the school district may affect the placement. Perhaps there are two physically handicapped children to be considered, and the agency would like the students in the same building so that the physical therapist, who consults with the public agency, will be able to serve both children more easily. Maybe there is only one program serving secondary students in the district.

These conditions must be so familiar to the agency personnel that they can describe them easily and thoroughly to the parent. If the parent can be told the complete reason, the parent may be able to help solve the problems. Parents may be able to "collect stamps" and purchase a school bus (it has been done) or attend the school board meeting to ask for more funds.

Parent Conference Summary

The notice sent to the parents must be in "language understandable to the general public" and provided in the native language of the parent. If the parent cannot read, the educational agency must communicate with the parent orally. There must be written evidence that the parent understands the content of the message, however. Translating information from one language to another can be done successfully only by a skilled individual who understands not only both languages but the cultural style of the two languages. It is clearly more difficult for most educational personnel to communicate with anyone who does not use standard English.

Most forms that have been developed for parents to sign, indicating that they have been told and understand what is to be done for their child, look like insurance forms with sections here and there of "fine print." Documentation of the parent's understanding would be clearer if the forms were open ended and had a place for a summary of the information exchanged and understood to be written (Exhibit 12-2).

If the educational agency needed to hire someone to translate information, it would be wise for that person to word the summary at the time of the conversation with the parent. It may seem to take longer to have the summary made at the time of the conversation, but, unless it is done that way, it is difficult to know what the

Exhibit 12-2 Sample Parent Conference Summary Form

Parent _____ Address _____ Phone _____

School _____ Date of Conference _____ Time _____ Place _____

Conference Initiated by _____ Purpose _____
                          name   title

Child's progress summarized on attached checklist?   Yes ( )   No ( )

Topics Discussed	Questions/Comments	Decision

Those Attending the Conference

Signatures   Title

_____

I have read this report, and it describes what
was discussed at the conference as I see it.

Signature   Title   Date

parent actually did understand. If there is a disagreement about what is understood, it is better for it to come out during the conversation than after the parent "thinks it over."

Prior Notice Given to Parents

After the child's problem has been initially evaluated and the child has been placed in special programs, it is necessary for the public agency to hold periodic review of each child's Individual Education Program (IEP). These meetings are to be held at least once a year, and efforts must be made to include the parents. There must be documentation that the parents have an opportunity to attend.

The meeting should be scheduled at a time that is mutually agreed upon and the parents must be notified of the meeting early enough to make sure that they have an opportunity to make arrangements to come. In addition to the time and place of the meeting, the notice must include the purpose of the meeting and who will be in attendance. It should also state that the parents may bring others to the meeting if they so desire (Exhibit 12-3).

If neither parent can attend, the agency may hold the meeting without the parent, but only when there is written documentation of (a) telephone calls and their results, (b) copies of correspondence and the answers, and (c) detailed records of visits to the home or work of the parent and the results of the visits. Since parent contact will be a continuing process, it might be wise to keep a record of all parent contacts.

The public agency is to take whatever action is necessary for the parent to understand the things and the decisions made at the meeting. A copy of the IEP is to be given to the parent upon request.

Prior Notice and the IEP Summary

Forms for recording the IEP are provided to most educational agencies by either state or local educational officials. Most of the forms include a summary of all informal and formal evaluations and are not necessarily a record of the things that were discussed in the meeting. It would appear that documentation of the IEP planning must be made by a copy of the minutes of the meeting that shows the give and take of the conversation and the alternatives that were discussed, even though the final decision did not include implementation of all the options.

One of the ways of accomplishing this might be to use checklists (see Exhibits 10-2 through 10-8) and write by each of the items on the list the summary of the conversation about that item. In addition to this, the more general options that were discussed in the meeting should be listed so the parent could review the process at a later time if desired. It is quite possible that the parent will think about the meeting many times within the course of the interaction with the child and the school. Since the meeting in which "my child" was discussed is far more significant to the parent than to the others who attend the meeting for less intense reasons, and since the terminology is far less familiar to the parent, it is important for the parent to have accurate "notes" to refer to later. A record of the proceedings of the meeting for the parent to review may be the best insurance that the parent will not become "suddenly" dissatisfied with the child's program.

The IEP conference could be summarized on the same form that is used for other parent conferences. The IEP itself is sometimes pages long and may be difficult for the parent to understand. A simplified IEP form (Exhibit 12-4) could summarize the services that are planned for the child, how those services will be implemented, and who will be providing the service to the child.

Parent Contact Form

A record of parent contacts should be kept, as mentioned earlier. All contacts with the parent should be listed on the form, even if they are not specifically related to the planning of meetings. The contact may have some significance later if there is some disagreement about the conversation with the parent. The contacts can be kept as a log and new sheets used as needed (Exhibit 12-5). It is important that any written correspondence to the parent or from the parent be attached.

The record of parent contacts should be a record of the contacts about an individual child. If the parents have more than one child in the programs, a record should be kept separately for each child. (See Chapter 6.) If, during the conversation about one child, something about another child comes up and is discussed, the information from that conversation should be entered into the record of each child. If written material from the parent includes information about more than one child, copies should be made and attached to the log of each child mentioned. The public agency should not set a conference for more than one of the parent's children at one time unless the conference is solely about such things as bus routes or qualification for free lunch. Most times, however, the school has more intense topics to discuss in relation to each child's progress.

CONFIDENTIALITY

In order to plan adequately for the exceptional children in the state, the state agency must have descriptions of the children, their handicapping conditions, and the types of services that are being offered to the children. The public agency is empowered to identify, locate, and evaluate these children and then devise a "practical method" to determine which children are receiving appropriate services and which are not. In the process of gathering this information, the state agency collects personal information about many children and their parents. This information is disclosed only to individuals who directly plan and implement services for the child and agency personnel who need the information for planning purposes.

Exhibit 12-3 Sample Notification of Meeting Form

NOTIFICATION OF MEETING TO PLAN INDIVIDUAL EDUCATION PROGRAM FOR:

Child _____ DOB _____

Parent _____ Address _____ Phone _____

Today's date _____ Parent contacted about the time for the meeting

Time set for meeting by phone ( )   note ( )   visit ( )   other _____

Meeting will be held:

_____ _____ _____
date   time   place

Those who will be in attendance:

Name	Title	Purpose/input expected

Discussion at the meeting will include:

a) present educational performance, b) writing of annual goals and instructional objectives, c) related services that the child will need, d) beginning dates and expected length of the programming, e) how the plan will be evaluated.

PLEASE BRING WITH YOU ANY INFORMATION THAT YOU HAVE ABOUT THE CHILD'S STRENGTHS AND NEEDS . . .

You may also bring anyone else that you would like to have with you at the meeting. If you have any questions, please contact _____ phone _____ See you _____ (date of conference).

Exhibit 12-4 IEP Summary Sheet

Child Name _____

Skill To Develop _____

This Task _____

Begin Date _____ Complete Date _____

Who Assist _____

When _____

Where _____

Materials _____

Methods _____

_____

Verbal Cue _____

Desired Outcome _____

_____

Evaluation _____

Reference _____

Child Name _____

Skill To Develop _____

This Task _____

Begin Date _____   Complete Date _____

Who Assist _____

When _____

Where _____

Materials _____

Methods _____

_____

_____

Verbal Cue _____

Desired Outcome _____

_____

Evaluation _____

Reference _____

Exhibit 12-4 continued

Child Name _Vivian_

Skill To Develop _strength in neck muscles (trunk rotation)_

This Task _side lying (lying on side with legs bent and moving body trunk)_

Begin Date _Sept. 1979_   Complete Date _____

Who Assist _teacher, teacher aide, parent/ward staff, OT, P.T._

When _Whenever it can be worked in, but at least before meals and snacks and bath time and after toileting. 4 or more times a day._

Where _On mat or heavy rug, in day room, classroom, bedroom, family room_

Materials _Mat or heavy rug approx. 5 ft. square. One or two of Vivian's favorite toys_

Methods _Lay Vivian on her side, keep arms in front of face, keep knees bent, keep head forward. Hold top leg gently with one hand and move the hip gently forward with the other hand, until the hip touches the mat. Then move the hip backward. Repeat by holding the top arm and moving the shoulder back and forward. Then roll Vivian to the other side and repeat the movement while she is lying on her other side._

Verbal Cue _gentle calm tone, "There Vivian, we are now moving forward/backward"_

Desired Outcome _Vivian will begin to relax and cooperate and initiate the movement and assist in the moving to the side lying position._

Evaluation _OT, PT evaluation, teacher observation, parent/staff observation_

Reference _OT, PT evaluation, Kimbo Education Record Developmental Motor Movement_

Child Name ___Vivian___

Skill To Develop ___head control___

This Task ___Holding head up and resting weight on elbow when placed prone (on tummy) on a wedge___
___and resting on elbows.___

Begin Date ___Sept. 1979___   Complete Date _____

Who Assist ___teacher, teacher aide, PT, OT, parent/ward staff___

When ___When not engaged in other programming, at regular intervals. At least four times a day.___

Where ___Classroom, day room, family room, living room, kitchen, bedroom___

Materials ___Mat or heavy rug, a wedge that is at the highest side the length of Vivian's arm from shoulder to elbow (4 inches)___
___and the sloped side the length of Vivian's trunk from shoulder to waist (20 inches). Toys.___

Methods ___Place Vivian on the wedge in a prone position (on tummy) with her shoulders and arms just above the wide part___
___of the wedge so that her arms are free to move and touch objects and so she can lean on them___
___and bear some weight. Place the favorite toys on floor in front of her and encourage her to reach for them.___
___Hang something from ceiling to encourage her to look up.___

Verbal Cue ___"Head up, Vivian" "Good girl" "See the (toy)"___

Desired Outcome ___Vivian will hold her head up for increasingly longer time.___

Evaluation ___teacher, aide, parent/staff observation. To be measured with a stop watch at least once each Monday.___

Reference ___PT evaluation, developmental scales___

Exhibit 12-4 continued

Child Name _Dean_

Skill To Develop _toileting_

This Task _will use toilet when placed there_

Begin Date _Sept. 1979_   Complete Date _____

Who Assist _teacher, teacher aide, parent/ward staff_

When _each hour during waking hours_

Where _school lavatory, home/ward bathroom_

Materials _toilet with adapted chair to support trunk, toilet paper, basin_

Methods _Take to bathroom each hour, assist in pulling down pants, say "good, you are dry"_
if he is dry. Assist onto toilet. Sit on toilet for 5 minutes. Assist in taking him off.
Assist in wiping and putting clothes back on. Assist in washing and drying hands.
Touch shoulder and say, "Good, Dean used the toilet", if he eliminated in the toilet.

Verbal Cue _"Go to toilet, Dean" "Good Boy, you are dry."_
"Pants down, Dean" "Good, you used toilet" "Pants up" "Wash hands"

Desired Outcome _Dean will eliminate on toilet 4 days out of 5_

Evaluation _Teacher records, parent/staff records_

Reference _parent/staff request, ARC Booklet, BCP, Marshalltown_
Kimbo Educational Adaptive Behavior Series

Child Name ___Dean___

Skill To Develop ___Self feeding___

This Task ___Independently scoop food with spoon___

Begin Date ___Sept. 1979___   Complete Date _____

Who Assist ___teacher, teacher aide, OT, parent/ward staff___

When ___all regular meal times, including evenings and weekends___

Where ___at meal table but away from distractions___

Materials ___Spoon with small, but rounded bowl, plate or bowl with small rim, nonskid material___
___to hold plate or bowl to table. Foods that Dean likes mashed or cut into small chunks.___

Methods ___Remind Dean 15 minutes before meal time, "Almost time to eat." Place Dean calmly at___
___table alone with adult if possible. Explain to him in a calm voice, "We are having _____ today."___
___"It is time to eat." Assist him in reaching for and grasping the spoon. Guide the hand when necessary.___

Verbal Cue ___"Let's eat, Dean" "Scoop" "Good (food)"___

Desired Outcome ___Dean will attend to eating and will scoop his own solid food at least ten scoops per meal.___

Evaluation ___O.T. evaluation, teacher, parent/staff reports___

Reference ___parent/staff request, BCP, Marshalltown, O.T. Evaluation___
___Kimbo Educational Adaptive Behavior Series___

Exhibit 12-5 Sample Parent Contact Form

Attach copies of written correspondence.

Child _____ DOB _____

Parent _____

Address _____ Phone _____

****

_____ Contacted by _____
date   name

Telephone ( )   Note ( )   Letter ( )   School Conference ( )   Home Visit ( )

Other _____
                                                              title

Parent Request ( )   School Request ( )

Purpose _____

Message _____

Parent Reply _____

_____

****

Contacted by _____
                          name

date _____   title

Telephone ( )   Note ( )   Letter ( )   School Conference ( )   Home Visit ( )

Other

Parent Request ( )   School Request ( )

Purpose _____

Message _____

Parent Reply _____

****

Exhibit 12-5 continued

****

Contacted by _____

_____   _____
date   name   title

Telephone ( )   Note ( )   Letter b))   School Conference ( )   Home Visit ( )

Other _____

Parent Request ( )   School Request ( )

Purpose _____

Message _____

_____

Parent Reply _____

_____

Only authorized personnel are allowed to examine the child's educational records, and a list must be kept of those who inspect the child's record and the agency that they represent. Since it is important to differentiate between employees of the agency who work with the child and other employees, it may be wise to keep a log of all of the individuals who examine the child's records (Exhibit 12-6).

Parent Access to Records

The parents have access to all records on the child, and they have the right to "reasonable" explanations and interpretations of the records. The parents may also have a representative of their choice inspect and review the records. The public agency may charge for copies to be made, unless the charge "prevents the parents" from exercising their right to inspect and review the records. Since many records of the child need to be studied to be understood, even by the professionals who are familiar with the terms and concepts, parents might need copies of much of the material in order to become familiar enough with the format and content to ask questions.

The parent's request to see the records (Exhibit 12-7) should be met without "unnecessary delay," especially if the parent is asking for the materials before an IEP conference or a hearing. In no case can the parent's examination of the records be delayed more than 45 days from the date of the request.

In most cases, of course, it will be more practical to have the parent look at the records at the time of a verbal request, since the longer the parent is delayed, the more anxious and critical the parent will be about the contents of the record. (See Chapter 4.) At times, however, it may be necessary to have the parent wait until a knowledgeable employee is available to make the required explanations and interpretations of the records. In addition, the parent should have a comfortable place to sit, look at the records, and perhaps spread the papers out on a table. It would not be appropriate to expect the parent to stand in the hall and merely flip through the file.

Amendments to the Records

The parents may have the child evaluated independently and have that information included in the child's educational record. The parents have the right to an evaluation by a qualified examiner at public expense if they do not agree with the evaluation made by public agency personnel. The public agency can initiate a hearing to determine if the original evaluation was appropriate. If it is determined at the hearing that the public agency evaluation is appropriate, the parents may still have the independent evaluation placed in the child's record, but the public agency will not be required to pay for the evaluation. Whenever the public agency is making any decision about the child's program, the independent evaluation must also be considered.

Exhibit 12-6 Access to Records Form

Name of Child _____ DOB _____

Parent _____ Address _____ Phone _____

Date	Inspected by	Title	Agency	Purpose

Exhibit 12-7 Request To Inspect Records

Child _____ DOB _____

Parent _____ Address _____ Phone _____

I/we would like to inspect the materials in my/our child's file of educational records.

I/we would like to inspect these materials on _____ (date) at _____ (time) in the _____ (location).

_____ parent
date

_____ parent
date

I/we have inspected the educational records of my/our child and have received copies of those records that I/we wanted to have.

_____ parent
date

_____ parent
date

If parents do not agree with some of the material in the child's educational records, they may ask the public agency to remove the information or to amend the information. The parent's request is to be implemented unless the public agency is prepared to have the situation examined by a due process hearing on the matter. It may simplify the process if the agency has parents approve items before they are made part of the child's educational record.

Personally Identifying Information

The reports and plans of the educational agency must include the number of children with different handicaps counted in a variety of ways. It is not permissible, however, to include in that information anything that would personally identify the child or the child's family. The child's name, the parent's name, or the names of any family members may not be disclosed. The address, Social Security number, or any personal characteristics may not be disclosed. The public agency must have the parent's consent before the information can be disclosed to anyone other than those authorized to work with the child.

From time to time, public organizations and even parent organizations request a list of the patrons of the school so that notices or other information may be sent to them. Although it is sometimes awkward to refuse, it is not appropriate for those names to be disclosed. In some incidents parent groups request a copy of the list so that the organization can send out information. The mere enrollment of the child in a special school setting may label the child as handicapped. If the information is of value to the parent, some educational agencies will take the stamped materials from the parent group and address and mail them. So that the parents who receive the information know that the agency did not disclose their identity, the notice might read: We heard about this program and thought that you might be interested so we addressed the envelopes for _____ (the name of the group or agency).

Persons who collect and maintain personally identifying information must have been trained in the state's policies and procedures for handling the information. An official of each agency is to have the responsibility of protecting the confidentiality of the personally identifying information. This single individual is to collect, store, and disclose information only to appropriate individuals and to destroy the information at the proper time. It would be ideal if this person kept the access to records form (see Exhibit 12-6).

When information is no longer needed to provide for the child's educational service, the public agency is to notify the parent and destroy the information if the parent requests. The public agency is allowed to keep a record of the student's name, address, telephone number, grades, attendance record, classes attended, grade level completed, and year completed for an unlimited amount of time, however.

KEEPING PROGRAMS CURRENT

Anyone who has worked with children knows that it is not possible to plan for a child a year in advance. Children's needs, interests, and skills change, and it is not realistic to expect that the plans once made do not need to be revised frequently. The public agency is required to determine at least annually whether the program that has been planned for the child is providing for the child's educational needs in the most appropriate way. Parents also have the right to ask that the program be revised at any time (*Federal Register,* 1977, p. 24291).

In order to ensure that additional planning time is productive, the teacher and others who work directly with the child must be free to alter the activities as seems appropriate. Penciled notes on the plan could tell of the findings during implementation. The notes might describe a method that worked well with the child, progress that the child has made, or maybe an observation that the child is not really ready to learn the skills described in the plan.

If the public agency personnel keep in touch with the parent, frequent small updates can be made to keep the plan appropriate. Updating and altering the plan does not weaken the concept of an IEP; it simply requires that the plan be flexible and that the parent is continually notified of the child's progress and consents to the school's programming for the child.

REFERENCES

Federal Register. Vol. 42, No. 163. Aug. 23, 1977.

Michaelis, C.T. Personal experience, 1974.

Overgaard, J. Personal communication, October, 1978.

Tallent, N. *Psychological report writing.* Englewood Cliffs, N.J: Prentice-Hall, 1976.

Turnbull, H.T. (Ed.). *Consent handbook.* Special Publication No. 3. Washington, D.C.: American Association on Mental Deficiency, 1977.

Chapter 13

Groups of Parents and Meetings

PTA TONIGHT

If teachers used cuss words "PTA Tonight" might be one of them. Seldom, if ever, did an educator look forward to a meeting with the parents as a group. For an educator, parent meetings are a little like a combination trial and coming out party. Without an attorney and a hostess, the whole experience can be exhausting.

First the classroom must be prepared. The bulletin boards must be changed, of course. It wouldn't be appropriate to have parents come and see last month's calendar. (Why didn't they have the meeting last month? My April Showers calender is much better than my May Flowers. . . unless I have the children make new flowers. . . .) The chalkboards, the students' desks, and, of course, the teacher's desk (and maybe even the closet, unless there is a lock on the door) must be cleaned. There must be some of the students' work on display; not so bad that it is embarrassing and not so good that it looks like the teacher did it. (I can't have them write about their mothers again. That went off so well, but I used it last time.)

The teacher must be ready also. Some scurry around and get their hair cut and perhaps a new dress or shirt. They will be looked over carefully by each parent. (Why didn't I go on that diet last summer?) The teacher must remember to check the records to be sure that the information given to the parent who casually asks about the child will be accurate, especially when the subtle message must be that the child needs further evaluation.

In addition, there are the extra behavior problems that crop up because the children, knowing their parents are coming to school, are concerned about what the teacher might say. The day before and the day after a parent meeting, the students act as if it were the day before and the day after a holiday. But for the teacher, the parent meeting is no holiday!

Father might agree. After having been at work all day, he is probably looking forward to taking off his shoes and watching the game on TV, jogging around the block, fixing the car, or having a game of tennis. Most fathers are not very excited about going to a meeting, especially when the meeting requires that they clean up and wear a tie. For fathers of children who have been experiencing some problems in learning, the meeting will be more than a nuisance. Since fathers gain satisfaction from the achievements of their children and this child does not achieve well at school (see Chapter 5), it is no wonder that many fathers offer to baby-sit and avoid the school atmosphere.

If it were up to educators and fathers, there would probably be very few parent meetings. But a mother's attitude about parent meetings is usually much different. Some mothers make a career of planning parent meetings. Perhaps the strongest meeting planning organization is the Parent Teacher Association. At the organizational meeting held in Washington, D.C. on February 17, 1897, the group was told:

> Let parents, particularly mothers, put in the list of their solemn obligations: (1) frequent visitation of the school attended by their children; (2) thorough acquaintance with the teachers of their children; (3) cooperation with the school plans. (*A Teacher's Guide to the PTA*, 1957, p. 18)

Parent organizations are usually run by the mothers who do not work, and the meetings are not only important as a way to understand the child's schooling but as a social event. For mothers, the trip to the parent meeting is often an opportunity to see and be seen. Since the bulk of the mothering responsibilities takes place in the home and the neighborhood, mothers can become very tired of "staying home."

Mothers can also become very tired of "wearing the same old dress" (or blue jeans). For mother the meeting may be a chance to dress up and have her hair done. An advertisement in a woman's magazine was captioned, "Imagine yourself leading the PTA meeting in this dress." One PTA founder's day program featured a quartet dressed in matching long gowns with matching parasols singing original songs created for the evening. Committees hold special meetings to discuss the refreshments: pink cookies and frappé.

For mothers of children who are having difficulties, the parent group meeting is an opportunity to find someone who has similar problems. Mothers of children who are having learning problems are even more likely to feel the need to meet together. In one midwestern state, mothers of learning disabled children wear long gowns to the annual state dinner.

Fathers and teachers haven't a chance of cancelling the parent meetings, because the mothers are going to "promote the welfare of children and youth in the home, school, church, and community" (*The PTA Organization*, 1944, p. x). And to do that they must meet. Of course the mothers are right (about the meetings, not the pink cookies and long gowns). It is important that the parents see one another and that the educators "report" and display school experiences for the parents, even if it is no holiday.

In order to please the educator, the father, and the mother, a set of compromise rules may be in order for parent meetings:

1. Schedule the meetings well in advance.
2. Plan the total meeting to last no longer than 1½ hours.
3. Have the talk/film/discussion at least as interesting as a TV commercial; have the children do something for or on the program.
4. Send a flyer home the week of the meeting; call the day of the meeting.
5. Have coffee/juice available during the meeting.

TYPES OF PARENT MEETINGS

Parent meetings come in two types: (1) those planned by the parents and (2) those planned by the school. The dichotomy is complete. Even though the same people may be there, meetings planned by the parents have little resemblance to meetings planned by the school.

Parent Meetings Planned by the Parents

Meetings planned by the parents are usually meetings that have been organized because the parents feel a need to be together to support one another and to share their problems. Frequently, at these meetings some improvement in the services for their children is discussed. Although the need for improvement may not be clearly recognized at first, it is clarified when the parents find that they have similar problems both at home and at school. Parents may find ways to solve some of their problems, such as trading baby sitting or taking the child to a doctor recommended by another parent. For the most part, however, parents find that the problem is larger than anticipated and parent meetings uncover more problems than they solve.

Parent meetings can be regular, advertised meetings, or they can be small "coffee in the living room" meetings. Whether the meeting is large or small, regular or occurring only occasionally, parent meetings organized by parents tend to be informal and are usually dominated by the social leader of the community, almost never by *Roberts Rules of Order*.

The advantage of the informal structure is that parents feel freer to express themselves. The problem is that meetings can easily become so disorganized that no consensus about what action to take and how to organize for that action can be reached. However, over time the parent meetings do accomplish important goals. For example, it was largely due to the efforts of parent groups that Public Law (P.L.) 94-142 was passed.

Parent Meetings Planned by the School

For many parents being "invited" to a meeting at school diminishes the desire to attend. Parent meetings organized by school systems are usually organized for specific purposes, such as to explain the new busing procedures, to orientate families to the school, or to explain the bond issue. Meetings organized by the school officials are often in the evening so that fathers can attend. These meetings, which usually have an agenda that is decided by the school administrators, are to last a specific length of time, usually not more than a hour and a half.

School officials usually start the meetings with formal introductions. There is a designated leader who recognizes the participants one by one. Discussions are conducted by the chairperson, who recognizes those who wish to speak and makes a judgment as to how long a topic will be discussed.

The formality of the meetings organized by the school may make parents uncomfortable about expressing themselves. The meetings almost always are presentations of information to the parents rather than exchanges of information between the school and the parents.

Dual Purpose Parent Meetings

Organizing a meeting in which both the parent and the school are comfortable and able to interact is a difficult process, especially since school personnel are frequently more familiar with the meeting procedures. Working toward the goal of meetings that meet the needs of parents as well as professionals would appear to be worthwhile. Although working with parents always requires that there are individual conferences with parents about the progress of their children, there are many kinds of information that can be exchanged with parents as a group.

Since a carefully structured group meeting can produce a great deal of information, it can be not only a problem-presenting situation, but also a problem-solving situation. The preparation of an annual program plan to describe the services to be delivered to the handicapped children of the state requires that the parents have input in the preparation of that plan. Parents have a variety of contacts with various businesses and suppliers, and they may be able to solve some of the school problems, if they have an opportunity to understand the problems. Meetings could cover the bus route problems, how to obtain funds to hire a physical therapist, or how to get a kitchen so that the handicapped students can learn to cook.

A CONTINUUM OF PARENT MEETINGS

Parent groups have a variety of purposes. There may be times when it is appropriate for the parents to meet without the professionals, just as the faculty of a school meets frequently, to define their problems and discuss ways of dealing with them. Other times, it may be important for the public agency personnel to meet with the parents in small groups so that more people can express themselves. Larger group meetings could be held to report the ideas generated in the small group meetings or present information to be discussed in the small groups. Some of the meetings might be led most effectively by school agency personnel; some, by parents.

The Small Discussion Group

The Classroom Group

The most likely group to form a small discussion group are the parents of children in an individual classroom. The needs and concerns of the children in that classroom can be discussed. Although back to school night presentations tell about activities in the classroom, parents seldom ask the teacher questions. One resource room teacher prepared for her meeting with the parents by taking 35-mm slides of the children working. She then showed the slides to the parents to help explain what she was doing in her classroom. When the parents saw the pictures of their own child, it was easier to talk about exactly what the child was doing.

Another special education classroom teacher meets monthly with the parents of the children in her class. They talk about what has been going on in the classroom, and the teacher asks for whatever help she might need. Sometimes it is an Indian costume for the school play; sometimes it is shelves or partitions for study carrells. Usually, she doesn't need to ask for help; the parents volunteer. They feel that they are working with the teacher since the planning of the projects is shared (Neal, 1970).

The Special Interest Group

The small group meeting could be arranged not for parents whose children are in the same classroom, but for parents who have similar interests. The preschool parent group met to talk about ways to discipline the child at home. The parents were interested in finding ways to get the child to "mind." The group discussed the need for continuous rules at home and some of the things that parents could have the children do that were "good."

Small Groups within Larger Groups

Sometimes large groups are divided into small groups so that all members of the group can share ideas. This has frequently been an effective means of gathering information. Someone is assigned to record the ideas that are spontaneously generated and report to the larger group. The information can be recorded on large chart paper so that the listeners can read the charts as the information is summarized. The information can also be written in notebooks or notecards. For some formal purposes the information can be summarized, edited, and published. This is a particularly effective means of collecting personalized information from a large group of people.

School-Sized Meetings

Parents who send their children to the same school share some camaraderie. The condition of the school is a source of pride for the families. Parents have been known to get together to help plant the lawn on the playground or to lobby for a street light on a busy corner. Parents have had bake sales to purchase a new projector for the school or a swing set for the playground. Parents have lobbied for more education funds and seat belts for the school buses. Parents cannot help solve the problem, however, if they do not know about it and feel part of the school.

Although these meetings may be organized by the school system, it may be wise to have one of the parents help conduct the meeting. The less formality, the more participation from the parents.

Formal Hearings for Gathering Information

In the long run, publicly advertised hearings are frequently the simplest way to gather information from the public. It is wise to have someone who is pleasant, but firm, to direct the meeting and to have another person to time each speaker's comments. If feelings about the topic have been explosive, it may be a good idea to have uniformed police in attendance.

If the purpose of the meeting is to gather information from the public, the meeting should be publicly advertised for several weeks before it takes place and should be held in a large, easily accessible meeting room. Tape recording of comments makes it possible to have an accurate record of the information presented. Recording equipment must be in good working order, and funds must be available to hire someone to transcribe the tape. Since it is a public meeting, the transcript of any recording must be available to the public. Although this process may appear complex, it may be one of the simplest methods of gathering information necessary to generate support for a state program plan.

COOPERATION WITH ORGANIZED PARENT GROUPS

To Meet the Parent's Need

Professionals attending meetings organized by parents are "guests." It is important that professionals attend, especially when they are invited to do so. Parents frequently invite a professional to attend a meeting and make a presentation on a topic of interest to the group. In this event, the professional should speak on the specified topic for the specified amount of time and give the parents an accurate summary of current knowledge on the subject under discussion.

Parent groups are very selective when they invite a speaker. The professional who rambles about "war stories" will probably not be invited back, and the agency that this professional represents loses status with the parents. If rapport is to be built between the agency and the parent group, professionals must approach a speech to the parent group with as much commitment as they approach a presentation of material to a conference of colleagues.

Professionals who attend meetings of parent groups without being specifically invited should be prepared to be welcomed by the group with perhaps less enthusiasm than the members welcome one another. Since the parents have usually shared life experiences and experiences within the group, they are likely to treat the professional as an outsider and may reject unsolicited opinions, just as educators frequently reject unsolicited suggestions from the parent.

To Meet the School's Need

There may be times when school officials want to contact the parents of children in the school to explain issues or ask for assistance with a project. One of the most efficient ways of doing this is to contact the parent groups. Many parent groups have organized a telephone chain system in which one member calls the next member. Professionals may also request an opportunity to talk to the parents at the parent meeting.

The parent group meetings are an ideal forum for discussing preliminary plans about new school buildings and equipment, proposed school lunch programs, or changes in the length of the school day. Since the meeting is organized and directed by the parents, it is more likely that the parents' true feelings will be discussed. Active members of most parent groups are also leaders of the community in other respects and can be influential in making arrangements for improvements in the school system.

Organizing Parent Groups

One of the most effective methods of counseling and training parents "to assist the handicapped child to benefit from special education" (*Federal Register*, 1977, p. 42479) is for the school agency to form special interest parent groups. Parents who need similar assistance or training could be grouped in small informal classes. To be effective the class must be small enough to permit open discussion.

From time to time, parents mention to the teacher that they are interested in having the child learn a particular skill or that they are interested in learning how to teach the child. (Parents are likely to ask for help in teaching the child by asking for help in "disciplining" the child.)

For new parents or parents who have not had much opportunity to learn parenting skills, it may be important to discuss the principles of child development and effective ways to train the child in social skills. Along with home training, the Marshalltown Project provides classes for the parent in general techniques of child rearing. The parent manual is filled with finger plays and suggestions for the parents to use with the children. The manual can be purchased from the project (Marshalltown Project, 1973).

In Omaha, Nebraska, there is a parent organization in which parents are trained to work with other parents. The more experienced parents are assigned to "parent" the new parents. The families share potluck suppers and lengthy telephone conversations. The Pilot Parent project has been copied in other places and has proved to be an effective model.

Having parents support one another can be very effective, but in some localities the parents need some assistance in becoming acquainted with one another. There have been some parent assistance projects that have received grant funds to provide transportation for the parent who cannot otherwise get to the school, the doctor's office, or the shopping center. It would not be inappropriate to offer payments to one parent for providing services to another parent.

If there is no active parent group affiliated with a larger organization in the area, it may be wise for the school agency to assist in the organization of such a parent group. The following list shows some of the national organizations of parents of exceptional children:

- AUTISM

  National Society for Autistic Children
  1234 Massachusetts Avenue, N.W.
  Suite 1017
  Washington, D.C. 20005

- BLIND

  American Council of the Blind
  1211 Connecticut Avenue, N.W.
  Washington, D.C. 20036

  American Foundation for the Blind
  15 West 16th Street
  New York, New York 10011

  National Association for Visually Handicapped
  305 East 24th Street
  New York, New York 10010

  National Federation for the Blind
  1346 Connecticut Avenue, N.W.

Dupont Circle Building, Suite 212
Washington, D.C. 20036

- CEREBRAL PALSY

United Cerebral Palsy Association
66 East 34th Street
New York, New York 10016

- DEAF

Alexander .Graham Bell Association for the Deaf
3417 Volta Place, N.W.
Washington, D.C. 20007

National Association of the Deaf
814 Thayer Avenue
Silver Spring, Maryland 20910

- DEAF-BLIND

National Association of the Deaf-Blind
2703 Forest Oak Circle
Norman, Oklahoma 73071

National Deaf-Blind Program
Bureau of Education for the Handicapped
Room 4046, Donohoe Building
400 6th Street, S.W.
Washington, D.C. 20202

- EMOTIONALLY DISTURBED

Mental Health Association, National Headquarters
1800 North Kent Street
Arlington, Virginia 22209

- EPILEPSY

Epilepsy Foundation of America
1828 L Street, N.W.
Washington, D.C. 20036

- HEALTH IMPAIRMENTS

Allergy Foundation of America
801 Second Avenue
New York, New York 10017

American Cancer Society
777 Third Avenue
New York, New York 10017

American Heart Association
7320 Greenville Avenue
Dallas, Texas 75231

The Candlelighters Foundation
123 C Street, S.E.
Washington, D.C. 20003

Cystic Fibrosis Foundation
3379 Peachtree Road, N.E.
Atlanta, Georgia 30326

Juvenile Diabetes Foundation
23 East 26th Street
New York, New York 10010

National Hemophilia Foundation
25 West 39th Street
New York, New York 10018

National Kidney Foundation
Two Park Avenue
New York, New York 10016

National Tay-Sachs Foundation and Allied Diseases Association
122 East 42nd Street
New York, New York 10017

- LEARNING DISABILITIES

Association for Children with Learning Disabilities
4156 Library Road
Pittsburgh, Pennsylvania 15234

The Orton Society, Inc.
8415 Bellona Lane
Suite 115
Towson, Maryland 21204

- MENTAL RETARDATION

Down's Syndrome Congress
1802 Johnson Drive
Normal, Illinois 61761

National Association for Retarded Citizens
2709 Avenue E East
P.O. Box 6109
Arlington, Texas 76011

- PHYSICALLY HANDICAPPED

  Arthritis Foundation
  3400 Peachtree Road, N.E.
  Atlanta, Georgia 30326

  Little People of America
  P.O. Box 126
  Owatonna, Minnesota 55060

  Muscular Dystrophy Association, Inc.
  810 Seventh Avenue
  New York, New York 10019

  National Multiple Sclerosis Society
  205 East 42nd Street
  New York, New York 10017

  National Spinal Cord Injury Foundation
  369 Elliot Street
  Newton Upper Falls, Massachusetts 02164

  Spina Bifida Association of America
  343 South Dearborn Street
  Room 319
  Chicago, Illinois 60604

- SPEECH IMPAIRMENTS

  American Speech—Language and Hearing Association
  10801 Rockville Pike
  Rockville, Maryland 20852

- ALL DISABILITIES

  Association for the Severely Handicapped
  1600 West Armory Way
  Garden View Suite
  Seattle, Washington 98119

  American Coalition for Citizens with Disabilities
  1200 15th Street, N.W.
  Suite 201
  Washington, D.C. 20005

  National Easter Seal Society for Crippled Children and Adults
  2023 W. Ogden Avenue
  Chicago, Illinois 60612

  National Foundation—March of Dimes
  1275 Mamaroneck Avenue
  White Plains, New York 10605

WHO SHOULD DIRECT THE PARENT GROUPS?

Informing without Insulting

Formal training in counseling does not automatically prepare a counselor to understand and work with people who have vastly different life styles and life experiences. After one public health nurse who had worked with parents of handicapped children for a number of years gave birth to a set of twins, she remarked that she would like to go back to the parents and apologize since she now realized that she was expecting too much from them. It is difficult for a young or inexperienced person to understand the intensity of parenting.

One elementary school principal remarked that, although there have always been edicts that mothers should stay home to take care of the children, he thought that mothers made better teachers and hoped that some would choose to teach when their children became school age. He felt that parents were better able to understand the children at school and build long-term relationships with them, and were better able to work with the children's parents (Bailey, 1969).

It may not be possible for someone who is not a parent to empathize with the parent. Relating to the complexities of parenting normal children requires skill and experience, but relating to the cognitive, emotional, and social pressures of parenting a handicapped child requires not only training, but personal and professional experience.

One preschool director expressed the belief that, although a certain person had the skills to work with the child, the child's mother would not accept the woman as a counselor. Working with parents in a group requires even more than skill and experience; counseling requires teaching and parenting. The leader of the class for parents and the speaker at the parent meeting should not be chosen casually. Care should be taken to ensure that the individual chosen has had as much personal and professional experience as possible. The individual should also have a life experience similar to that of the parents. Not only must the leader "speak the same language," but also the leader must have experience with a similar cultural life style.

In her book, *Children Who Should Not Be in School,* High (1957) states that one of the reasons she could be objective about excluding children who did not learn easily from school was that she was an "old maid" and did not have any children. Only then could she be objective. When working with parents, however, objectivity is a handicap. Interest in the exceptional child and personal experience in the parenting role are as important to success in working with parents as is the professional training.

Some agencies have created the position of parent liaison. Although all personnel in the agency have responsibilities to communicate with the parents of the children in school, this one carefully chosen individual coordinates the interaction. (See Chapter 14.)

Making and Keeping the Atmosphere Comfortable

To educators, the school building is as familiar as their own living rooms. Walking through the halls and sitting in the multipurpose room are mundane experiences. For most parents, however, the school carries a little of the same aura that it had when they were first graders; it is someone else's domain. If parent meetings held in the school are to be productive, the parents need to feel comfortable in the school.

Although many schools keep all but the front door locked for security purposes, this is not common knowledge among parents. To come to a meeting and find the doors locked can dampen the spirits of many parents. Someone should be stationed at each door to greet parents coming to the meeting. If it is not possible to have all the doors open, perhaps a poster showing a diagram of the school and indicating which doors are open could be placed at the locked doors. If parents have hurried to feed the children and organize things at home to come to school and then find they must walk around an unfamiliar building in the dark looking for an open door, it won't matter if the meeting inside is well organized.

It is also important to have someone stand by the inside door of the meeting room to welcome the parents. There are many doors inside a school, and all of the doors look alike to someone who doesn't walk the hall regularly.

Printed programs, even if they have only been copied on the ditto machine, are helpful. They might contain only the announcements and an outline of the program. Handing a program to the parents as they come in helps them feel welcome. Students may greet parents at the door and distribute programs, particularly if a school person serves as "head usher." Program covers can be made by the children. Having invitations written by the students and having students on the program have long been known as effective methods of increasing attendance.

Name tags help people become acquainted. A table in the hall or well inside the meeting room should be set up for them. They should include the parents' first names. If the group is to be divided into small groups, symbols or colors on the name tags can be used to designate the groups, although care must be taken to distribute them evenly so the groups will have similar numbers of people.

Of course, the meeting room must be an appropriate size for the meeting, not too large or too small. If chairs are to be set up, they should be in place well before the parents are due to arrive. Coming into a huge, cluttered room does not help the parent feel welcome in the school.

Although most parents visit with one another during the few minutes preceding the meeting, it is pleasant to have some background music before and after the meeting. The music could be recorded or played on the piano. If the music before the meeting is performed by children, however, parents may feel that they are late and the program has already started. The children's performance should be saved for the actual program. Slides of children working and playing in school could accompany the music for important meetings. Slides of parents participating in projects or at previous meetings could also be shown.

Making the meeting as enjoyable as possible can increase its effectiveness. For variety, parents can be asked to sit alphabetically, next to a paper banner with the teacher's name on it, or according to their zodiac sign. Sometimes a sing-along session can add interest. Awards can be given to parents for real or make-believe achievements. Door prizes donated by merchants or created by students can be given. Occasionally, the organizers of the meeting may want to plant some questions for parents to ask. Changing the format of the meeting is sometimes effective. Occasionally, a potluck dinner for the whole family attracts more participants. Obviously, these meetings have a short formal program and more informal interaction.

It might be helpful to have refreshments available throughout the meeting. A cup of coffee helps many people relax, but juice should be available for the non-coffee drinkers. Parents will probably be willing to take turns providing the refreshments if funds are not available, although money for simple refreshments for parent meetings is a legitimate budget item.

Topics for Parent Meetings

Parents are interested in two general topics: (1) how to help their children progress and (2) how to be effective parents without being consumed in the process. Programs planned to show the parents that the school is their ally in raising children can enhance the parents' image of the school.

Most professionals are serious about their work and tend to plan programs for parents that relate to the seriousness of the parenting role; however, programs should be much more than lectures. In order to carry the desired message, the program must be planned as carefully as the situation comedies and television commercials that it is replacing.

It is important to remember that parents are adults and have frequently had more life experience than the beginning teacher. The parent must be treated as a peer rather than as another student. Although the parent may not have had training in child development and child psychology and may not interact with the child in the most effective manner, the parent does have other skills that may be more sophisticated than the skills that the teacher has.

Parenting a handicapped child takes almost more than 24 hours a day and is an emotionally and physically exhausting experience. If program titles are catchy and the presentation is relaxed and entertaining, perhaps with some role playing and humorous lines, the families can think about applying the ideas to their own homes. If the presentation shows a household where no one ever spills the milk or runs out of clean socks, the parents will probably not be able to relate to it.

Topics should be worded in such a way that the parent can look at the child-rearing problems and smile. The age of their child is a cue to the kind of information that particular parents will be interested in hearing. Parents of young children may respond to a child development series called "Living with Toddlers. . . and Liking It!" with the following titles:

- Mealtime Madness
- Bedtime Blues
- Naptime Nuisance
- Playtime Problems
- Toileting Troubles
- Toys That Teach
- Regulating with Routines
- Knowing About "No"

Parents of school age children may be interested in a series called "Helping Your Child Succeed in School":

- The Morning Rush Hour
- Preparing for Reading
- Readin', Writin', and 'Rithmetic
- Dress for Success
- The Television Triangle: TV/the Child/Homework
- Foods and Behavior

Other individual programs could center around the parent's need to discipline or teach the child. Topics might include:

- How to get Johnny to go to bed at night (and get up in the morning!)
- How to keep Johnny and Betty from fighting
- How to get Johnny to eat his carrots (and beans, and potatoes, and milk. . .)
- What to do on a rainy day
- How much TV?
- Johnny is afraid of the dark
- How to get Johnny to take a bath
- He won't come when I call!

Programs designed to give parents more information about what they can do to keep the child "busy" with learning activities can be appealing to parents:

- story time: puppets, flannel stories, scrapbooks
- scissors, crayons, and colored paper

- tricycles, wagons, skateboards, and old tires
- wooden blocks of all sizes
- games to play in the car
- teaching by cooking

Other programs might give parents suggestions about how to train the child to be responsible for chores around the house:

- Who takes out the trash?
- Well, even puppies need to eat: pets in the house.
- I can make my bed, comb my hair, hang up the towel, and set the table!
- What is an allowance?

Parents are also interested in programs of general information:

- The History of Public Law 94-142 (and special class in _____district_____)
- What Is Adapted Physical Education?
- What Is an IEP?
- Friends at School: What Is a Peer?

Children on the Program

One of the most effective ways of getting the parents to come to a meeting is to have the children present part of the program. Since parents enjoy seeing their children perform, it is not necessary for the program to be elaborate, with costumes that cause more work for mother and expense for father. The children may perform for only a few minutes, and arrangements must be made to have someone, usually a teacher, supervise the children during the rest of the program. A Walt Disney or travel film from the media center and some light refreshment are usually enough entertainment for the children.

Having the children perform is usually considered an elementary school practice, and handicapped adolescents are seldom given an opportunity to perform. Programs planned to give them a chance to perform, usher, or serve could be most rewarding to the students and the parents, however. Handicapped students can also help prepare for the program by making invitations (Exhibit 13-1), programs, and advertising posters. Making the materials could be part of the language and art curriculum.

Parents of handicapped children usually enjoy watching the children of other parents perform also, particularly if they have been going to parent groups together for years, as many of them have. The parents "adopt" the other children and share the joy of their success with the parents.

Exhibit 13-1 Sample Invitation

Dear Mom and Dad:

The _____ School

Presents

TV or Not TV: What Is the Question?

Starring: Jane Anderson
        from Ms. Smith's room

    John Williams
        from Mr. Johnson's room

And an All Star Cast from the Third Grade

Tuesday,   January 31, 1980   7:30 to 9 P.M.

Love:

Your Child

Musical Activities for Children on Parent Programs

Singing is perhaps easiest for everyone, since it can involve either small or large groups and either a little or a lot of practice. If the children have difficulty pronouncing the words, they can sing along with the records. Kimbo Educational Adaptive Behavior—Self Help Skills (Michaelis, 1979a) and Adaptive Behavior—Socialization Skills (Michaelis, 1979b) albums have simple songs that children can pantomime as they sing. Children who cannot speak well can do the movements of the songs. Children with physical disabilities may be able to use bells or sand blocks to produce the rhythm.

Dancing, either round, partner, or square dances, can also be effective. There must be enough space for the children to dance, however; rather than move chairs back and forth to make a large dance floor in the multipurpose room, the same dance could be repeated with different children dancing.

Although the teacher will want to practice enough so that the children are not confused, it is not necessary to polish the production. Part of the fun for the children and the parents is the spontaneity of the program.

Reciting and Minidrama

Poems such as those in the basal readers can be recited or pantomimed. Dr. Seuss books have interesting messages. The teacher or one of the students could read aloud while the other students pantomime the actions. Classic children's stories could be altered for the occasion; for example, Mother and Father Bear could have gone to the local school while the porridge was cooling.

Role playing or miniplays can be interesting to parents. The Night the Crayons Talked has a cast of children who display the feelings of the colors (Spiegel, 1978). Other plays can be "written" by the children. Many exceptional children can express by acting what they find difficult to read and write. The following is a sample miniplay:

TV OR NOT TV: WHAT IS THE QUESTION?

Cast: Mother, Father, son Joe, and daughter Jane
All cast members could be students, a real family could be used, or a family could be created of one parent from one family and one parent from another. If students are used, practice is simpler, and "any resemblance" is not a problem. If students are too young or do not speak clearly, they can pantomime to a tape-recorded reading.

Living room, FATHER, JOE, and JANE *sitting on couch.* [A couch and overstuffed chairs can be created by using several folding chairs covered with a bedspread or a throw. Place a sofa pillow on the couch. A real TV set could be used or one could be made of cardboard. The set could be designed so that a student could kneel behind it and the face of the student could appear as the "picture." Several students could take turns being the "TV star."]

MOTHER: *(Comes from the kitchen, wiping her hands on her apron.)*
MOTHER: I'm hurrying to finish the dishes before the John Wayne movie starts.
JANE: Oh, Mother, I wanted to watch the beauty pageant. It starts at 7:30. You said you already saw that movie anyway.
MOTHER: I know, but there are so few movies that I like to watch.
JANE: Mother. . .
FATHER: Now wait a minute you girls, the football game starts at 7:30, and you know that Monday nights are the football nights.
JOE: Sure, Dad and I always like to watch.
FATHER: Sure, it is one of the things that I like to share with my son. *(Puts arm on Joe's shoulder)*
JOE: *(Beams)*
JANE: That's not fair; who wants to watch those dumb games every week?
MOTHER: John, I don't even want to watch most movies.
JOE: But tonight is the most important game of the season.
JANE: You say that about all games, and they are all the same. Someone takes the ball *(Picks up sofa pillow)* and runs this way, then that way—(JOE *tackles* JANE)
FATHER: Stop that. You two get up. Now look, I've worked hard all day, and I deserve a little peace and rest.

MOTHER: Well, I have been working hard all day and I deserve some relaxation, too.

JANE: You just don't want me to see how to be beautiful. No one around here likes me. . . *(Leaves room crying)*

JOE: Ah, gee, doesn't anyone understand? *(Walks out the other side of the stage)*

MOTHER: What was that all about? You would think that TV was everything.

FATHER: Well, sometimes we act like it is.

MOTHER: What else could we do?

FATHER: Well, I guess I could balance the checkbook.

MOTHER: I have some mending to do.

JANE: *(Walks in)* I'm sorry I was so nasty. I just remembered that I need to study my spelling. After I study for a while, will you give me the words?

JOE: *(Walks in with math book)* Well, I suppose if I can't watch the game, I might as well do my math. Can you help me, Dad?

(FATHER walks over to son and puts his arm around shoulders of both children. Family walks off stage.)

After the play, the chairperson might say:

> It is marvelous to have TV bring all those interesting things right into the living room, but it can also be a little like having a guest all the time; nobody gets any work done. There are some times when the TV set keeps the family from visiting with one another. There are also some shows that are not particularly good for children to watch. And, of course, some children watch TV so much that it interferes with their sleep, their studying, and even their learning to get along with the other people in the family and the neighborhood. We can't expect our children to use the TV set any better than we do.
>
> We are going to divide into groups now and talk about several things:
>
> 1. How much should children and parents watch TV?
> 2. What are good shows to watch?
> 3. What are some things that parents and children can do together that are fun, besides watching TV?

At this point in the program, the large group should be divided into groups of four to ten people. The groups can be made by giving each person a colored name tag as they come in, by counting off, or by assigning those who are sitting next to one another to groups. Husbands and wives should be in separate groups, however. It is wise to assign people to groups rather than to tell the audience to assign themselves. Frequently, this causes some people to leave since they feel that they are not needed.

The amount of time for discussion is usually limited to 20 to 30 minutes. A reporter for each group can record what is said. After the discussion, each recorder reports a summary of what the group discussed. A summary of the total thought can be printed in the newsletter, made into a handout or booklet, or presented at the next meeting.

Resources for Parent Meetings

Since parents have a variety of needs and interests, schools sometimes maintain a library of reference materials for parents. Some things that might be particularly interesting for parent meetings would be:

- Films: *Like Other People, Try Another Way, Graduation, A Day in the Life of Bonnie Consolo*
- Books: Smith, Landon: *Improving Your Child's Behavior Chemistry*
- Journals: *The Exceptional Parent*

SCHEDULING PARENT MEETINGS

Monday and Friday are busy days at home, just as they are in school. Tuesday, Wednesday, or Thursday are better days for meetings. Since parents must feed the children, etc., before they leave, meetings that start before 7:30 make it necessary for the family to rush. Most parents want to get home by 9:00 or 9:30 to be sure that the children are down for the night. It is helpful for the parent to know not only when the meeting will start, but how long the meeting will last.

Saturday afternoon meetings have been successful, especially when the whole family is invited. Since parenting is frequently seen as a spiritual experience, many parents are willing to attend meetings on Sunday. Parents of one boarding school had meetings on Sunday evenings when they brought the children back to the institution. Saturday and Sunday meetings have a disadvantage for the professional, however, since there is usually no additional reimbursement. Parents have difficulty attending meetings close to Christmas/New Year or Easter or any other religious or civic holiday.

MEETING NEEDS THROUGH MEETINGS

If the needs of the school are to be met through parent meetings, the school personnel must understand what parent meetings mean to the parent and organize the meetings so that the parent needs as well as the school needs are being filled. Parents who have not had contact with the school system since they themselves were students may have some leftover personal feelings about school personnel that they will transfer to the personnel of the school in which their child is a student. Even if the parents were successful in school, they remember that the role of a student requires respect for the teacher. One man tells the story of how disappointed he was when he saw his favorite elementary school teacher go into the ladies' room one day. He reported that until that day he had thought that she was immortal. Parents who themselves had difficulty as students may remember the feeling of defeat and feel as if the cards are stacked against them when they enter the school.

Parents and school officials must be comfortable with one another in order to work together. All school personnel know that there are no immortal co-workers. Although it is not necessary to portray the school personnel as inept, it is important to help the parent accept their strengths and limitations. Many parents are expecting the school to perform miracles for their children, particularly if the children are having learning problems. (See Chapter 4.)

Meeting together is one of the best ways to learn to understand and accept one another. Since all of the actions taken with an exceptional child are subject to parent approval and consent can be revoked at any time, it is important for the parent to feel comfortable in the school setting. Good parent meetings can create a "yellow brick road" to the school. So spruce up the bulletin board and go on a diet. The parents are coming!

REFERENCES

A Day in the life of Bonnie Consolo. (film) BARR Films, P.O. Box 7-c, Pasadena, CA 91104.

A Teacher's guide to the PTA. Chicago: National Congress of Parents and Teachers, 1957.

Bailey, J. Personal communication. 1969.

Closer Look Information Center. P.O. Box 1492, Washington, D.C. 20013, Nov. 1979.

Federal Register. Vol. 42, No. 163. Aug. 23, 1977.

Graduation. (film) Stanfield House, 900 Euclid, Santa Monica, CA 90403.

High, J. E. *Children who should not be in school*. New York: Exposition Press, 1957.

Like other people. (film) Perennial Education. 1825 Willow Road. Northfield, Ill. 60093.

Marshalltown Project. 507 East Anson Street, Marshalltown, Iowa 50158, 1973.

Michaelis, C. T. *Adaptive Behavior–Self Help Album and Teacher's Manual*, KIM 8055. Long Branch, N.J., 1979. (a)

Michaelis, C. T. *Adaptive Behavior – Socialization Album and Teacher's Manual*, KIM 8056. Long Branch, N.J., 1979. (b)

Neal, L. Personal communication. Oct. 1970.

Smith, L. *Improving your child's behavior chemistry*. Englewood Cliffs, N.J.: Prentice-Hall, 1976.

Spiegel, C. The night the crayons talked. *Teacher*, 1978, *96*, 44-45.

The Exceptional Parent. Psy-Ed Corporation. Room 700 Statler Office Building. Boston, MA 02116.

The Parent-teacher organization: Its origins and development. Chicago: National Congress of Parents and Teachers, 1944.

Try another way. (film) Film Productions of Indianapolis, 128 E. 36th St., Indianapolis, Ind. 46204.

Chapter 14

Presenting a United Front: Having Your House in Order

Professional literature is full of accounts of parents of exceptional children going from professional to professional to find one who will say what they want to hear. It may be that what the parents are actually shopping for is someone who will talk to them in the way they want to hear. Most parents don't mind hearing an honest "I don't know" (Schultz, 1978), and many times that is the most accurate answer.

Parents not only shop for professional comments, but also for nonprofessional comments. Since the social structure outside of the school system is not the same as the one inside the system, parents may have just as much or more respect for the opinion of the nonprofessional school personnel as for the opinion of those with graduate training in child development. The school secretary may be the banker's wife, the bus driver may have a farm, and the school lunch lady may have gone to high school with Grandma and returned to work after she raised her family. Parents are just as interested in these people's opinions about their child as they are the teacher's and principal's opinions. It is important to realize the impact of all of the school personnel on the parent.

There are two people in the school system that may be more important to the parent than the principal, the teacher, the therapist, or any of the other professional personnel. In sheer number of parent contacts, the bus driver probably has the most. The second highest number of parent contacts probably involve the school secretary. In order for the parents to feel good about the child's school program, they must feel good about all the people that are with the child.

GENERAL PROGRAM FOR PARENT CONTACTS

Since informed consent requires the public agency to provide education for the exceptional child with "satisfaction guaranteed" or the program is "refunded," the public agency should have a plan about how to deal with the parent. The parent is a combination depositor, client, patient, customer of the school system: all in one. The PTA's term is patron, which implies an honored guardian of the institution. In order to interact effectively with the "honored guardian," it is necessary that all of the personnel in the agency have training in (a) being open and accepting of the parent in spite of the child's problems and (b) maintaining confidentiality about those problems.

A secretary with a pleasant telephone voice and a bus driver who waves each morning can increase the parents' satisfaction with the school program. To be effective, school employees must know how the parents might be seeing them and how to respond. Employees also need to know the schools' organizational structure for dealing with children who have learning problems, something about what the parents are experiencing, and ways that they might be officially or informally helpful with the educational goals. Each school employee should be recognized for such services to parents.

Most professional and nonprofessional staff have some direct contact with parents, but even those who don't are sending nonverbal messages. It is important that staff people see how they can contribute to the total message sent to the parent. Some of the messages will be direct messages about the child's work at school; others will be subtle messages about how they see themselves in relation to those who are less than perfect. Parents will be receiving messages from professional staff, nonprofessional staff, from the PTA, and even from the other students.

INDIVIDUALIZED PARENT CONTACTS

Parents have individualized needs. Certain school agency personnel could be asked to perform more than the routine interaction with some parents. For example, the bus driver might be asked to keep the child's day-to-day notebook in a special pocket on the bus (built by the teacher to hold the notebook). The teacher could put the notebook in the pocket each day, and the bus driver could see that the notebook was given to the parent each afternoon and collected from the parent each morning. (See Chapter 8.) For a child on a special diet, the lunch lady might be asked to refrigerate and measure the child's special foods. As each role is listed, suggestions are given for potential interaction with parents. The activities can be mixed and matched, according to the combination of child and parent needs.

THE PROFESSIONAL CONTACTS

The Principal

The principal's willingness to accept the handicapped child in the school will set the tone for the general feeling about having "those children" in the school. If the principal is able to see the child as a challenge to expand the educational services of the school and his or her personal competence as an administrator, the child and the parents will be received as an opportunity rather than a burden. A principal who believes that the school is for the parents of the community is also likely to believe that it is necessary to interact cordially with all of the parents.

Facilities for Special Children

In a general sense, the principal communicates to the staff of the school and to the parents of handicapped children a personal interest in the children by the facilities that are assigned to the special students. For many years, the special education personnel have worked in restored broom closets and portable classrooms. They have had last choice on the schedules for lunch time and the multipurpose room. The special education classroom has usually been the one that was not wired for the intercom. All of these subtle messages tell the faculty, the children, and their parents that the children with learning problems are of low priority to the administration.

Attitude toward All Parents

If the administrator considers all parents an important part of the total school setting, it is easier to accept the parents of children who are having difficulties in the school system. The principal can communicate an interest in the parents' needs by returning their telephone calls as promptly as he/she returns telephone calls that come from the superintendent.

The principal can communicate an interest in the child's difficulties by discussing them in a nonjudgmental, objective manner. If the principal has not had an opportunity to learn about the child's problems, it would be wise to tell the parent and then investigate by discussing the child with the teachers involved and by personally observing the child, just as would be done in response to the superintendent's request for information.

Implementation of the Individualized Program

Unless the principal chooses to designate the responsibility to someone else, the principal is responsible for conducting the Individual Education Program (IEP) meeting. It is an administrative responsibility to process the forms and make sure that all the contacts are made. In order to be able to conduct these meetings and to ensure that the total plan is implemented, the principal must become personally acquainted with the child and the child's educational history. It would be vital for the principal to have read the child's Developmental History Form (see Exhibit 7-1) and Home Observation Summaries (see Exhibits 7-4 through 7-6) and to have observed the child in the classroom. The principal must make the necessary administrative arrangements to provide the related services that are planned in the meeting. If the principal does not participate in the planning and does not monitor the implementation of the plan, it is a message to the parent that the whole process is a charade. Parents who feel that they have been pacified may become dissatisfied and angry.

Monitoring the Child's Program

Programs that require a number of people to work together do not automatically run smoothly, even if the plans have been made carefully. The principal who drops in frequently to see how the program is going and makes a brief report to the parents shows respect for the parents and reaffirms interest. If the program is not going well, it is better to know before a crisis spotlights everyone's discomfort.

If in the observation, the principal sees that part of the program does not work well, a minimeeting can be organized in the hall, over lunch, in the workroom, or wherever the people involved can be pulled together. Telling the parents the results of a minimeeting can create a whole ledger sheet of brownie points. Mothers, especially (see Chapter 5), like to know exactly what the child is doing at each hour of the day and appreciate being told about even minor schedule changes.

One of the problems encountered by most children with learning problems is transportation to and from school. Some children with learning problems must ride a series of buses; others ride a different bus from the one that their siblings ride. Others cannot remember where the bus is parked or the number of the bus. Since the teachers and bus drivers are busy with many children at bus times, knowing that the principal will make sure the child gets on the right bus could make the parents feel more comfortable about the child's schooling.

In-Service Training for Faculty and Staff

Although there may be system-wide in-service training scheduled several times a year, it will probably not emphasize the routine procedures of the particular school building. The principal should have sessions for the faculty and for the staff to introduce the forms and routines to be followed in the school. Since teachers and others have so many responsibilities, these meetings must be brief to be effective. The sessions could be presented at regular faculty meetings or at other planned times.

Although the professional staff may have regular in-service training about child and family needs, seldom is this planned for the nonprofessional staff. When the impact of the nonprofessional staff on the parent is recognized, the need for "professional" interaction by nonprofessional staff becomes obvious.

If the principal directs or attends all sessions, it will be possible to discuss problems and misconceptions and keep them from growing. These sessions may also be appropriate times to discuss specific assignments for the faculty or staff for nonteaching or related service responsibilities toward a particular child.

Response to Misbehavior

There are times when any child's behavior is exasperating. If the child is exceptional, the times occur more frequently, and the behavior tends to disrupt the activities of others. It is easy to respond to the frustration with anger and to punish or suspend the child. Although parents are prone to respond to the same behavior in the child with the same "natural" response, the principal cannot afford such a personal reaction and must respond with the composure of a professional. It is never appropriate to set a punishment or impose suspension on the child without talking the situation over with the parents. If the principal does, the parents don't forget.

There are also times when parents' behavior is exasperating. Parents of children who are experiencing difficulties at school appear to have more of these times than other parents. The principal cannot afford to act in anger toward the parent, either. Expressing anger toward parents who are dissatisfied with school programs is a sure way to give the parent a reason to withdraw consent.

The Social Worker/Parent Liaison

If the school agency has a social worker, the social worker could serve as coordinator for parent services. If the school does not have a trained social worker, a person without specific professional training could serve as a coordinator to arrange for the professional service and to follow through on the administrative/clerical arrangements. If the liaison person attended the IEP conference and other conferences as requested, the individual would be able to see a clearer picture of the agency's needs in communication with the parents and the parents' needs in communication with the agency. For some families there will need to be contacts made to other agencies to assist with services to the families. Although the principal can assume this role personally, programming will run smoother if a specific individual is designated to follow through on those contacts.

Building Rapport with the Family

If the family feels that someone at school "understands," it is possible to discuss concerns and problems without anger and confrontation. It is important that the person have time to learn to understand. One of the ways to begin to understand is to make home visits as described in Chapter 7. A social worker or parent liaison person would be an ideal choice to make a structured home visit (see Exhibit 7-2) and to take a home history (see Exhibit 7-1).

Observe the Child at School

Since problems of handicapped children are individual problems, it is important that the social worker/liaison person know the specific needs of the child in order to discuss ways of having the family help the child with those needs.

Activities for the Parents/Families

Although many parent groups described in Chapter 13 are organized by the parents themselves, it is important that there be some activities sponsored by the public agency. The active members of the parent groups do not always represent the less verbal, less confident parents or families who do not have enough resources to volunteer the time. The social worker/parent liaison person could help to establish organizations that meet the needs of special groups, such as fathers or siblings of handicapped children. The social worker/parent liaison person could plan an excursion or some regular activity, such as swimming or bowling, that could be an interesting way for families to get to know one another and share their interests and problems. (See Chapter 6.) Grandparents could benefit from meeting together to share problems and solutions.

Although the social worker/liaison person may choose to direct some of the activities, it would be more appropriate to have considerable input from the families, even in the initial planning stages. Fathers and siblings may have different experiences than the professional and they can most clearly define what would be helpful to them and what would become a tedious burden. If the members of the group don't come willingly, the purpose will not be accomplished.

Parents Helping One Another

Some parents are not able to come to school easily because they do not have transportation, but other parents may be willing to pick them up. Taking a child to an evaluation is an emotionally exhausting experience (see Chapter 4); one parent may be willing to go with another parent. Some parents may feel more comfortable if another parent comes with them to the IEP conference. If parents get to know one another, they can support each other in these ways. They might even begin to trade baby sitting, since baby sitters are difficult to get for handicapped children. (See Chapter 5.) Some parents have been able to find time to go out together by taking turns caring for each other's children.

Sometimes parents of handicapped children need someone to talk to about their problems and frustrations. This frequently happens on the weekend or on a holiday. These are difficult times for parents, since the child continues to require additional help and the agencies designed to help are closed. Having someone available to "call anytime" is an important stabilizer. The social worker/parent liaison person can help parents become acquainted with one another so they can perform this role for one another.

Availability

Although concepts such as least restrictive environments or career education may be presented to the parents at a formal conference, or even in a group meeting, the concepts must be discussed to have meaning, particularly to the parent who is concerned about meeting both the handicapped child's needs and the family needs. Whenever there is personal involvement and emotional closeness, it takes more than one presentation to make the meaning clear. Most parents need someone they can talk to after they have thought for awhile about an idea presented to them. Since parents' needs are frequently spontaneous, it is difficult for them to wait for an appointment. It might be productive for the social worker/parent liaison person to make routine visits to homes and have open office hours at least one afternoon a week. Saturday would, of course, be the most convenient for most parents. Having open office hours and observing if any parents wanted to come could be an evaluation of the ability of the individual to make the parents feel comfortable and of the convenience of the time.

Assistance in Obtaining Other Services

Related services to the child and the family can be provided by other community agencies. In order to show that the services are being provided, the referral must be documented. Rather than waiting for the family to make the referral, the social worker/liaison person may make the referral or at least assist with the making of the referral. Information about such things as crippled children's clinics and mental health services is not easily available to parents.

In order to implement the appropriate services at the appropriate time, the social worker/liaison must be aware of crisis situations in the family. Homemaker services are frequently needed by families when the mother is ill, when there is a new baby, or when other stressful situations occur. The continuity of the child's progress at school is to some degree dependent upon the continuity of the child's care at home. "Working with those problems in the child's living situation (home, school and community) that affect the child's adjustment in school" (*Federal Register,* 1977, p. 42480) requires a constant understanding of what those problems are and a prompt response to the child care needs.

The School Nurse or Public Health Nurse

Since many of the learning problems of exceptional children are precipitated by or accompanied by physical problems, the role of the nurse in the education of the children is vital. Parent's satisfaction with the school program may rest on their confidence in the school's ability to meet the child's medical needs. Indeed, the fact that there is a nurse in the school may even be the reason that the child does not need a more restrictive educational setting. If the school does not have a school nurse, it may be possible for the school to receive assistance from the public health department. There are two types of services that the nurse can provide that are vital to the parent: (1) a structure and system to handle physical/medical problems and (2) direct intervention with the child.

Structure and System To Handle Physical Problems

Parents, especially mothers, are reluctant to turn over the care of the child's medication and nutritional needs to someone who is not trained to understand them. Having the nurse talk to the parent and show the parent where medication will be stored and how medication will be given can make the parent less concerned about the process. The same refrigerator that contains the medication could keep additional juice for the children who may need it or the special foods for children on special diets.

Parents of children who have seizures are very concerned about the child's care if there should be a problem. Since seizures can occur anywhere—in the lunchroom, on the playground, or in the classroom—it is important that all nonprofessionals as well as all professionals on the staff be trained to handle the situation in a calm and matter of fact manner. A seizure can be reported on a special form (see Exhibit 8-3) or on the daily activities form. (See Exhibit 8-2.)

Since many exceptional children have not yet acquired adequate toileting skills, the lavatory becomes part of the classroom. Appropriate toileting facilities and maintenance of sanitation in that area are of vital concern to the parent. If the toileting area is crowded and unclean, the parent will be dissatisfied with the setting. Sanitation procedures could be designed and monitored by the nurse.

Special eating equipment may also be needed for some children, and some children need special foods. The nurse could assist the principal and the parents in seeing that the appropriate food is either brought from home or obtained from the school lunch program.

Routine checking for rash, high temperature, and other signs of childhood illness could be done by the nurse. If the nurse understands the parent's continuing concern (see Chapter 5), information can be communicated to the parent in a sensitive manner.

Services to Individual Children

There are often times when a particular child is in need of direct help from the nurse. Some children need assistance in feeding programs. Other children may need medication during school hours. A number of children use wheelchairs or prosthetic devices that require attention. The parent will be more comfortable about sending these vital appliances to school if the parent knows that someone who knows (the nurse) will keep an eye on them. The parents will be more comfortable if the nurse is available to talk over these concerns and to get word to them immediately if there is some problem.

Having the nurse included in the IEP meeting can help parents feel more confident that the child's physical needs will be met. Having immediate access to the nurse when concerns are beginning can keep the parent from becoming unduly concerned later.

The Librarian

Most exceptional children have difficulty reading. Some have so many other developmental needs that they cannot read even when they are the age of secondary school students. If the child does not have the prerequisite skills for reading, it may be more appropriate for the child to be working on preacademic skills. It is difficult for parents to see this, however, and for many parents their child's use of the library is of vital concern.

There are many ways that the librarian communicates with the parent. If there are no books or magazines in the library that are interesting to the child, the librarian communicates rejection of that child to the parent. The librarian can meet the special needs of exceptional children by inviting their parents to visit the library, by getting materials appropriate for the children, by adjusting library regulations, and by helping the child make selections.

The Parent in the Library

The parent who comes to the library may be able to suggest ways in which the child could function in the setting. Maybe the child is interested in a particular subject, and some picture books can be found on that subject. Maybe the child is interested in magazines. Many exceptional children like to look through encyclopedias and atlases. Some exceptional children could benefit from a listening station. By brainstorming with the parent, the librarian can learn what structure and materials are appropriate for the child's needs. Parents appreciate genuine concern by the librarian to make the library accessible to their children.

During the visit, the parent may express an interest in helping the librarian by cataloging materials or reading to the students. There is more work in any library than the staff has time to do. A grateful parent might become a willing volunteer.

Materials Appropriate for the Child

Although the school budget is usually tight, some purchases can be made for those children who do not read well. There are any number of picture stories and magazines that would be interesting to these children. Since many children who are not identified as handicapped have reading problems, it is likely that the materials will become popular with other children also.

If the budget does not allow for the purchase of materials that are easy to read, scrapbooks can be created for the nonreading or slow-reading child. They can be made durable enough for library use by using light-weight cardboard and covering the pages with clear contact paper. The pages can be held in a loose leaf binder or by rings alone. These scrapbooks can be constructed by the children when they are studying vowel sounds, food groups, or things with wheels. Many teachers would enjoy cooperating with the project. PTA groups or other parent groups would also be willing to participate. Civic clubs are frequently looking for projects, and *everyone* is interested in the library.

Since exceptional children often have strong interests in one topic, it would be important to ask the parent about the child's interests. A few scrapbooks on special subjects may change disruptive behavior in the library to happy cooperation. Grant loved the library and the librarian, particularly after the librarian found books about World War II. The mother saw the librarian as Grant's only friend at school.

Library Rules

Since parents are aware of the child's slowness in learning, they appreciate it if the librarian alters the routine rules to fit the child's needs. Maybe the child needs to keep the book for longer than the regular loan period. Maybe it is important for the parent to be able to renew the book by telephone. Maybe it is important that some books from the library be kept the entire semester. Maybe the child keeps forgetting to bring the book back and the parent needs a call to be reminded to remind the child to bring the book back to school. Maybe the librarian should call to find out if the child enjoyed the book.

Helping the Child Make Selections

Many children are confused in the library. The cover of a book seldom is a clue to what is inside. For some children, the rows of book covers are not inviting. If the librarian does not have time to walk around the stacks with the child, perhaps another student could assist the child. A well-trained student helper could assist the exceptional child by suggesting books and opening them so the child could see what was interesting. The student helpers could sometimes sit with the exceptional child and read with him or her.

If the library is accessible to the child, the school will be less restrictive and the parent will feel that the public agency is helping the child be as "normal" as possible.

The Teacher

Referring Teacher

For a number of years, teachers have identified children with learning problems and suggested that these children be placed in another class for "special children." Telling the parents about the child's learning problem meant the beginning of the end of the relationship between that teacher and those parents. This is no longer true. Most mildly handicapped children will probably remain in the same classroom at least for part of the day. Now the relationship between the referring teacher and the parent is a continuing relationship and there is reason to cultivate it.

Before any comments are made about the child's difficulties, an observational record should be made of the child's activities. The record should include exactly what the child has difficulty doing, what the child did do, and what the teacher and children did in response. The behavior could be described in an objective anecdotal record, or with a graph or chart. The observation should be dated and the duration of the difficulties described. It would be easier for the parent to accept the information if the teacher made a brief telephone call to the parent to say that the child appeared to be having some problem and that the teacher would be observing the child to understand better.

If the observation shows a pattern of continued problems, the teacher may ask for help from the school psychologist or the special education teacher to see if minor changes in the structure of the classroom could help the child. If such changes are not enough, it would then be time to explain the referral process to the parent. The teacher could explain that more help might be available to the child if the child's problems were examined more closely.

Whenever a child is not learning as the teacher expects the child to be learning, the teacher has a natural desire to discuss it with someone. Although other faculty members can provide support, it is not appropriate to talk about the child's problems to anyone other than the child's parents. The difficulties that the child is having are confidential information and should not be the topic of general conversation in the faculty room. If it is, the parent will feel betrayed and the law will be broken.

Parents have access to all of the records about the child. Perhaps the most significant part of the child's record will be the reason that the child was referred for evaluation. The referral comment will guide the type of evaluation that is chosen for the child and the direction of the IEP. It is important that the referral teacher word the description very carefully so that it describes the exact difficulty the child is having and the observation that led to the discovery of the problem. A verbal discussion with the parent about the problem before the form is processed will help the parent accept the description and the wording on the referral form.

Regular Teacher

The parent may be more concerned about the regular teacher's opinion of the child than about the opinion of the special teacher or the evaluation team. Most parents are anxious for their child to be well liked by other children, and one way for this to happen is for the child to attend school with the other children. Most parents are aware of the teacher's influence on the attitude of the children toward handicapping conditions. The teacher must communicate an acceptance of the child to the parents if they are to be comfortable with the child in that classroom.

Creating a learning situation in which the child can spend part of the day with other children, if possible, is to be part of the IEP. It is important that there is parental input in the planning and feedback in the implementation. The regular teacher will probably be too busy to write in a notebook to go home each night, but a daily mini-report card (see Exhibit 8-5) can communicate quickly to the parent about the child's success or failure in meeting the specified goal of the day.

Resource Teacher

The resource teacher is responsible for the child's learning not only in the resource room, but also in other activities of the school. The resource teacher can serve as a translator of information to the parent about the activities in the resource room and the rest of the school. The parent can look to the teacher as a friend or "advocate" for the child in the school. A natural role for the resource teacher would be to send and receive messages for others in the school building.

Parents will probably prefer to discuss concerns with the resource teacher, who already is familiar with the child's problems, than with someone new. The resource teacher must speak openly with the parents but also must realize that the message will be considered a message from the school. Personal viewpoints about the activities of others in the school should not be disclosed. Any group of people working together will have personal and professional differences, but it does not reflect well on the public agency to have these discussed with the parent. The situation is potentially explosive when the resource teacher disagrees with some of the programming and the parents question the child's work in that area. If there is disagreement among the professionals about the child's programming, it is important that the agency personnel discuss the difficulties and make plans to deal with them without discussing their differences with the parents.

If the parent asks about something with which the teacher is not familiar, the teacher should say so and find the information that would be helpful. Ideally, of course, it would be best if each member of the school staff who has contact with the child discussed his or her interaction personally with the parent. With all of the time-consuming activities of the school personnel, however, it may not be possible for appointments to be made with each of these people. The resource teacher may be required to represent their positions. This can be a tremendous responsibility. The time consumed can be almost more than is spent with the children. But since the requirement of parent consent must be filled, it is a vital responsibility.

The resource teacher may also play a vital role in helping the referral teacher to explain special services that may be available. This information might be given to the other school personnel by having the resource teacher present the materials at the faculty meetings or at the parent meetings.

Self-Contained Special Education Teacher

Normal children go home and talk about school. They tell what they are studying and how the teacher wants the work to be done. Most children assigned to self-contained special education classes are not able to express themselves easily. They do not go home and describe the social studies unit or the program that they are preparing. In order for the parents of the children in the self-contained class to support the school program, however, they must know what the programs are. The newsletter and notebook sent back and forth can be a good method for sending the information home to the parent. (See Chapter 8.)

The self-contained classroom teacher may also need to let other school personnel know what is happening in the special class so that they can give the information to parents of other children who may need referral. Information about the class structure and curriculum could be presented at the faculty meeting, or the children themselves could help present a program about the self-contained class to the parent group meeting so that the parents could understand more clearly. (See Chapter 13.)

The Psychologist

It is important that the parent understands the purpose and format of the psychological examination and the reports that the psychologist makes. Most parents are somewhat concerned about having the child's abilities evaluated and need to be reassured by being told exactly what will happen during the evaluation and the purpose for the evaluation. It may also be helpful for parents to visit the examination room ahead of time to see the test protocol. Suggestions for explanations of the test and testing procedures and materials are given in Chapter 11, Parents Must Understand: Technical Concepts in Nontechnical Language.

For some parents who do not read, the psychologist must sit down with the parent and explain the report, even though the parent may not have asked. Parents may have a variety of questions about the testing procedures and meanings. It is important that the psychologist listen carefully and explain simply. When the child is tested, the parent also feels tested. The psychologist must appear as nonthreatening as possible when interacting with the parent.

The psychologist should also be prepared to discuss the ultimate educational goals for the child and such topics as career education and trade schools.

Since many educators have not had training in the administration of individual psychological tests, it may be helpful to have the psychologist give in-service training to the faculty on the purpose and procedure for testing. This will make it possible for the teachers to explain the procedures more clearly to parents. The psychologist could also present this information to parent groups. One psychologist has a set of cartoon overhead transparencies that explain the developmental problems of children. It has been the focus of entertaining discussions about child needs.

The Speech Therapist

Since the speech and language of the child are closely related to the speech and language of the home, it is not possible to implement a successful therapy program without the cooperation of the parents. A speech notebook, newsletter, or mini-report card explained in Chapter 8 might be good tools for the therapist. The parent needs to hear how the child is progressing in the therapy sessions and about the activities of the sessions.

Special therapy programs that include tongue thrust or special feeding programs require a continuous interchange between the therapist and the parents. Most such programs will not be successful unless the therapist teaches the therapy directly to the parent and observes the parent giving therapy from time to time. If nonverbal communication techniques are being taught to some children, these techniques must also be taught to the parent. The communication system for the child will not be effective unless it is shared by the child's parent.

It is important that the therapist explain the need and purpose of screening for speech problems to the teachers who may be making referrals. The methods of evaluation and treatment of speech and language difficulties should also be explained to the teachers and might even be an interesting topic for a parent group meeting. The children could demonstrate the activities of the therapy session as part of the program. (See Chapter 13.)

The Physical/Occupational Therapist

Since more of the severely handicapped children will be served in the public schools, the public agency will be responsible for more children who need physical and occupational therapy. Therapists must communicate closely with the parent in order to show the parent how to handle the child in the routines of daily life. The parent will need assistance in planning and implementing safe, practical ways to bathe and toilet children who have physical problems that inhibit normal development. If the therapist goes into the home to assist the parents, practical, individualized suggestions can be made.

All of the therapy recommendations for the child should be demonstrated for the parent as well as the teacher. The parent should then be allowed to practice the activity while the therapist observes. Physical therapy must have a doctor's order, and information about seizures and other medical concerns must be secured by asking the parent for access to the child's medical records.

NONPROFESSIONAL STAFF

Nonprofessional staff in the educational system are significant to the programming for exceptional children. Many services and types of support that exceptional children need are not directly related to the organized curriculum of the school system. The bus driver, school secretary, custodian, food service personnel and teacher's aides may be providing more of the intimate and personalized services to the child than the members of the professional staff.

The Bus Driver

Many mothers of exceptional children wait for the bus each morning with the child and wait for the bus and the child each afternoon. When her son was a student in a self-contained class for trainable children in Granite School District in Salt Lake, and she was "just a mother," one mother wrote (Michaelis, 1969):

THE SCHOOL BUS

I'm in love with the school bus.
I know that sounds ridiculous,
But it is big and strong and always comes.
We organize our day around the school bus.
We must be ready when it comes,
And we plan things for after it leaves
    . . . Jim and me.
When it is time, Jim stands and waits,
    then it comes.
The door opens and he steps up;
Each time it seems like the culmination of a miracle.
He steps up into his world,
 from my world to his. . .
And the engine turns and the noises come
 and the big yellow miracle takes Jim to school.
At school Jim has a place, Jim has a teacher, Jim belongs. . .
And when his belonging is through the
 big yellow miracle brings Jim home again.
I'm in love with the school bus.
It is golden evidence that someone cares about Jim. . . and me. . .

The person on that bus is the driver. Parents trust the skill and patience of the bus driver to transport the family treasure back and forth each day. Most parents know the bus driver on a first name basis and sometimes make holiday treats for the bus driver. The crossing guard holds the same position when the children walk to school. Bus drivers and crossing guards offer concrete, obvious service to the parents. Bus drivers and crossing guards can help see that the handouts, flyers, notebooks, and notes don't get lost on the way home.

Perhaps the bus driver is most appreciated by parents for being at the assigned bus stop at the assigned time, day after day after day. Parents of exceptional children are understandably protective of the child. (See Chapter 5.) In order to feel good about sending the child to school, they must feel comfortable about the skills and interest of the driver of the school bus. Of course, most important is knowing that the bus driver will drive carefully. Whole communities are concerned when the school bus is in an accident. Parents of the children on the bus are more than concerned. If the children also have difficulties, the parents are even more concerned about their safety.

Bus Aide

Many school systems are arranging to have an aide on the bus so there will be someone to attend to the children's needs while the bus driver concentrates on driving. If there is no aide on the bus, one of the more responsible students could be asked to "take care" of a handicapped child. Parents of exceptional children and other parents have volunteered to serve as bus aides in some localities.

It is difficult for all children to remember to take jackets, lunch boxes, and books off the bus; exceptional children have more difficulty remembering. The bus driver, or aide, can assist by reminding the child or actually handing the item to the parent at the bus stop. The driver or aide could be responsible for delivering a special note to the parent or returning a form signed by the parent to the school. Some parents are not in the habit of using the mails and may see the bus as the most efficient way to send information to the school. One school system has the bus aide collect the lunch money from the parent and take it to the office at school. This may be helpful for young or severely impaired children.

Busing Arrangements

Even before the parent meets the bus driver it is possible to make the situation more comfortable for the parent. For example, parents can be told the exact time and location of the pick up before they meet the driver. The names and telephone numbers of the bus driver, the bus aide, and the other children who will be on the bus are also important. This information should be communicated to the parent well in advance of the beginning of school so the parent has an opportunity to take the child on some bus stop drills.

Organizing the household in the morning is a task for any parent. For the parent of an exceptional child, the duties are multiplied, especially if the parent or one of the siblings must take the exceptional child to the bus stop and wait for the bus to come. Standing on the corner waiting for the bus that has been detained or doesn't come is a frustrating experience. It is even more frustrating if the mother has rushed and left things half-done in the house and other children who are still getting ready for school. There should be a system to notify parents if the bus must be late for some reason. Parents would not mind calling other parents if they had the phone numbers. Some fragile children should not be standing out waiting for the bus in marginal weather. And neither should "fragile" parents.

There might also be a system for the parent to notify the bus driver if the child is not going to school that day. One district that picked up special students at their door gave parents a large yellow card with a large black arrow on it. If the child was not going to school, the card was put into the window and the driver knew that the bus should not stop.

Since school bus problems usually occur before the secretary is in the school building, parents should have a number that they can call when there is a bus problem. Parents are understandably concerned about such problems, and it is important that the phone is answered by someone who has some answers and gives those answers as if the questions were about the safety of their own child.

Transportation services delivered by the school system are usually administered from a completely different structure than are the educational services. There is usually little personal contact between employees and little interaction about programming. To the parents, however, "the school" is "the school," and if they are sent to another administrative office to talk about busing problems, they may feel that "school" personnel are disregarding or neglecting administrative responsibility. The principal should understand the structure of the transportation department so that any interaction necessary could be done by the principal and coordinated services could be provided.

The School Secretary

The sign on the door of the school usually reads, "All visitors report to the office." (The sign even says where the office is, sometimes.) When visitors get to the office, it is not the principal, but the secretary who greets them. In some very significant ways it is the secretary that runs the shop, because the secretary is always there. The secretary's interaction with the parents of children who are having learning difficulties is vital to the parents' satisfaction with the school program.

A good secretary can make or break a banker, an attorney, a physician, or a corporate executive. It is the secretary whom the depositors, clients, patients, and customers talk to most. Having the secretary follow through and process the papers is almost more important than seeing the "boss."

Parents feel the same way about the secretary at school. If a call to the school results in a pleasant, "Hello, this is your Public School, Ms. Brown speaking. May I help you? . . . Oh, yes, Mrs. Jones, how are you?" the parent feels more comfortable, even if the answer to Mrs. Jones' question is not exactly what she wanted to hear.

"Just the way they talk to you on the phone," the parents of one special secondary school student said, "it is as if they don't want you there" (Dove, 1978).

Although the parent may be known to the whole staff as "the pest," the secretary must act as if that parent were the "best customer." In a sense, this might be true, since the family is in need of more of the school's product than other families. No matter how frequently the parent calls and how rude the comments, the secretary must still be cordial. The secretary must be dependable in getting the messages to the principal or other staff and must not ignore or respond impulsively to the parent, even if the parent's messages are about a due process hearing or some other formal complaint.

There may be times when the parent only needs to talk to the secretary about forms for field trips, dates of vacation, or the price of lunch tickets. It is usually appropriate for the secretary to handle these routine requests without consulting others.

Record Parent Contacts

Since Public Law (P.L.) 94-142 requires documentation of parent contacts and signatures on many documents, the secretary must be prepared to handle some of the routine paper work. The process of arranging for parents to inspect the child's records and making copies of the records could be the responsibility of a trained secretary. The time of the public agency personnel is used more efficiently if the secretary can take a significant role in parent contacts. Written documentation of contacts and phone calls about parent contacts can be handled most adequately by a secretary who understands both the procedures and the parents.

Assistance with the Referral Process

It is important that the secretary understand the referral process: what papers need to be completed and in what order. If the parent understands the content of the messages and the way in which the referral system is organized, the secretary can implement many of the details. If at any time the secretary feels that the parent does not understand, arrangements should be made for the parent to talk to the teacher or psychologist or social worker or whoever might know about the situation.

Arrangements for Related Services

The related services that are necessary for many exceptional children can frequently be coordinated by the secretary. The secretary should have the schedule so that the parent can easily find out what day the therapist comes and when the adaptive physical education teacher works with the child. The secretary may be the ideal person to call and remind the parent of the appointment with the neurologist and to ask for the insurance forms.

Other in-house services to the child may be coordinated by the secretary. Follow-through on the purchase of special educational, eating, toileting, or play equipment may be the responsibility of the secretary. Before the equipment is ordered, it may be necessary for the secretary to contact the parent about measurements or other details.

During all of these contacts, the secretary should communicate an attitude of acceptance of the child and the parent.

Confidentiality

Secretaries have access to a great deal of personal information about fellow employees. School secretaries also have access to a great deal of information about the children in the school and their families. Since the secretary types the reports and letters to the parent and processes the information coming from the parent but has no active role in the interaction, the secretary may be able to look at the situation more objectively than either the parents or the school personnel. It is important, however, that the secretary not sympathize with the parent about the child's condition or the school's services to the child. The secretary must remain uninvolved and talk to the parent as if the content of the communication was not known to the secretary. Any personal comments to the parent would be a breach of confidentiality, and talking about the child's condition or the parent's concerns to the bridge club is not only a breach of ethical standards but also a violation of the law.

In addition to maintaining personal confidentiality, the secretary may be responsible for keeping the record of those who have access to the child's confidential records. Although there may be a temptation to comment about the content of the record to those who come to read it, information about the child and the family is not to be casual conversation.

The Custodian

In spite of equal rights, there are not usually many men around the school setting. One special school referred to the custodians as "the men" and described how they had helped to build some things for physically handicapped students. To all children the custodian is a key person, but to the exceptional child the custodian is not only "the man" but also a model for possible imitation. There are many things that the custodian can do for, with, and to the exceptional child.

Cooperation in Special Services

Children with special problems may need to have the side door unlocked early so they can bring the wheelchair in; maybe extra equipment must be installed in the lavatory, or maybe the doors on the lavatory need to be fixed so they will open and close easily. A stand may be needed under the water fountain so the child can sit down while drinking, arm rests may be needed on the desk, or the lower windows of the classroom may need to be painted so the child won't be distracted by the children on the playground.

Exceptional children are more likely to throw up on the newly waxed floor, spill the shavings from the pencil sharpener, write on the chalkboard with crayon (an accident, of course), or flush too much paper down the toilet. If the custodian accepts the additional work as part of the services, the parent will appreciate the extra interest. If the custodian complains about the "damn kid and all that extra work," the parent is likely to be personally hurt and become dissatisfied with the total school program.

Career Education and the Custodian

The custodian who understands the concept of career education (preparation for real life) may choose to cooperate by allowing exceptional children to help with the dusting, cleaning, and maintenance of the school. If the school prepared the custodian for the role, such an experience could be included on the child's IEP. It would be appropriate to pay the custodian for the additional service, just as a coach is paid for additional responsibilities.

The Food Preparation Personnel

The last few years have seen an increasing interest in the relationship between the child's diet and the child's behavior and general health. Even before the current attention to diet, a number of exceptional children have been on special diets. Food preparation personnel may have direct contacts with parents of exceptional children as the diet of the child is planned and the food either brought from home or specially supplied by the school kitchen. Mothers especially (see Chapter 5) are likely to be concerned about the child's lunch. If food service personnel communicate an acceptance for the child and the child's problems, the parents will be more comfortable about the child's schooling.

Cooperation with Special Diets

Many exceptional children have weight problems. Learning to eat appropriately to maintain health and proper weight may be part of the child's IEP. Children with weight problems, allergy problems, and metabolic disorders may not be able to eat the regular school lunch. Although undoubtedly the parent will begin by explaining the child's needs to other school personnel, it would be simplest if eventually the food preparation personnel and the parent talked face to face, preferably in the school kitchen, about what was needed, how it would be stored, and how it would be served.

Cooperation with Special Eating Arrangements

Most of the learning problems that children have show in their eating skills. Children with motor problems have difficulty getting the food to the mouth and closing the mouth. There is likely to be food on the child and on the floor. Children who are slow learners may also be slow eaters. Children who find sitting still in a classroom difficult also have difficulty sitting still in the cafeteria, maybe even more. Those who throw spit wads in the classroom have a heyday when peas are served in the cafeteria.

In order for a child with learning problems to eat in the cafeteria, it may be necessary for the lunchroom procedures to be individually designed. It would be helpful for the parent to come to the school to see how the noon meal is handled so that the parent could participate in the design. For cerebral-palsied children, the distractions of the other students' noises may cause more spasticity and make eating more difficult. Children with behavior disorders may need to eat when the lunchroom is not crowded. Mentally retarded students may need to have an extended time for eating. Some students may need to eat with special utensils rather than the usual plastic tray. Some children may not be able to handle the tray without repeated spilling.

Help in the Cafeteria

One of the best learning experiences for a child who is older but has not learned the preacademic skills is to work in the lunchroom preparing the room, serving, or cleaning up. Although this "help" is frequently more "trouble" for the food service personnel, it is one of the few accessible places for the student to have some practical experience. The patience of the food service personnel in allowing the child this learning experience can be seen in the way the child is treated and the way the parent is treated. If the child does work in the cafeteria, the parent should speak directly with the food service personnel about the child's progress rather than hear it second-hand from someone who has talked with the food preparation personnel but can't answer all the questions about the child's progress.

THE PARENT ORGANIZATION

Although it may be assumed that a parent organization works toward the needs of exceptional children, some parent organizations have specific missions; the needs of handicapped children are not fostered by these groups. Just as some professionals within the field campaign for categorical treatment of learning problems, so do some of the parents. Some categories of disability are more generally accepted by the public and, therefore, also by the parents. Parent groups have not only been successful in getting services for particular children, but in creating new categories of learning problems with more titles (Retish, 1977). Not realizing that many of the services required by children with one type of learning problem are very similar to those required by children with another type of problem, parent groups usually focus their interest on the needs of "my" child and those who are like him or her.

The official organization of the parents of the school should include in its mission statement a commitment to work to make the school a comfortable place for the exceptional child and the child's parents. The Parent Teacher Association has listed an Exceptional Child Chairman as a possible officer. If this person is active, the needs of the exceptional child could be made known. One of the ways to help people understand the needs of the special child is to have at least one official parent group meeting about the needs of the child with learning problems and the school's services to the child. (See Chapter 13.)

Volunteers

Some school districts do not have funds to hire teacher's aides or bus aides. The parent organization could secure and assist in the training of volunteers to perform these roles. The parent group could also recruit volunteers to assist with field trips or other special activities for the exceptional child. There are times when the exceptional child could be included in such activities with the other children if the teacher had additional help.

Sometimes exceptional children need special equipment that is not readily available or is too expensive for the school to purchase. Parent groups might raise the money for the prone board, the extra high table for the typewriter, or the floor mats, or the members of the parent group might make and donate the smocks for the work experience in the cafeteria or the peg boards for hanging woodworking tools.

Direct Service to Other Parents

The parent group can organize itself to offer rides to parents who need assistance to come to the school program or conference. They may also offer to help the family when there is a new baby or a child is sick. Parents may also help each other through parent-to-parent counseling.

Parent groups sometimes sponsor Boy and Girl Scouts. It is important to make sure that exceptional children are not only invited to participate, but truly made welcome.

STUDENT SERVICES TO STUDENTS AND PARENTS

In many schools the student officers meet regularly; some schools even have a student government class. Although the students themselves sometimes plan projects, frequently the projects are "suggested" to the students by the faculty sponsor. The projects usually range from keeping the school grounds clean to getting more attendance at the school games. If the sponsor presents ideas with enthusiasm, most are accepted readily by the students. If the sponsor suggested that the students work with handicapped learners, the students would probably be willing to help. Frequently the students want to help and don't know how. One of the greatest compliments that the school can give to the parent is to organize the students so that the exceptional child is part of the ongoing activities.

Vickie was assigned to work with Jim. She helped him play with the other children on the playground and sometimes ate lunch with him. Jim was thrilled with the valentine that Vickie put in his valentine box, but not nearly as thrilled as Jim's mother. It meant that Jim had a "real" friend (Michaelis, 1975). Students can help a handicapped learner by (1) assisting the student in the school setting and (2) extending the relationship into the neighborhood. In order to do this, the staff must show the student how to help.

At School

A special responsibility of the safety patrol could be helping exceptional students get back and forth to school safely. This might mean having another student stop by and walk to school with the child or meet the bus when it arrived at school. It would be important for someone to show this student just how much help the child needed. A natural role for the safety patrol would be to assist the handicapped child when there was a fire drill.

Some handicapped students also need assistance in the lavatory and getting the tray to the table in the lunchroom. Students could also be recruited and trained to assist in the feeding of children with severe motor problems. Of course, there is always the tutoring. One of the best ways to help both students is to assign one student to help another. If these student-to-student interactions are to be optimal, it is important that the students are trained and that the services are monitored by an interested, supportive adult.

In the Neighborhood

Exceptional children may not be good at making friends. Many children with learning problems would be helped by an opportunity to visit in the home of a child who has status in the school system. Such a child would probably not invite the exceptional child home unless encouraged to make such an invitation and given some training in how to interact comfortably with the handicapped child.

One former vice president of her high school class remembers with some pride how she was asked to help orient a new girl who had moved to the community. The new girl became not just a part of the established student's school routine, but also part of her group of friends outside of school. The school personnel are in a unique position to promote community acceptance of the child and the family by helping the other children understand and by having the children help the exceptional child.

Parents should be introduced to the students who are assigned to help their child so that they can personally communicate with them. Since the student's world is more similar to that of the handicapped child than is the adult's world, the student may be able to do more for the child than the adults can. If the school personnel arrange for the exceptional child to have pleasant interaction with the other children in the school and the neighborhood, it is a message to the parent that there is a genuine desire to fill the exceptional child's total developmental needs.

PRESERVICE AND IN-SERVICE TRAINING

What you don't know can hurt you, especially if you infringe on what the parent sees as the "rights of handicapped children and their parents." Since legislation requires the services to the child to be in the regular school setting, all persons in the school system may have contact with the handicapped child and the child's parents. It is important to know what the regulations are, what the parent's experiences have been, and how the parent is likely to approach the school setting.

There are people who have been working in the school setting for many years who have not had contact with the parents of handicapped children except to tell them that their child was to be transferred to the special education class. Special education personnel have not been accustomed to explaining the evaluation procedures or the curriculum of the self-contained classroom. The new requirements make most of the old interaction patterns obsolete, even for those who have worked with parents of handicapped children for years. There are new procedures to follow.

Organization for Training

Preservice sessions could be regular university course work, special workshops, or independent study. In-service sessions could be given on the in-service days, in special summer workshops, or bit by bit in faculty meetings. The course could be taught by a university faculty member or designed as a seminar in which students presented various topics to the group. Since much of the information is emotionally laden, not only for the parent but also for the public agency personnel, the information should not be presented solely in lecture format; discussion is essential. Preservice and inservice sessions could be designed around the topics in each chapter of this book.

The training sessions could be planned for an entire district or for the personnel in a single school building. Professional and nonprofessional staff could attend all sessions together, or some sessions could be held for each group separately. The sessions could be organized by district for all bus drivers, all teachers, etc., or by building. There are some advantages to both groupings. The content would be easier if the sessions were organized by the job role, but more cooperation may be generated if the sessions were organized for the people who would be working together.

Learning to know and understand the needs of parents of handicapped children generates a great deal of self-evaluation and self-examination of attitudes, goals, and values, both personal and societal. In a democratic society the values of the society are the missions of the educational system. People who share this personal exploration frequently feel as if they have shared some of their own childhood with one another.

Study Format

Training sessions could be designed around the content of each chapter in this book. The concepts in some chapters can be learned as abstract concepts; others require concrete personal experience for understanding. Some chapters require more student work than others, but the content of each of the chapters could be covered in a three-hour class time.

It would be helpful during the study process to bring in the specific forms or regulations that are used in the district or school such as a Parent Services Questionnaire (Exhibit 14-1). Suggestions are given in the following study format for each chapter. Suggestions for experiences with parents are also given, as well as for presentation and student activities.

Chapter One
Goal: To understand the due process procedure

- Supplementary Materials/Information
  Council for Exceptional Children
  (CEC) tape of due process hearing
  NASDE hearing officers manual (1978)
  Forms, regulations for hearing in state of residence
  List of names for hearing officers

- Learning Activities
  Gather materials in list
  Role play a hearing
  Watch the CEC tape, except for the decision, then write a decision

Exhibit 14-1 Parent Services Questionnaire

Please circle the most appropriate answer or add the answer if none are appropriate.

1. Who originally told you that your child was handicapped?

   1. MD
   2. Nurse
   3. Social worker
   4. Other

2. What terms were used to describe your child?

   1. A little slow
   2. Retarded
   3. Developmentally disabled
   4. Mongoloid
   5. Down's syndrome
   6. Brain damaged
   7. Cerebral palsy
   8. Neurologically impaired
   9. Other _____

3. What was the age of your child when he/she first received educational evaluation?

   1. At birth
   2. 3 months
   3. 6 months
   4. 1 year
   5. 2 years
   6. 3-4 years
   7. Kindergarten
   8. First grade
   9. Other _____

4. Did you request to have your child evaluated?

   1. Yes
   2. No

Exhibit 4-1 continued

5. Did someone tell you what the evaluation procedures would be?

    1. Yes
    2. No

6. Did someone explain the results of the evaluation to you?

    1. Yes
    2. No

7. At what age did your child begin to receive schooling regularly?

    1. At birth
    2. 6 months
    3. 1 year
    4. 3 years
    5. 5 years
    6. 6 years
    7. Other _____

8. At what age did your child no longer receive educational services?

    1. Preschool
    2. Elementary school
    3. High school
    4. 18 or over
    5. Higher education

9. Were you invited to participate in setting goals for your child's education?

    1. Yes
    2. No
    3. Somewhat _____

10. When you suggested to school personnel what you wanted your child to learn, did they listen to you?

Exhibit 4-1 continued

1. Yes
2. No
3. About some things; specify _____

11. Has your child had a vocational evaluation?

    1. Yes
    2. No
    3. Partial; explain _____

12. Has your child had vocational training?

    1. Yes
    2. No
    3. Partial; explain _____

13. Do you (or did you) pay tuition for your child's schooling?

    1. No
    2. Yes, under $20 per month
    3. Yes, between $20 and $40 per month
    4. Yes, over $40 per month; specify _____

14. Does your child ride the bus to school or work?

    1. No
    2. Yes, under 5 miles one way
    3. Yes, over 5 miles one way
    4. Yes, over 20 miles one way
    5. Yes, over 30 miles one way

15. Has your child been evaluated by a physical therapist?

    1. No
    2. Yes, within the last 2 years
    3. Yes, more than 2 years ago

Exhibit 4-1 continued

16. Does your child need physical therapy?

    1. No
    2. Yes, a little
    3. Yes, a lot
    4. Don't know

17. Has your child been evaluated by a speech therapist?

    1. No
    2. Yes, within the last 2 years
    3. Yes, more than 2 years ago

18. Does your child need speech therapy?

    1. No
    2. Yes, a little
    3. Yes, a lot
    4. Don't know

19. Does your child belong to any organizations for children/young people?

    1. Boy Scouts
    2. Girl Scouts
    3. Campfire Girls
    4. Boys Clubs
    5. Other _____

20. Does your child participate in regular recreation?

    1. No
    2. Yes, weekly
    3. Yes, monthly
    4. Yes, during the season; specify _____

Exhibit 4-1 continued

21. Is there transportation provided for the recreation?

    1. No
    2. Yes, at no cost
    3. Yes, at less than $2 per session
    4. Yes, at more than $2 per session; amount _____

22. Who organizes the recreation?

    1. Individual parent organizes own
    2. Regular city recreation department
    3. Special recreation organization
    4. Parent organization plans
    5. Other _____

23. Does your child swim?

    1. No, child is afraid of the water
    2. No, swimming is not available
    3. Yes, splashes in water
    4. Yes, can float
    5. Yes, can dog paddle across pool
    6. Yes, other _____

24. Is there a charge for the swimming?

    1. No
    2. Yes, less than $1
    3. Yes, more than $1
    4. Yes, more than $5
    5. Yes, but only for transportation; amount _____

25. Does your child need medication regularly?

    1. Each night
    2. Each morning
    3. Each morning and night
    4. Morning, night, and noon

Exhibit 4-1 continued

26. Who pays for the medication?

    1. You
    2. Medicaid
    3. Other insurance
    4. Other _____

27. Where does your child live?

    1. At home
    2. In a public institution
    3. In a private institution
    4. In a group home
    5. Other _____

28. How long has or did he/she live at home?

    1. Not at all
    2. 6 months
    3. 1 year
    4. 5 years
    5. 10 years
    6. 15 years
    7. 20 years
    8. 25 years
    9. Still living at home; child is _____

29. How long has the child lived outside the home?

    1. Not at all
    2. 6 months
    3. 1 year
    4. 5 years
    5. 10 years
    6. 15 years
    7. 20 years
    8. 25 years
    9. Still living outside the home; child is _____

Exhibit 4-1 continued

30. At what age did he/she leave home?

    1. At birth
    2. 6 months
    3. 1 year
    4. 2-5 years
    5. 5-8 years
    6. 8-10 years
    7. 10-15 years
    8. 15-25 years
    9. Over 25 years of age; specify _____

31. Does your child receive SSI payments?

    1. Yes
    2. Applied and was refused
    3. Have not applied

32. Does your child have a Medicaid Identification Card?

    1. Yes
    2. No
    3. Have not applied

33. Has your child been evaluated at a medical clinic?

    1. Within the last year
    2. More than a year ago
    3. Never

34. Has your family received genetic counseling?

    1. No, not offered
    2. No, not wanted it
    3. Yes, public expense
    4. Yes, private expense under $50
    5. Yes, private expense over $50

Exhibit 4-1 continued

35. Can your child take care of his/her personal needs?

    1. Toilet adequately
    2. Toilet and feed adequately
    3. Feed self but not toilet self

36. Can your child take care of his/her personal things?

    1. Dresses self
    2. Dresses self and makes bed
    3. Makes bed but does not dress self

37. Can your child get around the community?

    1. Walking
    2. Bicycle
    3. Public bus
    4. Automobile
    5. Only when someone takes

38. How many other children do you have?

    1. None
    2. One older son
    3. One older daughter
    4. One younger son
    5. One younger daughter
    6. Two other sons
    7. Two other daughters
    8. Specify _____

Chapter Two
Goal: To become familiar with the *Federal Register* and the terms describing
services to handicapped children

- Supplementary Materials/Information
  Copy of the *Federal Register*, Aug 23, 1977 for each student (obtainable from
  congressman or the office of education, but it usually takes some time)

- Learning Activities
  Find the terms described in the chapter or in the *Register*, mark them to be
  turned in for grading
  Make a list of the references in the register for each concept/term

Chapter Three
Goal: To understand how the parent feels about the services delivered to the child

- Supplementary Materials/Information
  Parents' description about the services that they and the child have received
  Questionnaire to structure the inquiry with the parent (Exhibit 14-1)

- Learning Activities
  Interview the parent of a handicapped child and make a brief report of the
  responses or turn in the questionnaire
  Fill out the form or use the form to structure the presentation when talking to a
  parent

Chapter Four
Goal: To understand the extended family and neighborhood situation

- Supplementary Materials/Information
  Parent/neighbor/friend of parent of handicapped child speak to class and
  describe their role relationship to the child and the parent

- Learning Activities
  Listen to the description and participate in the discussion

Chapter Five
Goal: To understand how the mother of a handicapped child feels and how the
father of a handicapped child feels

- Supplementary Materials/Information
  Personal experiences of mother and father of handicapped child, either a
  couple or parents of different children; both mother and father together or at
  separate times

- Learning Activities
Listen to descriptions by each of the parents and write what appears to be most important goals for the child as seen by each of the parents

Chapter Six
Goal: To understand the role of the sibling of a handicapped child

- Supplementary Materials/Information
Panel discussion by siblings of handicapped children: some adults, some teenagers, and some elementary school students

- Learning Activities
Listen to description and make a list of the positive elements of the role and the negative elements of the role

Chapter Seven
Goal: To learn to gather a home history and make a home observation

- Supplementary Materials/Information
Practice experience with parent/family

- Learning Activities
Gather developmental information using Exhibit 7-1
Make a 12-hour home observation and analyze the data (Exhibit 7-2)

Chapter Eight
Goal: To learn to be creative about sending information to the parent

- Supplementary Materials/Information
Data about real children

- Learning Activities
Create a newsletter, make copies (perhaps with the help of the children), and distribute it to families and other class members

Chapter Nine
Goal: To understand how counseling techniques suggest effective interaction

- Supplementary Materials/Information
Vignettes about real situations in which names are changed

- Learning Activities
Role play the interaction with the parent using each of the counseling techniques and taking the part of the professional and the part of the parent

Chapter Ten
Goal: To become comfortable about communication with the parent about the
    child's progress

- Supplementary Materials/Information
  Copies of the checklists that are appropriate for children in the school who are
  currently or potentially students in the school

- Learning Activities
  Conduct a conference with a parent using the checklist to create the agenda

Chapter Eleven
Goal: To communicate special educational needs in "language understandable to
    the general public"

- Supplementary Materials/Information
  Contact with housewives/businessmen or the nonprofessional staff of the
  school

- Learning Activities
  Prepare descriptions of learning problems/child needs/materials; put descriptions on paper, and draw out descriptions for nonprofessional educator to read
  and comment on the style and language

Chapter Twelve
Goal: To be comfortable using the compliance procedures and forms

- Supplementary Materials/Information
  Forms used by the district/school for referral, consent, etc.

- Learning Activities
  Examine forms and fill out sample forms

Chapter Thirteen
Goal: To plan, organize, and present a successful program to parents

- Supplementary Materials/Information
  Program chairman, dates of parent meetings
  Interests of parents

- Learning Activities
  Present a program to a parent group either individually or in small groups

Chapter Fourteen

Goal: To be able to explain special education to people in the community

- Supplementary Materials/Information
  Program chairman and schedule of civic club and ladies club meetings

- Learning Activities
  Present a description of home-school relations to a ladies club or a civic club
  Present one chapter of the book at a faculty or staff in-service session

TIME TO LEARN

Whether a child is learning to walk or to multiply, or an adult is learning to listen and understand, growing takes time. No child learned to multiply in only a few days, and no adult learned to understand another adult in only a few days. There will be times, many times, when the meaning of messages will not be clear and understanding will not be reached. There will be many times when the message received is not the one that was meant; understanding, like consent, is revokable at any time. Even when the message is well sent, it is possible that the receiver has not had the same life experience and does not understand the message in the same way.

There are many lists of developmental skills and age levels at which children usually learn such skills; however, there are no lists of skills and sequences for the development of adult skills and no age levels for attainment. Some parents and some professionals are much better able to build relationships than others. Some can listen well, and some can express how they feel and think; others have not yet learned how. But whether the communication is with someone who is skillful and fluent or with someone who is withdrawn and unaware, the response is the same: (1) listen carefully to all messages that are sent; (2) send careful, personal messages; and (3) patiently keep sending and receiving. Relationships, both with other professionals and with parents, take time to grow.

REFERENCES

Dove, K. Personal communication, 1978.

Due process in special education: A step-by-step resource manual for hearing officers. Washington, D.C.: National Association of State Directors of Special Education, 1978.

Federal Register, Vol. 42, No. 163. Aug. 23, 1977.

Michaelis, C.T. The school bus. Unpublished poem, 1969.

Michaelis, C.T. Valentines and Vickie. Unpublished editorial, 1975.

Retish, P.M. Mental retardation in the suburbs. *Education and Training of the Mentally Retarded,* 1977, *12* (1), 60.

Schultz, J. The parent-professional conflict. In A.P. Turnbull & H.R. Turnbull (Eds.), *Parents speak out: Views from the other side of a two-way mirror.* Columbus, Ohio: Charles E. Merrill, 1978.

Index

Note: Page numbers in italics designate
exhibits.

About the Author

DR. CAROL MICHAELIS can remember listening as a college freshman to a grandmother explain the speech problems of her grandson as they waited outside the therapy room during his treatment. Since that time, some 30 years ago, Dr. Michaelis has listened as a professional to parents explain the trauma of trying to help a handicapped child develop, and she has listened to educators explain the trauma of trying to work with parents of children who are having problems.

Dr. Michaelis has felt the frustrations of both situations personally, because her 24-year-old son, Jim, has Down's syndrome. She has organized and attended parent groups as a parent as well as a professional. She has presented programs through the PTA, the ARC, and the LD parent group, as well as through the school district. She has worked with parents as a regular teacher, a resource teacher, and a teacher trainer at universities in Utah, Iowa, Virginia, Washington, D.C., and Louisiana. This book reflects not the a priori model of a flow chart, but a practical model developed from having been field-tested in life.